/ life as a
92

THE SKY WEPT FIRE

MIKAIL ELDIN worked as a journalist before taking up arms in the conflict with Russia. He eventually left Chechnya in fear for his life and secured political asylum in Norway, where he now lives.

ANNA GUNIN read Russian at Bristol University. She has translated stories for anthologies, plays for the Royal Court Theatre, German Sadulaev's novel *I Am a Chechen!* and film scripts by Denis Osokin and Yuri Arabov. Her translations of Pavel Bazhov's folk tales are included in *Russian Magic Tales from Pushkin to Platonov* (Penguin Classics).

The Sky Wept Fire

My Life as a Chechen Freedom Fighter

Mikail Eldin

Translated from the Russian by Anna Gunin

Portobello
BOOKS

Published by Portobello Books 2013
Portobello Books, 12 Addison Avenue, London W11 4QR

The publication was effected under the auspices of the Mikhail Prokhorov
Foundation TRANSCRIPT Programme to Support Translations of Russian
Literature

This book has been selected to receive financial assistance from English
PEN's Writers in Translation programme supported by Bloomberg.
English PEN exists to promote literature and its understanding, uphold
writers' freedoms around the world, campaign against the persecution and
imprisonment of writers for stating their views, and promote the
friendly cooperation of writers and free exchange of ideas.

A CIP catalogue record for this book is available from the British Library

9 8 7 6 5 4 3 2 1

ISBN 978 1 84627 318 6

Typeset by Avon DataSet, Bidford on Avon
Printed in the UK by Page Bros Norwich Ltd

www.portobellobooks.com

To those who fell undefeated, for whom the Sky wept

CONTENTS

Preface

It is only possible to write beautifully about war if you have never witnessed it from within. It was my fate, though, to spend long years seeing war from the inside. And so much happened that perhaps would have been better forgotten, but it was my duty to remember. Yet this book is not a chronicle. After all, memories can be messy … For a chronicle, you need the utterly cold and impartial mind of a historian. Whereas I have followed my memories haphazardly … Listening more to my heart. Trying to understand just what it was that happened to me – a man far removed from the blood and romance of war. I have tried to be as neutral as possible in my account of these events, yet at the same time I remain deeply partisan. Partisan about everything I saw.

   This is not a seductive story of war for the adventurous or the romantic. I've merely recounted to the best of my ability what I was fated to witness and what my memory deemed important. I've omitted the names of persons with whom I crossed paths – some are still alive, and those who are dead have relatives who are still alive. Though on second thoughts, I don't know if I could have resisted the temptation, for the sake of historical record, to name 'names, addresses and safe houses' (as President Putin once urged his citizens to do) had it not been for my strange memory, which has blotted the names from my mind, leaving only the faces and their actions. Indeed, history is made up not of names, but of the personalities behind them.

I

Ragnarok

And the wanderer enquired of the people, 'Tell me, what has brought about your strife?'

'We're quarrelling over a pearl,' someone replied.

'What is a pearl?' the wanderer asked.

The people replied, 'A pearl is precious, you can buy anything with it.'

'For the love of God! Give me the pearl,' entreated the wanderer. 'I would buy mercy from God …'

'You can't buy feelings with them …' responded the people in surprise.

'And what is their value if they cannot bring mercy?' said the wanderer, walking away.

From a Sufi parable

1

Everything began with two huge blasts rocking the centre of Grozny, capital of Chechnya, a country enjoying its fourth year of independence. It was 26 November 1994 and dawn was breaking on an unusually warm autumn morning. There had already been occasional explosions rumbling through some of the city's districts in areas targeted for their industrial and strategic importance, but it was this morning's blasts that would mark the beginning of the terrible tragedy. Three years had passed since Dzhokhar Dudayev had been elected the first president of a sovereign Chechen state. From the moment independence was declared, Russia began hatching schemes to meddle with and destroy Chechen autonomy. Hoping to exploit the Chechen people's grievances, Russia created and bankrolled military, rather than political, opposition to Dudayev's rule. This Armed Opposition – essentially, armed groups hired by Russia and headed by Russian Army officers and intelligence agents – tried several times to take the city in the hope of ousting President Dudayev. Saboteurs had also committed the odd terrorist attack within the city limits, blowing up facilities of strategic value, such as electrical substations and oil depots, but, despite the ferocity of these acts, they had inflicted little damage on the city, and even less on the government of the day. So the residents of Grozny were getting used to sporadic explosions and bursts of gunfire and were not unduly alarmed on that November morning.

At the time I was cultural editor for the Chechen literary periodical *Vast* and wasn't particularly interested in the military side of politics, although I'd been closely following the events unfolding in Chechnya and kept abreast of political developments. I had my own views on the artificially engineered showdown between the Armed Opposition and the 'dictatorship'. Rather than rallying around their president and building a sovereign state, the political opposition, acting on personal grievances and ambitions – or most of them, at any rate – went into open confrontation, thus paving the way for Russia's squalid meddling in Chechnya's internal affairs. The President's administration made no special effort to win over those members of the opposition who were intelligent, educated and devoted to their nation – and there were many such people – to join in building an independent state. While both sides were fervently proclaiming their willingness to unite and accusing the other of being uncooperative, they were also busy laying down conditions that were unacceptable to the other side. The Armed Opposition was incapable of listening to anyone but the Russian intelligence services funding their mission to stir up tensions and unleash conflict. Such was the situation that had arisen in Chechnya by that momentous day. The political background and root causes of this tragedy are themselves deserving of a book. But let us return to the first day of all-out war.

2

The moment I heard the blasts, my journalistic curiosity got the better of me and I ran straight into town, heading in the direction the sound had come from: Freedom Square. I lived quite close to the city centre – around twenty minutes on foot – and before long I had come to the site of the detonations. As I was approaching the square, I saw a large number of armed men standing around the building of the Department for State Security. Several tanks from the Chechen Armed Forces' Shali Tank Regiment stood on Ordzhonikidze Avenue. Beyond them, a hundred metres from the Presidential Palace, were the carcasses of two tanks that had been ripped apart by the massive explosions. The turret of one tank lay a few dozen metres from the burnt-out hull. An anti-tank shell from a Russian-manufactured RPG-7 must have pierced the armour and detonated the ammunition inside, tearing up the tank as if it were a papier-mâché toy. As they came out on to the square in front of the Presidential Palace, these tanks clearly hadn't had time to fire a single round. Chechen Army soldiers had taken up position in all the streets and alleys leading to the Presidential Palace. Glass splinters from the panes shattered by the blast were crunching under my feet. Civilians mingled with the soldiers, naïvely huddling around the tanks, completely oblivious to the danger a tank posed, even if it was one of ours. There were no dead or wounded to be seen and I still had no idea what was going on. I imagined two Armed Opposition tanks must have strayed into the city, most likely because their crews were drunk, and they'd been hit. That type of thing had happened before. And the crews, I was almost certain – the number of times I'd seen it in the movies – must have fled their burning vehicles and been taken prisoner. I went up to some armed young men – special forces, judging by their uniforms – and asked, 'What's happening? Whose tanks were hit?'

'The opposition have come into the city with the Russian Army. They're Russian tanks,' one of them told me.

'When did they come in? By which route?'

'They came this morning at dawn, down the Staropromyslovskoye Highway, from that side,' the soldier said. Neither he nor I paused to reflect on the absurdity of my question: after all, there had plainly been no tanks in the city the day before. The information given by the soldier did not worry me unduly. In 1993, the opposition had also entered a district of Grozny, but they had left without a fight. We continued our conversation.

'Are they far from here?'

'They're in Druzhba Narodov Square.'

Reassured by this information, I headed off down the avenue, past the gutted tanks, making for the square.

'Hey, don't go that way! The road's under fire, they're not far,' the soldier hollered at me.

'But you told me they're in Druzhba Narodov Square.' I replied, puzzled.

'That's right, they're in the square. But that's not far from here.'

'Well, I've got to get there.'

'Why?' he asked, suspiciously.

'For work.'

'Work, today? Look, go on home.'

'But I'm a journalist.'

'Oh, I see … Well, take the street running parallel, if you must.'

He most likely rated my chances of survival as nil, yet all the same didn't want to watch me die from sheer folly. I was excited that my profession would give me something interesting to reminisce about in old age – oh, silly and naïve thoughts! – and decided to follow this kindly advice. I walked past bewildered civilians who were flocking around the gruffly rumbling tanks.

'What are you doing out here?' I couldn't resist asking.

Two young guys smiled at me awkwardly and shrugged. 'We heard the blasts and came over to find out what was happening. Well, it looked pretty serious and we decided to stay,' they said, as though explaining themselves to me.

With them were a number of women, some with children, who were stranded on this side of the city.

'Young man, who are you?' an elderly man asked me.

'He's a journalist,' the soldier answered on my behalf.

'Well, if you're a journalist, then you'll know. These attackers – are they Russian or Chechen?'

'What's the difference?' I replied. 'What matters is they're shooting.'

'Maybe you can't see it, but there's a massive difference!' The old man spoke crossly. 'See, I've got my son here in the National Guard,' he added, somewhat more gently. 'I came to get him, but he's refusing to leave. Says he doesn't want to desert his comrades. Well, I can understand that. But I'm not going to let him shoot at fellow Chechens,' he said firmly.

'Of course, I understand. But I actually don't know,' I tried to explain.

'You're a journalist, and you don't even know who's shooting?' he responded, his tone implying that he was quite sure Presidents Yeltsin and Dudayev reported their plans daily to journalists in general, and to me in particular.

'No, listen. I don't know,' I mumbled, shaken by his persistence. People around us began smiling. 'But the tank crews were Russian!' I offered.

'Yes?' His face brightened. 'Well, if they're Russians, then let him fight. And if he chickens out, I'll ruddy well kill him myself.'

At this point, one of the fighters began swearing blind to the old man that the soldiers in the tanks were Russian, and I went on my way. I was still under the illusion that this wasn't genuine military engagement – I hadn't heard any small-arms fire yet – but merely the same old sabre-rattling we'd seen before. And it wasn't just me: most people failed to grasp the full gravity of what was unfolding. On that first day and later too, when things were quiet again, you could hear people discussing the assault excitedly.

'If it's the Russians starting a war, then more fool them. After all, the Chechens are hardly going to start killing each other.'

'Just you wait, those opposition soldiers will take their weapons and go over to the Chechen side.'

'In fact, I bet some of them only enlisted so they could arm themselves at Russia's expense.'

Seeing this naïve faith of ordinary Chechens in the Chechen sense of national consciousness and comradeship made me well up with a feeling of pride and pity for them. All too soon, though, events would shatter their illusions with terrifying speed. Just as they had in the Caucasian War more than a century earlier, Chechens would take up arms to serve their enemies. Chechens would serve their enemies as mountain guides; Chechens would serve in law enforcement; they would even create a state, complete with all its institutions, and hold mock elections, although there would also be cases of opposition soldiers, sometimes entire units, switching sides and joining the resistance. But in the early days naïve convictions held enormous sway, and people treated the activity of the occasional pro-Moscow armed group as an exception. For a long time we stubbornly refused to believe that the Chechen spiritual world had imploded at the moment when, for the first time in modern history, ordinary Chechens took up weapons against their fellow Chechens. And when we finally accepted the blunt truth, we ended up losing countless lives, and many of the living would lose what was most precious of all: their Chechen spirit.

But at that time, early in the morning of 26 November, I walked down Rosa Luxemburg Street in the direction of Druzhba Narodov Square truly thrilled at my luck. Before long I was stopped by some armed men who were taking up positions calmly, confidently and soberly. Their commanding officer walked up to me and asked where I was going. I explained that I needed to 'cross over to the other side'.

'Why do you need to?' he asked with interest.

'I'm a journalist. I want to interview them. I've already interviewed your side.'

I had not actually interviewed their side, but then there was no need. After all, the motives of the defending side were plain enough. They were defending because they had been attacked. Well, that was their job. What interested me was the motive of the attackers. The commander looked over my papers, and, satisfied I was telling the truth, said, 'Of course you're just doing your job, but we're going to start shooting soon and you could get hit by a stray bullet. And you do realize their side could kill you? They'll see you as one of Dudayev's journalists.'

'A journalist cannot belong to Dudayev, or indeed to any side!' I declared loftily, and he smiled sadly at this. Here I was, trying to pass into enemy territory just as engagement began, yet it is the duty of a commander not to let such things happen.

'Do you think you could hold your fire until I reach them?' I asked – a question utterly idiotic in its selfishness.

He looked me in the eye and replied, 'All right, we'll wait, only be quick. Will a few minutes be enough?'

'Oh, yes. I run fast when frightened,' I quipped, making a sprint for it.

A chorus of laughter followed me. Perhaps they were laughing at my folly: we both knew that if the fighting started, no one would hang around waiting for some unknown journalist to finish running. Yet I needed the commander's promise for my own peace of mind. *There you go, an entire unit is delaying the start of the battle just for me.* All the same, I ran as fast as my legs could carry me. When I caught sight of a group of armed men, I stopped and said hello. They said hello back.

'Who are you?' I asked, noting the white bands on their sleeves.

'We're the opposition. Who are you?'

'I'm a journalist. I want to interview your commander.'

A stocky soldier leapt forward and pointed his assault rifle at me: 'We don't recognize journalists. You've all sold out to Dudayev! Get out of here while you can!' he shouted.

Things weren't looking good for me, and I figured the best thing I could do was square up to him. At that time, an unarmed man could still dare to act tough in front of an armed Chechen. 'Look, you can see I've come unarmed. What, you think I'm frightened of you? Put down your gun and let's step over there if you want to discuss whether I've sold out,' I goaded him. Just then a man in uniform, aged about forty-five, came to my rescue, defusing the situation, which had been on the verge of exploding into a hail of gunfire.

'Aren't you ashamed of yourself, pointing your assault rifle at an unarmed man!' he chided my opponent. Then he spoke to me: 'Who are you? What do you want?'

'I am a journalist,' I repeated for the umpteenth time that day, as if it were a magic formula. 'I'd like to interview your commander. It's my job.'

'Sure.' He nodded. 'Wait here, I'll go and ask him.' My unexpected ally went off, while the stocky soldier threw me a hostile glance and fired a long burst towards the empty balcony of a nearby five-storey building. In response to his superior's disapproving stare, he said, 'I saw something move up there!' My new friend soon returned and told me to go with him to a kiosk that stood in the square. By a large crowd of soldiers there were two tanks with what I thought were Chechen flags on their turrets.

These flags threw me somewhat. At the time I didn't realize that the opposition flag consisted of red, white and red bars across a green background, while Chechnya's official state flag had bars of white, red and white, also across a green background. To me the flags looked identical. The front part of the gun turrets had been painted white. It turned out white was the Armed Opposition's identifying colour. A man in his mid-thirties sporting a luxuriant black moustache sat leaning against the kiosk. Barely responding to my greeting, he asked for my papers.

He looked at my ID. 'But you're one of Dudayev's journalists! You're not getting any interviews, now leave!'

'No, it's an independent newspaper,' I protested. This was an outright lie, but there was nothing else for it.

'Really? You're sure about that?' Upon hearing my affirmative answer, he consented. 'OK then, fire away. What do you want to know?'

'Could you start off by introducing yourself?'

'Tolstoy-Yurt Militia Commander Idris!' he barked, as though reporting to a superior officer.

'What was your objective in entering the city, and when do you plan to withdraw your men?'

'We aren't budging until Dzhokhar leaves. Now that's it!' he snapped.

'Do you think he will go?' I continued.

'He'll have to. His people hate him.'

'Which people?'

'The entire Chechen nation. Except the mafia, whom he's financing with the nation's petro-dollars. He's surrounded himself with mafiosi and thinks that the Chechen people are going to put up with it indefinitely!'

I wanted to probe: And why do you think the discontent of the Chechen people is so convenient to Russia? Why is this dis-content being nurtured with Russian money and Russian tanks? But instead – my survival instinct must have kicked in – I asked a standard question: 'In view of your profession, do you think war is the best way and the only way to help your beloved nation?'

'That's a question for the politicians. And indeed … If only Dzhokhar had listened …'

'Listened to whom?'

Here he became ill at ease, but he answered all the same: 'To us. We're the Chechen people too, you know. Look, I've told you the interview's over, but you keep asking questions! Ah, but maybe you're one of Dzhokhar's supporters?' he then said, eyeing me suspiciously.

I'd bargained on arousing suspicion, accepting it as a hazard of the job. So I calmly replied, 'I'm not on anyone's side, neither his nor yours. My profession requires neutrality.'

'Did you come here from the town centre?' he asked, more mildly.

'Yes.'

'What's been happening there?'

'Two tanks were hit.'

'We know about that … Did you see any other tanks?'

'Yes.'

'How many tanks? And how many men?'

'I didn't count them.'

'What make were the tanks?'

'Russian-issue military-industrial Mercedes!' I quipped. 'What makes do tanks come in?' I hadn't the foggiest notion of the different tank manufacturers and whether tanks even had makes. And despite the awkwardness of the situation, I was deeply affronted by his assumption that I'd willingly share information about their adversary if I'd had any. This was not yet my war, and I still hadn't taken sides. I was trying to remain an impartial observer.

Again I provoked a heated response: 'What, are you making fun of me?' the commander asked, while someone grabbed me by the shoulder. But once again my new ally came to my aid.

Apparently my naïvety had made an impression on him and, being a good-natured guy, he didn't want to see me die needlessly. 'Oh, he doesn't know one tank from another,' he intervened. 'See those ones?' he asked, pointing to the tanks in the square. 'Now, did the tanks you saw have the same shape turret or a different one?'

I told him that the turrets were as alike as two peas, although to this day I have no idea whether they were, in fact, the same. I was simply interested in seeing how they would react.

They became nervous. 'Are you sure?'

'I'm certain.'

'But they don't have any T-76s, they've only got T-65s.'

'Could it be Labazanov?[1] He has T-76s,' someone suggested.

I couldn't resist asking a question that in the circumstances was entirely unnecessary: 'If Labazanov is over there, then what are you doing here? Go and seize the Presidential Palace.'

'He isn't a journalist! He's an agent provocateur!' a voice called over my head. Someone's hand alighted on my shoulder and deeply hostile expressions came over the faces of the men around me, but again I was in luck. This time it was the commander who helped me. Probably because we had not yet learnt to spill the blood of our own civilians. A little later on, Chechens would start killing, and for much smaller misdemeanours, indeed just for the heck of it. At that time, though, the commander said, 'Leave him alone! He's not an agent provocateur. They're all like that …' He turned to me. 'You'd better find yourself some place to shelter. We're going to attack now, the fighting will start. No job, not even a journalist's, is worth that kind of risk.'

I saw he was right. The infantry of the Armed Opposition was going in to attack. They were advancing by bounds, in straggling columns, just like in the movies. I took cover in a nearby building, along with the other civilians who found themselves there, some by chance, others by choice. Given the jumpy nerves of the Armed Opposition soldiers as they grilled me, their restless

13

animosity, the excitability of their commander, as against the Chechen Army soldiers' composure and faith in their cause, I felt almost certain that the latter would emerge victorious. In this combat sector, at any rate. But at that time, I did not take victory or defeat (or indeed the battle itself) too seriously; it all felt like one of those war games we used to play as kids at Pioneer camp. The opposition infantry going into attack, the intense gunfire breaking out closer to the city centre – it felt like we'd stumbled on to the set of some Soviet war film. Everyone here felt the same elated thrill and privilege to be witnessing this. It was as if even the soldiers (who were products of the same school of Soviet patriotism) could not quite comprehend that there was going to be a battle and people would die.

Yet just a couple of hours later – far too soon for those rallying to topple the 'hated dictatorship' – the Armed Opposition were forced into a retreat which quickly turned into a rout. The tanks pulled out of the square, taking a few random parting shots at the Presidential Palace. The fighters of the Provisional Council (as the opposition styled their political body) abandoned several dead comrades and withdrew from Press House, where they had set up headquarters, under pressure from the advancing Chechen special forces. Hot on the heels of the retreating opposition forces, the Chechen special forces and Presidential Guard were now securing the square. A middle-aged man who'd been hit by a stray bullet was being treated by a Chechen Army doctor. There were as yet no corpses or blood to be seen.

3

Deciding that the operation to overthrow Dudayev had now ended, I turned back and headed for the city centre. As I was passing the Presidential Palace, I saw the same tank crew sitting on their tank. Their commander was saying into his radio, 'Four! Four! What's the situation?'

Through the hiss and crackle, I could hear a voice replying: 'We've got two of their tanks surrounded. We're telling them to surrender. They won't surrender.'

'Are you out of ammunition?'

'No, we've got ammunition. But we're hoping to avoid bloodshed.'

'Look, if they won't surrender, then take out their tanks and complete the operation!'

I enquired about the situation in the city.

'The enemy are retreating in all directions, we've taken lots of them prisoner. Luckily we've had far fewer losses than we might have expected,' he told me.

This news was reassuring, and I headed home with the blissful nonchalance common to newcomers to war. Filled with exhilaration from my bloodless adventure, and secretly rather pleased with myself for my interview scoop, I was walking along the platform at the station whistling the tune of a popular song when a girl called out to me. She was peering out of the window of a three-storey building overlooking the platform.

'Hey! Don't go that way! There are tanks!' she warned me.

'Tanks? But they're already leaving the city,' I told her confidently – but I was wrong. I had barely taken a couple more steps when two tanks came speeding around the corner, and one of them fired a round. The shell landed twenty paces from me (I went back and measured the paces later), but I was strangely lucky: it didn't explode, merely kicked up dust and chunks of tarmac. I don't know whether the tank gunner had decided to be merciful with the first round or it was just sheer good luck, but the shell turned out to be a dud. Almost at the very moment the tank fired, a hail of small-arms fire broke out. From nowhere some men from the Department for State Security sprang up behind me and they opened fire at the tanks. The tanks in turn began pelting all around with their heavy-calibre machine guns. And in the middle of this mayhem, numb with fear, I stood rooted to the spot.

To say I was frightened would be a lie: I wasn't just frightened, I was terrified out of my skin! I'd stumbled – for the first time in my life – straight into crossfire. Crushing fear paralysed me to the point where I could not move, let alone run. It felt as if everyone was aiming directly at me, and this was only made worse by the eerie whistling of bullets. All this was happening with unreal speed, but how strange is the human brain, nature's finest computer, for my mind captured every detail with amazing precision. 'Run over to us! If you don't move fast, you'll be killed!' the Department for State Security soldiers shouted to me. And to my utter surprise, I suddenly became calm. I couldn't understand why, but I had a wave of certainty: these tank gunners and soldiers were not going to kill me. It was as if I'd made telepathic contact with everybody firing and I'd understood no one would harm me. Of course in reality there was no telepathic contact. I'd simply found myself in a situation (as I realized later) where

I was faced with the choice: conquer your fear and stay alive, or surrender to it and die. Rather than fleeing for dear life, as most people in my place would have done, I spun round and quickly climbed down the railway embankment, taking cover behind the three-storey building. I chose to stay put not from any desire to act bravely – that was the last thing on my mind. No, I'd simply remembered that if you run during combat you'll be taken for a target. No sooner had I got behind the building than half the top floor was blown out by a round from the tank. Almost simultaneously a grenade launcher fired, knocking out the first tank, which was left to burn on the railway crossing, while the second tank made straight for the Department for State Security building. In an instant I transformed from frightened civilian to daredevil journalist. I climbed over the fence and ran down a parallel street in pursuit of the tank, although I could not explain to myself why I was chasing after it. I must have thought that was what I had to do, being a journalist and all …

It must have been the speed of the tank, which was too fast for me, that once again saved me from death. I'd run out into a square by the station where a market used to be held when I was stopped by the taut, drawn-out sound of an explosion. Instinctively dropping to the ground, I saw the massive gun turret of a tank rotating above me in slow motion. This turret gave me an incredible fright. It seemed as if it was about to fall straight on to my head. The daredevil journalist reverted to a terrified young man. Whirring shrapnel was sinking into the ground with heavy sighs, like weary travellers. Then deathly silence broke out. Some time elapsed before I heard voices and came out into the square. I was stunned by the scene that met me. The tank that a few minutes ago had failed to kill me had been transformed into something that defied imagination. The warhead from the RPG-7 had detonated the tank's own ammunition supply, which in turn had ripped its way through the hull, twisting the tank inside out. That had been the long, drawn-out explosion. And the turret had been torn clean off – that's what I had seen falling towards me. But it was not the mangled tank that threw me into a cold sweat – I'd already seen two that day. It was the sight of the corpses. Or rather of what remained of them. Seeing people who had died in war up close shook me so deeply that I lost all sense of reality. On a nearby tree hung naked human hips, unnaturally deformed, with pinkish-white bones jutting out of them. Around ten metres away lay a head that had been ripped off together with a piece of meat running down the spine, and from another tree innards were hanging. A bit further off lay an entire severed shoulder with lots of little chunks of flesh. The scene looked like a giant cannibal had decided to make lunch and had been chopping up plenty of meat. And the intolerable salty smell of blood fused with the smell of molten metal. Here was all that remained of people who'd been alive a few moments ago. I could not make sense of the nakedness of the corpses at the time; only later did I find out that the force of the blast completely strips people of clothing.

So all those Soviet war films had been nothing but lies. The hero had always died beautifully with a smile on his face and with time to bid farewell to his comrades. And the enemy had died ugly deaths, falling face down, arms and legs sprawled out like spiders. The soldiers here on both sides had been raised on the same films as I had. They too had believed in these beautiful wartime deaths. Some time later in the war, one such child of the school of Soviet patriotic cinema, a Chechen fighter, was wounded in combat. His injury was not life-threatening, but there was a lot of blood. Believing himself to be fatally wounded, the fighter decided to 'die beautifully'! To this end, he assumed a pose befitting the occasion, bade us farewell, smiled and lay motionless, waiting to meet death with a smile on his lips, just like in the movies. His plans were dashed by the doctor who suggested he 'get up and quieten yourself down, and save your pose for a more serious occasion.' The war would later make cynical combat professionals out of all these men, but at that time there was more romance and adventure than hatred or malice.

Here, however, I saw no beautiful deaths and no ugly ones. Just hunks of bodies that a moment ago had been living. Unlike the film heroes, these tank gunners hadn't had time to think their last thoughts, let alone bid anyone farewell. It was as if they had never even existed. A keen foreboding came over me that it would not be the last time I witnessed a scene like this – and that I'd better learn to handle it. But I never did. Because, unless you are a maniac, you can never learn to handle the sight of mangled corpses. I was jolted from my stupor by the sad and weary voice of a soldier: 'Hey, you'd better get out of here. There could be more tanks on the way.' I silently nodded and turned away.

Before long I met a large group of young people who, like me, were trying to escape from the combat zone. Despite being total strangers, we joined together and formed a long, colourful convoy of civilians, unprotected by camouflage, heading out via the railway depot towards Grozny's Oktyabr district. Soon – it was around lunchtime – a number of Russian ground-attack planes appeared in the sky. They must have wanted to survey the scene of combat, and spotting our brightly coloured convoy, mistook us for the enemy. Or maybe they knew perfectly well that we weren't combatants, but all the same one of the planes turned around and unleashed a long burst from its rapid-fire gun. Luckily, nobody was hit. In our naïvety, it simply hadn't occurred to us to disperse when the planes had appeared. After a while the planes departed, there was a lull in the shooting, and with a clean conscience I headed home. So now I had witnessed war: I had seen its blood and its corpses, I had heard small-arms fire and had even been fired at myself – or so it had seemed, at any rate. I was naïve, and didn't have the vaguest notion of what lay in store for me. Yet of all the horrible deaths I was destined to witness in this interminable and brutal war, the image that is seared deepest in my memory is the death of the tank gunners who just minutes earlier had almost killed me. Maybe because they were the first real wartime deaths that I witnessed – the first living people to be snuffed out by war, or perhaps it was because they hadn't killed me when I stood stock still in their tank's field of fire. Many moments from that day are etched in my memory as isolated fragments: the opposition infantry going into attack. The calm absorption of the Chechen special forces and the Presidential Guard. The excitability of the commander of the 'Tolstoy-Yurt Militia'. The three drunken men with Red Cross armbands sobbing, 'I don't want my people to die!' For some reason those three stood out as the most openhearted of everyone I saw that day. The woman with her two twin boys in her arms, fleeing from a building that had been set alight by a tank round. And the crowning touch: the ghastly episode with the deaths of the tank crew.

Arriving home, I switched on the television and was completely stunned. On the main Russian channel, the presenter was announcing, 'The Armed Opposition forces have taken control of Grozny with Ruslan Labazanov's troops seizing the Presidential Palace. But Dudayev loyalists are not ready to accept the situation, and we can expect an intense night ahead in Grozny, for they're sure to try to win back the city …' Events which I had witnessed myself were being presented as if exactly the reverse had occurred, and it all sounded so convincing that I even began to doubt my own eyes. Since they knew I worked as a journalist, my neighbours soon came round for 'the truth', and I told them openly about everything I had witnessed. They began angrily cursing the Russian media: 'Those lying parasites,' and they immediately went off to tell the whole neighbourhood the 'real truth, straight from our own Chechen journalist'. So the Russian government's disinformation campaign was an instant flop with our neighbours. Over the coming days we would discover what rules the Russian Army played by. Tanks began opening fire on residential areas of the city and civilians were killed in large numbers. Some tank men surrendered to the Chechens without a fight when they received orders to fire on residential buildings from which no one had been shooting. Almost every building in central Grozny suffered some degree of damage, with the Presidential Palace getting off the lightest; untouched by a single round, its windows were merely shattered.

4

At that time, along with plenty of Chechens, I supported neither Dudayev's government nor the opposition. I was an ordinary young guy, no different from thousands of others across the vast Soviet Union. I listened to Modern Talking and Abba, loved going to discos, where breakdancing was all the rage, and in my spare time I read books. Up until perestroika my life had been uneventful. I had gone to school, then college. Then came mandatory service in the Soviet Army, after which I got a job, studied at university and so on. It must have been my innate curiosity that led me into journalism, which I hadn't considered initially. Yet even as a journalist, I had little time for politics. Soviet ideology had the most amazing ability to disappoint the moment you opened your textbook, because of the glaring discrepancy between the official picture and the reality. People who earnestly believed the stories printed by the government press were considered soft in the head. It was only when the USSR's political processes were freed from Party control and things started moving in a new direction that I began to take an interest in politics. And then Chechnya declared independence, unleashing events that simply couldn't be ignored. Yet I always remained impartial and apolitical, as a journalist should. Following independence, Chechnya faced huge economic problems. These were to be expected for such a young state but they were also artificially fuelled by Russian interference. The Chechen people had more than their share of woes, and so the Chechen government faced mounting discontent. The majority of Chechens didn't regard Russia as an enemy state; they saw her at the time (as they still do now) as a country rich in culture, a country that would make a good neighbour. After all, they had imbibed not just their own cultural tradition, but Russia's too. Ordinary Chechens saw the clash between the opposition and the government as nothing more than the resentment of those left out in the cold after the division of revenue and power. But this one day turned thousands of neutral Chechens into ardent supporters of Dudayev. No matter how noble their intentions, the opposition had arrived under the aegis of a military that for centuries had been deployed against the Chechen people. Accepting assistance from an army reviled for decimating the Chechen nation every fifty years or so over the past few centuries was not the cleverest move. In securing the help of the Russian Army, the opposition committed a fatal blunder. And it was this, along with the Russians' indiscriminate targeting of civilians and the wanton cruelty of their soldiers, that turned many Chechens into supporters of Dudayev. The blatant lies of the Russian authorities, the killing of civilians, the bombing of homes – all this illustrated Russia's true intentions and methods so graphically that within days I too had gone from being a genuinely impartial journalist to a partisan witness to yet another – history was littered with them – Chechen tragedy.

We should give credit where credit is due; among the opposition leaders were honest men who sincerely desired prosperity for their homeland. But the following story reveals that there were other types too. The Chechen elders had by this point entered the political fray. A delegation of these elders decided to visit the home of one of the Armed Opposition leaders. In Chechen tradition, they wanted to entreat this man's father to talk some sense into his son before human blood was spilt in vain. The meeting took place and the father replied to the delegation that he'd be happy for his son to quit politics but the son had already invested too much money from his own pocket into this 'project' and he couldn't just drop everything without at least recouping his investment. So while for some the 'overthrow of the regime' was a matter of blood and death, others simply saw it as a profitable and cynical business venture.

By the evening of that first day, news had spread not only of the failure of the military operation, but of the wholesale collapse of Russia's Chechen policy. For President Yeltsin and Defence Minister Grachev[2] had formally renounced their own soldiers and officers captured in Chechnya, branding them deserters. Public interviews and addresses made by the Russian captives via the media to their command, in which they confirmed their military-unit numbers, the locations of their bases, and the recruitment methods of their counter-intelligence officers, were dismissed by Russian officials as 'lies and propaganda'. Defence Minister Grachev, meanwhile, got so carried away as to boast that he would never have made the mistake of sending tanks into Grozny: 'A single parachute regiment would have got the job done in two hours.' Just a few weeks later, of course, he himself would give the order to send tanks into the city, and we know how long it took for several army groups to capture Grozny. But for now Chechnya froze in uneasy suspense.

With the arrival of Sergey Yushenkov's[3] team of deputies to negotiate the release of the captured soldiers and officers, people began to nurture the hope that the conflict could be resolved through peace talks. But sadly their hopes were soon dashed. The government representatives in Moscow refused even to entertain the idea of negotiations with the Chechen side. Amid almost daily statements from Dudayev conveying his willingness to negotiate, Russia's preparations for the approaching conflict were steaming ahead. Russian politicians had pretensions to being Roman senators, seeing Russia as the Third Rome; their approach to Chechnya was that 'Carthage must be destroyed'. Sergey Shakhray, the Russian deputy prime minister at the time and an ardent opponent of negotiating with the Chechen side, actually used this phrase of Cato the Elder during a television interview. The Chechens too were quietly preparing as far as their modest capabilities allowed. The inevitability of all-out war was palpable. The rounds of discussions, the march for peace organized by the residents of Chechnya and Ingushetia, the Duma deputies' promises to 'prevent bloodshed' – all this was seen as the inevitable overture to the coming tragedy. And then the tragedy began.

5

On 11 December 1994, three Russian Army columns – 23,000 men according to the official Russian Ministry of Defence figures, although independent sources suggest 60,000 – crossed the border into Chechnya. They were subsequently redeployed into four columns: Group North, Group North-East, Group West and Group East.

Two days later, I set off with a party of Chechen, Russian and foreign journalists for the village of Pervomaysky,[4] which lay right on the front line. We left in a bus graciously provided by the President's press centre. A small group of armed men in uniform also loaded into the bus – for our protection, we were told. We arrived at the site and, brushing off the warnings of the Chechen fighters, we naïvely walked almost to the first defence line. By that point I quite seriously considered myself a battle-scarred veteran war correspondent, and I was acting the part. My confident manner and my use of the odd military term impressed some of my colleagues, further bolstering my self-image as an old hand and encouraging the other journalists to stick close by me. We left the bus and walked on ahead until suddenly we found ourselves in the first line of Chechen trenches; the Russian troops were just over a kilometre away. Their main force was on the mountain ridge, but as soon as we got to the trenches, the forward infantry and tanks slowly began to move downhill. It was as if the whole scene had been specially set up for journalists wishing to photograph real combat. The Chechen fighters were sitting in trenches, slightly ahead of them were two crews with automatic grenade launchers, and behind the trenches stood a few Chechen tanks. A soldier stuck his head out of a tank and addressed us: 'Anyone here a tank gunner?'

'No, we're journalists,' I replied on our behalf. 'Why, what's wrong?'

'We've got no gunner for this tank. I'll have to stand in as one, but I'm not a gunner by training,' he explained amiably.

'Sorry we can't help you,' I said. After my experience on 26 November, neither love nor money could have persuaded me to climb into a tank. At that point firing broke out, and the soldier told us to run for it as he disappeared into the hatch. The bombardment rose to a horrific pitch. The advancing Russian tanks were firing, the Chechen tanks were returning fire, and in the spaces between was the thumping of the automatic grenade launchers, all accompanied by assault-rifle and machine-gun fire. I sat in the trench with the militiamen. Little remained of the 'battle-hardened veteran', but I tried desperately not to betray my fear. It is hard to believe that very soon this terrified young man would become almost indifferent to gunfire and shelling of far greater intensity. And a little later still, he would be living his life under conditions that would seem completely unfit for humans. Now the Russians were firing furiously. The air was thick with the whistle of bullets and the whirring of shrapnel. As if in mockery of my fear, I found myself right next to a deafening tank. I had, of course, 'seen combat', but I wanted like mad to jump up and flee for dear life. Such a rush of adrenalin came to my legs that it felt as if I could outrun even the bullets. It seemed impossible that anyone could withstand such intense fire. But these fighters had no thoughts of fleeing, whereas I could think of nothing else. Two things were holding me back from such an act of craziness: the fear of poking my head above the trench to make a dash for it and my self-respect. After all, I was a 'veteran', and it would be unseemly for me to panic. Although this second argument was clearly preposterous, I'd come up with it for my own consolation. To make matters worse, it seemed as if I was the only one struck by panic. This was nothing like our games of war, so beloved among us when we were little boys. If anyone tells you that in a moment of fear he thought of a loved one, don't believe it. He didn't. He thought of no one but himself. In fact, he wouldn't have had any thoughts at all. Fear is your mind's survival signal. This instinct is concerned with you alone. At such moments, it simply doesn't enter your head to be frightened for some other person. All my fear was focused purely on me – on my beloved self.

The Chechen resistance were successful in repulsing the attack. On the slope of the ridge, two Russian tanks and an infantry combat vehicle were left burning – the work of the tank man who wasn't a gunner by training. One of the automatic-grenade-launcher crew had died in combat, and the grenade launcher itself had been hit. Around half a dozen men were wounded to varying degrees. When the fighting was over, I looked around to find that the journalists, the bus, and our armed escorts had all fled. This helped to soothe my injured pride: so I hadn't been the only one gripped with fear. Only one Russian journalist and a young Chechen had stayed. We started walking away from the front line. Soon some aeroplanes appeared, dropped their bombs and disappeared over the ridge. Moments later some Grad multiple-rocket launch vehicles drove out from somewhere, fired several volleys towards the ridge where the Russian units were dug in, and slunk back to their hiding places in the nearby garages and farms. No sooner had they hidden than several ground-attack planes emerged from behind the ridge. They circled the skies, searching in vain for their targets, then they bombed the outskirts of the village and left. Hot on their heels, the Grad vehicles re-emerged from their shelters for a new volley of fire. And this went on for almost the whole day: the Grad vehicles would fire at the ridge and vanish, the planes would search for them, fail to find them, then drop their bombs on some decoys and fly off again. In the evening, some men who'd noticed we were missing from the group and had set out in search of us finally tracked us down at the trenches near the village. Our runaway comrades were a little surprised to see us back at the press centre, but we did not give them a hard time for their very human response to such an unexpected and inhuman situation.

Following three weeks of fierce fighting, the army was closing in on the capital. The city had long been under bombardment; the Russian Air Force pilots had total dominance in the air, and they had tried every possible method of bombing Grozny. On the night of 31 December 1994, the majority of the fighters defending the capital had been discharged for New Year's Eve. The city had been left with a small but battle-worthy group, which included two of the Chechen Army's most effective units: Hamzat Gelayev's[5] special-forces regiment and Shamil Basayev's[6] Abkhaz Battalion, a volunteer force formed in 1992 to assist Abkhazia. I'd been working tirelessly for a good many days: I'd been at a rally that had disbanded just before New Year's Eve; I'd been at the front line; and, alongside journalists from a number of Russian and foreign news agencies, I'd been meeting various ranks of military and political functionaries. There had been little time for relaxing and thinking about mundane matters. And so on the evening of New Year's Eve I'd decided to give myself a well-earned rest and was sitting at home in front of the television (thankfully our power station had not been blown up). But there was to be no rest for me that night.

Countless words have been written about the New Year assault on Grozny. And each side has advanced its own version of events. The Chechen command, of necessity – as this was a war not just for freedom, but for the right to live on their own land – milked the most graphic aspects of the assault for propaganda purposes; in the process, they were able to spin their mistakes into a deliberate strategy. The truth is that Grozny had been left poorly defended on New Year's Eve. Even though in the first days of the assault the Chechens smashed the Russians with minimal losses, nevertheless the Russian forces gained a foothold at various points on the city fringes, and this accelerated Grozny's fall. The Russian generals – those who participated in the storm and those who didn't – later came out with ever more absurd explanations for their failure to take Grozny. The best excuse that Gennady Troshev[7] could come up with was to announce to the whole country, 'We hadn't expected such resistance on the part of the Chechens. After all, they were up against a proper army!' – though the events of 26 November had clearly hinted at what was to come. Yet the truth was the Russian generals sent their troops to storm the capital without even equipping them with detailed maps or proper intelligence. They'd hurried the operation because Grachev had wanted to celebrate the New Year with Grozny's capture. And the generals had wanted to hand Grachev the city as a present on his birthday, 1 January. The Russian press wrote so at the time. The Chechen command had known that sooner or later an attack was coming, but they hadn't expected it on the night of 31 December, and they had no multi-layered defence system, as the bungling Russian generals said and as my account of that night's events will bear out. On these pages you won't find the parroting of either side's views; you'll find the account of an eyewitness, with what may seem, at times, like too many fine details. But because this is an eyewitness account and not an analysis, such detail is inevitable, for when someone is caught in the thick of things, it is the details he relies on to build his picture of what is happening.

6

It was around noon when I heard the Chechen television presenter's voice through the crackle: 'Everyone out there! Everyone out there! Whoever is listening! Russian troops are storming Grozny! The Presidential Palace is surrounded! Everyone out there! Everyone out there! Russian troops are storming Grozny! The Presidential Palace is surrounded!' The Presidential Palace was indeed surrounded: clearly the Chechens had been taken by surprise, though they did later manage to break the encirclement. As the Russian special forces closed in on the palace, they were met by a surprise barrage of Chechen fire from just fifteen metres away. Up until then the Russians had been moving under a smoke screen, but at the last minute a gust of wind had blown in from the Sunzha (the river that cuts through central Grozny, with the Presidential Palace on one bank), sweeping away the smoke and sealing the battle's outcome. Yet even if the Russian special forces had stormed the palace successfully, who knows how the assault might have ended. Later, their special forces stormed many Chechen-held buildings, only to retreat from them with heavy losses.

I was walking towards the railway station with some journalists and a group of Chechen fighters we'd run into when we stumbled into a horrific firefight. Two of the fighters were killed on the spot. The Chechen Army units were engaged in the first serious clash with the Russian armada of tanks. We were witnessing the beginning of the famed demise of the Russian Army's tragic 131st Maikop Brigade, who were trapped at the station. Later, when the brigade was fully encircled, a battle erupted in which both sides fought impeccably, shining examples of valour. We could clearly hear the voices of Chechen fighters calling on the Russians to surrender and of Russian soldiers trying to keep their spirits up.

'Don't send your lads to their deaths, Commander! Surrender, we have you surrounded! If you give yourselves up, we guarantee you'll live. And we'll help you return home!'

'I have orders!'

'I don't have the authority to make decisions like that!'

'Vasily! Let's fight to the death! The Chechens will only kill us anyway!'

These shouts reached us from the area of the depot held by the Russians. All these exchanges, the groans of the wounded, the smell of gunpowder – they evoked in me a feeling of … Perhaps it was impending doom?

By now groups of resistance fighters were fast making their way from every corner of the republic to help defend the capital. Each came armed as best he could: some had an entire arsenal of state-of-the-art small arms, some were armed with a hunting rifle, or a single hand grenade, or a petrol bomb, while others had no weapon at all. On the roads into Grozny, signs announcing 'Welcome to Hell!' proved prophetic. The militiamen armed themselves to the teeth with trophy weapons taken from the Russians and, without the least training in the theory of warfare, they became a genuine nightmare for the Russians.[8] According to the official figures,[9] in the space of twenty-four hours on 1 January 1995 in Grozny 1,426 Russian military servicemen were killed and 4,630 wounded. But you have to remember that armies traditionally hugely under-report their losses. As well as the 131st Brigade, almost the entire contingents of the 81st and

74th Motor Rifle Regiments and the 276th Brigade were taken out. The units were virtually annihilated. The Chechen fighters knew every last alley of their capital like the back of their hand, which is critical in urban combat. But their adversary was by no means weak. The Russian Army may have already been a piteous shadow of its former self – once one of the world's mightiest militaries – but it remained one of Europe's finest armed forces. And its officers, particularly the mid-ranking ones, fighting on the front line alongside their soldiers, were imbued with the spirit of the Soviet Army. You won't hear stories of mass cowardice on the part of the Russians except from people whose knowledge of the war comes merely from hearsay. I myself witnessed them on several occasions during the assault showing true martial prowess and bravery. The very fact that they secured several sites within the city bounds attests to their strength and courage as opponents. Later, on the television, I saw shots of Grozny filmed by journalists: all was white snow and the Chechen fighters in their white camouflage suits. It really was like that. But that came later. On that first and most horrific night there was no snow. Just black earth – as if soaked with grief and horror at the nightmare to come – and above it, a black sky hung low. It was strange and terrible to see a southern city at one o'clock in the afternoon almost entirely cloaked in darkness, as if the city were trying to hide its defenders. Daylight could not penetrate the vast storm cloud of black smoke that covered the burning city. And in this gloom the only way to see anything at all was to crouch down below the hanging smoke.

7

Modern man, raised on the ideals of goodness and compassion to all beings, aware of the sanctity of life, naïvely assumes that he's frightened of blood and the sight of it will make him queasy. Yet he is deluding himself. It is only when you find yourself in a situation where death and blood are as natural as life itself that you realize that anyone can cope with the sight of blood – and if you can't, then something is wrong with you. What's more, the sight of fresh blood awakens man's primordial instincts, boosting his chances of surviving in extreme circumstances. For it is no coincidence that the nations of antiquity, accustomed to fighting in close combat, survived and thrived and even created great civilizations in conditions which would be fatal for most people today. When man is faced with a situation where there is only one law, one instinct, 'Kill or be killed, if you want to survive,' he takes a leap backwards into the psychology of his ancestors, and all talk of the sanctity of life seems like a dim memory of something beautiful but unreal. Obeying an ancient instinct, he tries to survive by killing his own kind. The only difference is that the warrior – a sacred class – will kill only warriors, whereas a coward will try to wipe out everyone, anything that breathes, life itself, because the worm of a tremendous fear is gnawing at his heart, making him wantonly cruel. Once you have cultivated a calm, philosophical approach to death, you start to view blood and corpses as mundane, humdrum even. And when that happens, the only thing that can save you is a deep, sincere faith in God – and it doesn't matter which God, or even whether it is God at all you believe in, so long as your belief is sincere and is not a belief in Evil, otherwise you'll become a slave to instinct. It is instinct that helps you survive, but faith is what keeps you from turning into a beast, what helps you stay human. If you give yourself up to instinct without faith, you'll soon turn into an animal, while if you nurture only faith without instinct, you'll end up a crazed fanatic. Our ancient ancestors began praying to stones and trees not from boredom, and not because they were terrified of unexplained natural forces, as we were taught in our Soviet schools, but to preserve their distinction from the animals which served them as food.

Although when you see human bodies ripped apart, corpses mashed by the treads of tanks, when you see dogs and cats feeding on the remains of people who only yesterday were just as alive as you … When you know that tomorrow a stray dog might come down the street gripping your severed arm in its jaws – after all, you've already seen dogs carrying other people's arms … When you're washing your shoe and suddenly realize with a shudder you're rinsing away human blood … When you have to nudge somebody's severed head aside with your foot to avoid stepping on it … then it becomes horribly hard, almost impossible to remain a human being, to preserve your faith in God. It is terribly difficult to get used to the horrific smell of corpses that lingers in the air. No, not the stench of decaying bodies, for it is winter. Rather, the unique, indescribable smell of corpses. That smell will haunt you for the rest of your life. You will dream of it far more often than all your other dreams of the war. And each time it will jolt you from your sleep and you'll wake up in a cold sweat with a foreboding of something dreadful. Something beyond the bounds of what is human. Speaking of dogs brings to mind the story of one of the Chechen fighters, a friend of mine, a poet and artist who lay wounded for several days in the ruins of the Petroleum Institute until he was found by his comrades.

'Well, I was unable to move, and there were feral dogs circling and waiting. Waiting for me to stop stirring ... And the most horrible thing wasn't that I might get gangrene in my wound, it wasn't Death breathing near me. It was the repulsive stench of dogs that had tasted human flesh. And what you fear more than anything is not death ... No, you are terrified of falling unconscious. Because you know that if you fall unconscious you'll be killed. You won't die in battle. You'll die through being eaten alive by dogs. When I tried shooting at them, they ran off a bit, but they wouldn't leave, they knew I had no way out. I was their catch. I know that for Muslims there's no greater sin than suicide ... But I decided to save the last round in my gun. For myself. I believe God would have forgiven me my sin. What kept me from doing it was hope. The hope of being buried in the earth, rather than in the stomachs of dogs.'

It is the knowledge that faith alone can save you from turning into a fiend that forces you to believe, and the more horrific the picture, the fiercer your faith. Of course, you could always use drugs and alcohol to numb yourself into a state of oblivion where only one feeling is left: hatred of the enemy. That's what many of the Russian soldiers did. According to one Russian officer, every single soldier was issued Sydnocarb[10] pills. But that would simply have turned you into a vicious and cowardly beast. You'd have been a zombie, unable to take your own decisions.

So, abstaining from synthetic stimulants, you wander like a ghost through the ruins of your capital city, begging God to save your mind. You witness the ferocious close combat between Chechen fighters and the Russian special forces storming a building. And you realize that during this moment, this lethal encounter, no fighter can ever remember what his trainers in hand-to-hand combat taught him. They won't remember in whose name and for what reason they are fighting; they'll have no thoughts of their soldierly duty; they remember neither God nor the Devil, and it is not the best fighter who survives but the one with the greatest desire to live, the one whose life force is the strongest. Those whose genetic memory has endowed them with more defiance of death are the ones who will survive. And the abundance of blood and corpses everywhere only intensifies your desire to avoid becoming dead meat yourself.

There was one other path out of this hell: to flee the combat zone, which was easy enough for the Chechens to do; those that stayed were all fighting of their own free will. Indeed, some Russians and Chechens did flee, and it would be heartless to condemn them for it, but that was not the way of the warrior. And so, in this city, the finest warriors of this once-united great country came together in lethal battle. A battle from which no one could emerge as victors or vanquished; merely as survivors or corpses. A battle where to survive meant victory: victory not over the adversary, but over death. And which side would eventually gain control of these ruins may have mattered to the politicians and the Russian generals, but it didn't to the combatants. There were sites which would change hands four or five times in a day. No one here was fighting for the Russian Constitution any more than they were fighting for the city. The Russians were fighting for the right to stay alive, while the Chechens were fighting for all the former generations who had fallen in combat against this Empire; they were fighting for all those who had been unable to retaliate during the period from 1944 to 1959;[11] they were battling with Death for Life itself. And the battle was brutal and majestic; it was a hymn to human courage and valour.

Since the days of Peter the Great, the leadership of the Russian Army had been wont to bombard its enemies with the corpses of its finest sons, and now in Chechnya it held true to this tactic. The generals inundated the city with the corpses of its soldiers and the carcasses of burnt-out vehicles. While thousands of Russian soldiers and officers were dying in Grozny, a song by Oleg Gazmanov[12] called 'Officers' was playing on the radio day and night (I have hated his songs ever since); it included the words, 'Officers, officers, your hearts are in the crosshairs, for Russia and for freedom, to the bitter end.' This song rang out like a sardonic Satanic requiem for the thousands of dead soldiers pulverized by the tracks of their own tanks, torn limb from limb, devoured by feral dogs. Meanwhile, the city began to resemble the set of an apocalyptic horror film.

8

It was staggering to see the attitude of the Russian command towards the corpses of their own soldiers. These were young men who had fulfilled their duty to the homeland honourably, and they were hardly to blame if their country had been taken over by a band of traitors and misanthropes. The Chechens appealed to the Russians many times proposing a few days' truce for the sole purpose of clearing the soldiers' corpses from the streets of the city. The Russian generals, though, in their infinite wisdom, decided that this was a ploy by Dudayev to buy time to reposition and they rejected the offer. Yet the dead, whatever their nationality or faith, no matter what they were fighting for, by virtue of their death had fully exonerated themselves before the living. A man who has beheld God's great mystery ahead of you cannot be guilty before you. Only a coward who doesn't have it in him to face his fate in open combat could dishonour an enemy corpse. Yet the Russian authorities dishonoured the corpses of their own soldiers.[13] Rest in peace, boys! You fell on the battlefield and you are free of blame. This battle has reconciled its fallen fighters with the world and with one another. In pagan times, the Chechens had an ancient custom: whenever there fell in battle sixty-three of the enemy (a number that was sacred to the Nakh),[14] the last enemy corpse would be stood on its head. This was a signal to the enemy: 'Sixty-three of your warriors have been slain. Perhaps it's time for us to pause and bury the dead?' The ancient Nakh tribes believed that leaving sixty-three dead warriors unburied on the battlefield would invoke the wrath of the heavens upon the earth. By standing the sixty-third corpse upside down, they hoped to trick the heavens and at the same time send a sign to the enemy. So, from the viewpoint of ancient Nakh philosophy, Russia should have been struck by the sacred number of sixty-three major calamities for this abomination. Russia should have invoked the wrath of the heavens.

Even in this dead world, swathed in winter's shroud, where the only living creatures were the combatants and the dogs grown fat on human flesh, life could still be discerned. Life lurked timid, deep below the earth but stubbornly clinging on. One moment a woman would run quickly down the ruined street carrying a water canister; the next, a man's sallow face would appear for a minute, shyly checking out 'the situation in the city', as though he lived not in the city but somewhere deep in the countryside. I remember two colourful characters, a Chechen and a Russian. Sitting in the courtyard of a wrecked five-storey building with an open bottle of vodka and a jar of pickled tomatoes, in the company of a giant Caucasian sheepdog, they posed excitedly for my camera: 'For the journalist, for posterity.' They united in cursing the attacking forces and Boris Yeltsin for starting this 'colonial war'; they vowed to unleash the sheepdog on the Russian soldiers 'if our side runs out of ammunition and the Russians reach us'. And they wanted me to get their photo into some newspaper or magazine, for some reason deciding, 'Best choice would be *Forbes*, of course.' What became of them I don't know – chances are they unleashed the sheepdog on some soldiers and all three were shot dead, but their carefree candour left a deep impression on me. Then there was the old man feeding his hens to the thunder of guns and the drone of attack planes. One very uplifting scene was vividly seared in my memory. It happened in

January 1995 when the battle for the capital had reached its peak. The relentless roar of guns was echoing through the city. You were wearily walking through the streets of the devastated city when you saw a remarkable scene. A young guy around the same age as you was standing on the street corner with two very striking girls. They had slim, elegant figures with classically beautiful faces. One was blonde with deep-blue eyes, the other had raven hair and a limpid expression. Meanwhile ground-attack planes were whining overhead, flying so low that you could make out the figures of the pilots in the cockpits. They were not just doing air reconnaissance of the warring city, they were pounding it with missiles and fire from their aircraft guns. But these three seemed oblivious. They were chatting quietly and laughing, artlessly, gaily. A woman walked past carrying water and, seeing them, she remarked, 'How happy you look!' But they didn't hear her. You realized that this guy must have left his post defending the city (this was clear from his attire) and come to see these girls. And stifling their natural fear of death, the girls were standing with him under this blitz and laughing. They knew that this moment might perhaps save their friend's life when he has nothing left to keep him going. Like the daughters of Dadi-Yurt,[15] who, on the day their village was destroyed, performed a last dance for their menfolk defending the doomed village to the roar of Yermolov's[16] guns. Overcome by what you saw, you declared, 'As God is my witness! As long as our women can laugh in the face of death, our people will remain unconquerable!'

'Brother, you're right!' laughed the guy.

Of course there were looters, too, who plundered the ruins and the houses that still stood. The Chechen soldiers and militiamen executed them as mercilessly as they shot the man-eating dogs, but, like all evils, they were ineradicable. There was also the occasional lone drug addict roaming the streets.

I remember one I'd often encountered in this part of the city before the war. He was small and dark-haired and he used to wander about the market quietly in search of something sweet. Soft-hearted women-traders would give him free chocolate. I last saw him in January 1995. His bare feet were in slippers, he'd covered his naked body with tracksuit trousers and a jacket, and he was shivering fiercely from the cold as he walked down the devastated street. What brought him to mind was his death, which came later, in February. By then the occupation of the city was complete. In full view of passers-by, Russian OMON (Special Designation Police Detachment) paramilitaries had been savagely beating a Chechen boy of around fifteen. The entire time they were beating the boy, the swarthy drug addict was studying them in silence, spellbound. The paramilitaries knew he was a drug addict and they paid him no attention. That night he slipped into their quarters with a knife. The city had no electricity and so it was dark indoors. How he managed to steal into the badly damaged building remains a mystery. He must have known every last alley of that district, where he'd lived all his life – drug addicts usually know all the hidden nooks and corners in their locality. Once inside, he plunged the knife into the first paramilitary he encountered. He managed to knife two or three more before the petrified OMON were woken by the screams of their comrades and opened fire randomly in the pitch dark. They killed and wounded more than twenty of their own before they realized what was happening. The junkie was taken alive. After they'd tied him up, beaten him viciously and promised him 'the most horrible death ever invented', his adversaries began gathering their dead and wounded. At that point a seasoned colonel walked up and shot him once in the heart, quickly and painlessly. He handed the corpse over to the Chechen women: 'Bury him decently. He may have lived like a bum. But he died like a man.' Unfortunately his name is lost from my memory.

It was not easy to tell the attackers' positions from the friendly ones. There was no front line as such, battles were raging across the whole city and the districts which the Russian troops could not push through were being pounded night and day. Sometimes Chechen soldiers would pass with convoys of Russian prisoners.

I often wondered why the Chechens favoured death over captivity whereas the Russian soldiers were surrendering in droves. There were reports that on just one day, 26 November 1994, seventy Russian privates and officers surrendered, while among the Armed Opposition fighters the number was still higher: 200 men. Later in December of that year an entire squadron of Russia's elite Spetsnaz GRU (the special forces of the Main Intelligence Directorate of the General Staff) surrendered, all forty-eight men. Yet when thirty-three Chechen Army fighters encircled near the village of Alkhan-Kala[17] were invited to surrender, they replied with fire and were killed to a man. It was only later that I understood why, and it certainly wasn't because every last Chechen rebel was a fearless warrior who sneered at death and spurned the shame of captivity, as the propaganda would have us believe. Among the Chechen fighters you came across all sorts, as in any conflict, though the vast majority of volunteers taking up arms were genuine patriots and courageous warriors. No, the roots of this phenomenon went far deeper. The fact is that when a Russian soldier gave himself up into captivity, he hoped not to be executed or tortured. President Dudayev had outlawed the torture and abuse of prisoners. There were, of course, cases where captured Russian soldiers were summarily executed, and I certainly wouldn't wish to idealize all the Chechen resistance fighters. Humanity has never been short of monsters. But among the Chechen resistance such cases were in the absolute minority and never found sympathy or support among the population or the army command. Quite the reverse, the Chechen command widely employed a policy of returning captured soldiers to their mothers. This was done, of course, in the interests of propaganda, but for the soldiers released, that hardly mattered. But a Chechen fighter taken captive stood no chance of being treated with even the basic clemency usually shown to prisoners of war.

Chechen militiamen were able to capture the elite GRU troops in mid-December 1994 because the landing of this Russian reconnaissance and sabotage unit had been badly bungled. They were dropped into an area where they were completely unable to operate effectively; to reach the nearest road connecting the highlands with the capital they would have had to pass through villages where people were going without sleep day and night because of the war. And even if they had made it to the road, they'd have been powerless to stop the movement of Chechen militia forces, as there were dozens of alternative routes. The militiamen had stopped using the main highways ever since the Russian planes began zeroing in on them. What's more, no pre-mission intelligence had been gathered about the landing site or the area covered by the operation. So the Russians relied for intelligence entirely on data from Armed Opposition fighters, who in turn gathered this data from rumours that were growing ever more fantastical. And their command had left the unit with virtually no support on the ground. Two peasants, who had gone out to the woods to fetch firewood, discovered the Russian unit by chance. The special forces captured and held the peasants, but some local people came out in search of the missing villagers and found the unit. Alerted to the Russians' presence, around fifteen militiamen turned up from the nearest villages of Komsomolskoye and Alkhazurovo.[18] Without having the haziest idea what kind of unit this was or the number of soldiers in it, the militiamen closed in on the special forces and proposed they surrender. The militiamen told the Russians that they were surrounded, that they had several snipers, and that the Abkhaz Battalion, which never took prisoners, was on its way. They were bluffing, of course, but engaging in combat with this unit would have meant certain death. Among the militiamen was a professional hunter; he killed a couple of members of the unit with two clean shots to the head when they tried to open fire. Whereupon the Russian special forces accepted the militiamen's story and everything was sewn up. State-of-the-art weapons were seized that hitherto had been shrouded in secrecy. There was so much booty that it had to be loaded up on carts. When the commander of the unit saw who had captured them, he wept with mortification.

9

For the first three days of the assault the incessant flashes and the roar of guns made sleep impossible. But with time I got used to it and learnt to sleep like a baby to the thunder of gunfire. To unwind I would go to a nearby cellar, which the owner and his two elderly neighbours were using as living quarters. They had remained in the city to guard their homes from looters. This trio left an indelible impression on me. It was a complete mystery how these unarmed men planned to shield their houses from the looters, who were frequently armed, and indeed from the Russian soldiers. Happily, though, all three survived and later made it safely out of the captured city. They were often to be found in the cellar with a bottle of something warming, which they drank with sour faces giving toasts 'to victory'. 'We don't usually drink,' they told me, 'but here we have to tackle the stress.' One of the trio found the bombardments terrifying: the mortar attacks and tank rounds, any kind of weapon frightened him. He preferred sitting in the cellar. But his lively elder comrade would pull rank and was constantly sending him out of the cellar on errands. The younger man would protest that he was trying to get him killed, but the elder comrade would say, 'Your problem is that you let your fear walk ahead of you. But it's you who should walk ahead of your fear.' From time to time they would offer me – to help with the stress – a drink of some liqueur or wine from their stash (one had a wife who traded in alcohol before the war). They would pull long faces when I refused and shake their heads. 'If you can cope with all this stone sober, you must be a strong man,' they would say, in an attempt at admiration, although judging by their eyes they considered me terminally mad. Indeed, there were moments when I came close to agreeing with their unspoken opinion of me. During an air raid, one of the men's homes was hit by a bomb, but he decided to remain with his two comrades 'for company', as he explained. All we had to eat were jars of tomatoes pickled in brine, unaccompanied by bread or anything else. The salty tomatoes caused intolerable thirst, but there was no water. We lived on these preserved tomatoes for so long that I've been unable to abide the sight of them ever since. Some time later, an item of great luxury was added to our diet: pigeons. Untold numbers of them appeared in the city. Or perhaps they had always lived there but we'd never noticed. The neighbours caught them with ingenious snares. What cruel irony: the emblem of peace became food for the pale shadows of former men who found themselves at war, once again confirming my theory about the might of man's instincts.

Sometimes, amid a rare lull in the fighting, it was even possible to wash, with water heated on a small kerosene stove. We obtained water for basic hygiene and drinking from melted snow. Even after boiling it five times, the smell was revolting and it was undrinkable, but somehow we drank it. And the effect of washing with it was more psychological than sanitary. You could comfort yourself that the human urge for cleanliness had not died in you. It meant you were still of lucid mind, you had not become an animal. I remember I had a snow-white scarf from my life before the war, now so distant and unreal; it was the only white item in my wardrobe. I'd never managed to change out of what I'd been wearing when the assault began. And I became unhealthily obsessed with preserving the whiteness of this scarf. No doubt I had gone a bit barmy in these extreme conditions. Rationally I understood that it couldn't be done in a city where even the snow fell grimy with the soot of gunpowder residue, but for me the cleanliness of at least one piece of clothing served as proof I was still of sound mind. A similarly sacred meaning was given to the poor imitation – for you could never actually wash off that smell of soot – of bathing in the frost.

Over the first few days of the assault I listened intently to the news on my portable radio. But observing the huge discrepancy between the reports on the news and actual events in Grozny, I stopped listening. And whenever they broadcast classical music and their regular programmes, it sounded like voices beamed from another planet. Everything that existed beyond the boundaries of this small piece of land seemed like an inane television show where people merely acted out their roles till the day they dropped dead. Real life existed only on this patch of the planet, because here you were vividly aware of each second of life granted to you by fate. Here, each breath might be your last and for that reason each breath was bursting with life. Here, each moment lived was filled with the most profound sense of purpose. Life here was real.

After a month of bitter fighting, at the end of January 1995, it was time for the Chechen defenders to retreat from the city. Yet it was the Russian Army, with General Grachev at the helm, that had conclusively lost the battle for Grozny, just as Marshal Zhukov in his time had lost the battle of Berlin. The victor on the battlefield is not the side that wins control of a particular territory (which sooner or later will fall to the numerical majority, as happened in Grozny), but the side that inflicts the greatest damage on their opponent while sustaining the fewest losses themselves. In the battle for Grozny, the losses on the Russian side simply bore no comparison with those on the Chechen side. And perhaps the only people not to understand this (or who made a pretence of not understanding) were the Russian soldiers hoisting their flag over the ruins of the Presidential Palace and taking their pictures against its backdrop; the Russian President and the Minister of Defence handing out decorations to those men who'd survived the bloodbath; and the team of craven officials whose howls of delight filled the chambers of the Kremlin. The entire civilized world shuddered upon seeing the price Russia had paid, and what's more without even bargaining, for a city that had little strategic value in a war without front lines.

I slept right through the Chechen fighters' withdrawal from the city. Along with three resistance fighters with whom I wasn't acquainted, I was resting in some cellar when we awoke to the thud of boots and the voices of Russian soldiers entering the yard looking for loot. Our cellar had been cleverly camouflaged: it was under a lean-to and the top of the trapdoor had been concreted over, as had the ground below the lean-to. Unless you were inspecting the area closely, you would have been hard pressed to notice it. The soldiers who'd come to steal just gave the place a cursory scan, and that alone is the reason we weren't discovered. Of course, if it had been not the regular infantry but 'the Dogs', a special squad from the Interior Ministry, out on a 'cleansing operation', they would have found us fast and killed us just as quickly. But at the time we didn't even know that 'the Dogs' existed, and so we decided to stay put until dusk. Having decided to flee the occupied city, we emerged from the cellar. We were kitted out with just enough weaponry for an honourable death. The militiamen had assault rifles with a small supply of bullets, an anti-tank hand grenade, a single-use RPG-18 'Mukha' type anti-tank rocket launcher and two anti-personnel hand grenades each. As a civilian in a peaceful profession, I was armed more simply: with a hunting knife and an antipersonnel grenade – to blow myself up should the need arise, but the need to perform this heroic deed did not arise. The idea of surrendering didn't enter our heads, and had we been discovered, the natural outcome would have been death. There had been no snow for a long time, and every few minutes the entire city would be lit up by bright flashes, from the masses of illumination rounds fired by terrified Russian soldiers. There was a continuous rumbling overhead, and from time to time the planes too would shower the city with parachute flares. There were so many of these flares, on top of the illumination rounds from the ground, that the greater part of the city remained well lit. After their chastening experience of enemy night attacks, the Russian Army was feeling deeply unnerved, each moment expecting to hear the Chechen war cry, 'Allahu Akbar!' heralding death. Whenever the illumination rounds flashed, we dropped to the ground, thus losing much of the night during our exit from the city. Dirty and fatigued, we finally made it out and by dawn we had reached Urus-Martan, a small town around thirty kilometres south-west of Grozny. As Urus-Martan was considered an opposition town, where the pro-Moscow Provisional Council was based, as well as the headquarters of Bislan Gantamirov, the former mayor of Grozny who had gone over to the opposition, there were no Russian Federation soldiers here. What's more, all of us had friends or relatives living here, so overall it seemed a good choice for us. We stopped at the home of one of the fighters' relatives on the edge of the town to wash ourselves of mud, as our appearance might have attracted unwanted attention. When we had cleaned up and slept a little, we went our separate ways.

10

It was strange to find, at such a short distance from the hell of Grozny, a town that was buzzing with life. There were a number of markets in the centre where you could buy everything needed for daily life, and a weekly market was held in the suburbs where they sold not only the goods needed for life, but also the weapons and ammunition needed for death, and they did so openly. Provisional Council fighters and Russian Army officers alike were selling weapons and the buyers were their opponents. True, there were no major consignments of weapons changing hands – other channels existed for that – but all the same, weapons were being sold quite brazenly. Meanwhile, the Provisional Council held regular meetings, which the leaders of the opposition would attend, to convince the locals of the sheer futility of resisting the Russian Army and the righteousness of the Provisional Council's path. Although the town's administration was pro-Moscow, it had given shelter to large numbers of refugees. In hosting this huge quantity of residents from the ruins of Grozny, the locals in Urus-Martan had illustrated that 'Oppositionists' and 'Dudayev loyalists' were artificial labels that had nothing to do with the Chechen people. International refugee agencies were operating there too, helping with the evacuation and relocation of refugees to the neighbouring republics.

During my first few days in Urus-Martan, my insomnia returned with a vengeance. This time it was the silence that I was finding oppressive. My relatives had a house on the main road, where the traffic was fairly heavy for wartime. At night the beams of passing cars would sweep across my window, just like the flash that comes before a blast, and after each flash I would instinctively wait for the explosion. I spent several nights in horrible tension, until my nerves ceased sending alarm signals to my brain. If each flash had been followed by a thunderous blast, my mind would have automatically determined which sector of the city was under fire and I would have fallen asleep without any trouble. Going crazy from the lack of sleep, I tortured my hosts with the question, 'Why aren't there any explosions after the flashes?' Finally my brain stopped responding so violently to the headlight beams and I could fall asleep, though during the night I would often dream of the dead city.

After Grozny I could not get rid of the feeling that there was a chasm between those of us who had witnessed and participated in that hell and the people here, the civilian population, for whom life went on as usual. It was as if that war-torn city, overrun by two-legged and four-legged curs gone wild from the scent of blood, had never been. Here people were living, loving, marrying and divorcing, dying of natural causes and being buried with sumptuous funerals. Young, healthy guys were sitting about at home at the very time kids the same age in Grozny were fighting for their motherland's freedom, knee-deep in their own and the enemy's blood. While the corpses of thousands of young people at the dawn of their lives were being left unburied in my city – where there was nobody to bury them, and they were eaten by dogs in violation not just of religious law but of the moral laws of humanity – here in this town some doddering old man would be buried with the utmost solemnity, as if he were a pillar of the nation's wellbeing. Of course, in my mind I understood that this was life, and that everyone had his own personal fate, separate from the fate of the nation and of humanity at large, and these people too were helping our warriors in their own way – by giving birth to the next generation. But as for my heart – it could not understand them, nor did it want to.

Living in this town and meeting the Provisional Council's representatives and supporters only intensified my antipathy to their stance. It was chilling to see their joy at the fall of Grozny, which they expressed passionately at their meetings in Urus-Martan. After my long contact with its members, I began to look upon the Provisional Council as a gang of Satan's servants. Whenever an opposition political activist or fighter would start extolling the mighty arsenal and bravery of the Russian soldiers, who had 'smashed Dudayev's men, and quite right too', a terrible searing surge of fury and hate would well up in me, and it took a superhuman effort to keep myself from uttering a wild, primal scream and sinking my teeth into his throat till this bloodthirsty traitor choked on his own blood and fell silent. But man's most powerful impulse, the impulse for survival, restrained this crazy desire. For in this town, where both ardent supporters of Chechen sovereignty and supporters of the Russian side had flocked, I was meant to be just a journalist who had fled the war, though in fact I had abandoned my neutrality on the first night of the attack on Grozny. Here the psychological pressure was so monstrous that Grozny's hell now seemed like a picnic site. At least there you were free to respond to people's actions, be they friends or enemies. Here all you could do was grit your teeth and keep quiet. Stay silent to safeguard the people who were sheltering you.

11

After a couple of months I finally managed to find some acquaintances who were travelling to the Shatoy district in the mountains, and I set off with them for southern Chechnya. By that time, the Russian troops had slowly but stubbornly pushed into the southern and eastern parts of Chechnya, and fighting was already underway in the villages of the foothills. When I arrived in Shatoy, where my relatives were living as refugees, I ran into quite a few fighters and special-forces soldiers of my acquaintance. They had their base in the town, along with the headquarters of Hamzat Gelayev, who'd just recovered from being heavily wounded in Grozny. Here too was the Office for the Prosecutor General of the Chechen Republic, headed by Usman Imayev.[19] A few days later I rode in Imayev's car to Vedeno.[20] After passing the village of Ulus-Kert, we drove for a long time along the bed of a small mountain river, the Vashtar, until finally coming out on to the road to Vedeno. As Vedeno was the seat of the Chechen resistance military headquarters, Chechnya's key government bodies were located there too. Despite many agreeable moments, the trip to Vedeno left me with a bad feeling. Some men flashing their military secret service ID had begun to pay close attention to my presence there. Their professional interest in me came down to the questions, 'Who are you? Where are you from? Why aren't you at your workplace? What are you doing here?' And so it went on. They grilled me with an admirable obstinacy, despite my equally obstinate and consistent replies.[21] What irked me was that these secret agents never once invited me to their office. They'd approach me in the street in pairs or threes and keep on asking the same old questions, and if I carried on walking, they'd walk by my side. Of course, I was disgruntled at their attention. After all, I'd grown used to the fact that, since Grozny, the vast majority of the fighters already knew me by sight. In the end I decided to bring it up with Zelimkhan Yandarbiyev[22] and Imayev, whom I'd known since before the war, and with their help I broke free from the beady eye of the independent state.

In Vedeno I met Shamil Basayev, who came across as rather pleased with himself, but, this weakness aside, he was a fine warrior and strategist, and especially congenial to journalists. His thinking on the future of the Chechen state showed no hint whatsoever of the Islamic radicalism which he would later be said to espouse and personify. Unfortunately I never got to watch his transformation into a 'radical', as I had no further dealings with him. After a few days working as a consultant to some Russian journalists, I quit Vedeno for good and returned to Shatoy. There I joined a special-forces unit which was about to set off for the villages of Bamut, Stary Achkhoy and Yandi (Orekhovo)[23] in western Chechnya, where the Russians were stepping up their offensive. The regiment's commanding officer was Hamzat Gelayev, who some time ago had been appointed commander of the south-western front (the south-eastern front being commanded by Basayev), and he was sending the special-forces fighters into the fiercest zones. After a long and strenuous trek, we arrived at our position near the village of Yandi, which the militiamen were fighting desperately to defend.

It was interesting to see the men fighting in these conditions. They did not show the slightest sign of jumpiness or nerves during the air strikes or shelling, nor during combat. These special-forces fighters were professionals of war, and, like all professionals, they did their job with ease and skill. Over time, the militiamen too became quite professional, as their enemy had plenty of occasions to discover. Here entirely different people, with divergent views on life, with different dreams and aspirations, were united by war – or, more precisely, brought together by the fact that they cherished their nation's freedom. In conversation after conversation, my questions would elicit the following response:

'I'm not really fussed who's president, so long as it's someone chosen by the people, like Dzhokhar was. I don't care what agreement he signs with Russia. Ultimately I'm fighting because I don't want the Russians, or some soldiers or bureaucrats, to lord it over us on this God-given land of ours. We didn't come sword in hand to their country, they came to us, and not for the first time in history. Russia's been laying waste to our nation ever since the Russians first stepped foot in the Caucasus. And as a human being I have a right and as a man I have a duty to protect my people as best I can. I have a right to do everything in my power to see that this campaign will be Russia's last.'

'Do you think Chechnya has enough military might to punish Russia?'

'It's not about punishing Russia. And it would be ridiculous to compare Russia's military might with ours. It's about the fact that for every yard of earth they'll pay an extortionate price; it's about the fact that at this point in history the blood of the Chechens will cost the imperialists dear. The Russian leadership has got to understand once and for all that they're better off being our allies than our enemies. And that's exactly what our president Dzhokhar was offering Russia, but Yeltsin's brains are permanently fuzzy with drink, and the majority of the Russian politicians are traitors to Russia. The Russian people, who are feeding, clothing and honouring an army that's destroying our nation, they've got to understand: it's not the generals' sons who will die in this war, it is their sons. And when that happens, the people can stop this war, which brings nothing but sorrow to us ordinary folk, and all for the sake of some ambitious pack of traitors to Russia.'

'Do you believe the Russian Army will leave our land?'

'Why would we be fighting if we didn't believe it? The ones who don't believe it are busy serving the Russians.'

And this was how the vast majority saw it. During our stay in the area, enemy troops tried several times to storm Bamut, Yandi and Stary Achkhoy, but on each occasion they retreated with heavy losses. I managed to befriend many special-forces fighters, and over the course of the First and Second Chechen Wars, I lost nearly all of them.

In early May 1995, fighting flared up on the Shatoy and Vedensky axes, and the special-forces fighters were redeployed to the area near Shatoy. I arrived there two days before them. Along this axis the special forces were sustaining their heftiest losses, although the Russians too lost a good many men, at times entire units. And they were dumping large numbers of their own soldiers' corpses from helicopters into remote gorges to cover up the number of fatalities. That area near Shatoy was where Hamzat Gelayev would again be severely wounded. But that came later. Whereas now ... Now my journalistic dream came true.

12

With the help of Gelayev's personal patronage, I managed to join a group leaving to buy arms and ammunition. Most of the party knew neither the route we were taking nor our final destination. We were a small group, with just enough manpower to defend the cargo, two UAZ jeeps and an all-terrain Ural motorcycle with a sidecar. Heading the group was a colourful old character, armed with a short assault rifle, a pistol and a long sabre, who was nicknamed 'Daddy'. We set out in the evening. We passed the site where the fighters were digging their positions straight across from the federal forces, then we drove deep into the forest. In the dead of night we arrived at a village in the opposition-held Urus-Martan district. We stopped for the night with friends, planning on an early start in the morning. The next day we had our meeting with Russian Army officers on neutral ground, mediated by supporters of the Provisional Council. Due to the endless monetary reforms brought in by the Russian government, I no longer recall how much money changed hands, but I remember the transaction went smoothly. Both sides were pleased with the deal: 'Daddy' purchased a large consignment of arms and ammunition at a good price, and the officers successfully offloaded their 'wares', mumbling in an attempt to ease their consciences, 'Of course, we realize you've got to defend yourselves too. We didn't want this war. It's an unjust war which Yeltsin unleashed to distract people from the crimes of his own team. You Chechens are good guys! And you're not just defending your own freedom; you're defending ours, too.'

One of the fighters, who'd already taken part in these operations a few times, commented that the officers weren't usually so talkative. 'They must have decided you didn't look like a militiaman and gave that speech for your benefit.' 'Daddy' stayed on with some of the other fighters to buy another consignment of weapons. Meanwhile, we left in two vehicles, weighed down with arms and ammunition. Our return to Shatoy was uneventful, not counting the close call with enemy artillery, who fired rounds at our convoy. A few days later, I was summoned for a chat with one of the leaders of the resistance. They offered me a role in the counter psy-ops team they were putting together. I agreed without a second thought – acquiring this kind of experience was a dream come true for my career but I asked the team's leader why it had taken us Chechens so long to think of it.

'Up till now we've been running quite a successful psychological operation against the Russians. But there's been no centralized control over the programme, like we have, say, in the information war run by Movladi Udugov[24]. So we decided to create a team to plan and coordinate the psychological warfare effort.'

As the leader of the team was a man of keen intellect (he was an academic) and dedicated to his nation, I accepted the offer and began work. But a few days later our campaign headquarters was bombed. All the files were burnt in the fire, and we did not get a chance to start afresh.

13

Life is easier for fatalists – because fatalists find it easier to die. And how else could you die 'with a smile on your lips', as General Grachev described the Russian soldiers dying in the meat-grinder of Grozny? If you are not a fatalist, then you'll arrogantly assume that you are master of certain things in your life – of your fate, for example. You'll assume that man shapes his own destiny, and so on, in the finest traditions of atheist ideology. But if you are a fatalist, then you know that whatever happens to you has been ordained by God, and the only choice open to you is which path – the righteous or the sinful – to take on your journey towards destiny. If you are a fatalist, war too will be easier.

You were sitting over a cup of tea with your wounded comrade, a cheery special-forces fighter. You noticed that today he is unusually sad and pensive; you joke with him about this, but, realizing that the joke has not elicited the usual chirpy response, you fall silent. He answers your puzzled question with a wave of the hand and indescribable grief in his eyes: 'You know what? I'm tired. I can't make sense of it all.' There are planes in the sky, but you pay no attention to their tiresome whine; you've grown used to their continual presence, and you start fretting whenever they fail to appear at their usual time. Planes are a confirmation of life for you, like mosquitoes are a confirmation of summer.

And as for the fact that they bomb you – well, that's life, you may not like it, but you're not bitter about it. Mosquitoes bite, after all, but you still love the summer. What's more, over the past few months you've become a professional. You're now an expert person-under-bombardment, and you know exactly when and where each particular plane will drop its bomb or fire its missile. So rather than panic, you continue to gaze at your comrade in surprise, and with an inexplicable ache in your soul. He draws your attention to the planes; you nod absent-mindedly, as though he were telling you about the good weather. Your wounded comrade again says, 'They're close,' you dismiss him with a wave of your hand, someone shouts, 'Drop!' and at that instant you hear the blast of a missile, but you leap up, rushing towards him and … The silence is deathly, almost perfect, only somewhere far away there is the faint roar of water. No, you haven't lost consciousness, you can see everything fine … well, no, you cannot see. But you can see that you cannot see in the dense billows of smoke and dust … You fumble about on the bed where your wounded comrade had been sitting. He's not there. You call out. He does not answer. Or maybe he's answered but you cannot hear. After taking some paces towards the door, you see the wall collapse, and something burns your outstretched hands. You find a window and jump through it into the street. For some reason a special-forces fighter is standing there moving his lips but no words come out. You ask, 'Can you hear me?' He nods. You shout, 'I can't hear you!' repeating this over and over, wanting to satisfy yourself that he can hear, while you can't. He makes some gestures, but you don't understand, and you stand there bewildered in the middle of the street. He grabs you, presses you to a tree, pressing himself against you, covering you with his body, and almost instantly you see a missile explode right where you were just standing; you note this fact as unexciting but significant. The special-forces guy who saved you is pointing to your chest and your head, moving his lips. You look. Blood is pouring from somewhere near your ear, and the binoculars round your neck have been smashed to bits, with one eyepiece dangling from the strap. For some reason those smashed binoculars, a gift from a comrade who died a week earlier in hand-to-hand combat while trying to break out of an encirclement, bother you more than the blood issuing from your head. Well, you've already understood it's nothing much. People collapse from serious wounds, but you're still standing, it's just you can't hear anything. When will that water ever stop gushing! You're grabbed by the arm and dragged into the air-raid shelter. You try to break free, without really knowing why, but they won't let you go, and catching sight of your wounded comrade, who is also being led there, you call out to him joyously.

The air-raid shelter is packed: there are wounded fighters and civilians. A military nurse runs over to you, and, true to her professional duty, draws out a small piece of shrapnel lodged near your ear. A few fighters leave the shelter; you follow them. People try to stop you, they're saying something to you, pulling you back by the arms. But you smile at them and leave. You know the planes must have flown away, otherwise you would hear them. As for those people – well, you cannot hear them because they're talking so softly. In any case, you are a fatalist. If your hour has come, then there's nothing that can save you. You take a few steps and notice a fighter desperately waving his arms, trying to tell you something. You stop and look at him. He runs to a tall tree, continuing to gesture at you; you run after him, but don't make it in time. You see an explosion. Yes, first you see it ... Then the dull sound of a blast reaches you. No, not a missile ... It is the powerful blast of a bunker-buster, a bomb specially designed to destroy enemy air-raid shelters. You are sure of this, because you've become an expert on bombs. It falls at the very spot you've just left.[25] In slow motion you see an enormous piece of iron come flying towards you. Desperate to move out of its path, you realize that you won't make it. But for some inexplicable reason it doesn't hit you. Later, a number of fighters swear that the blast wave flung you a good two metres, and you believe them only after measuring out the flight path of this chunk of iron blown from the second floor of a building. You come back to your senses as you jump through the window of a school standing a hundred metres from the air-raid shelter. Running into the school cellar and seeing the people there, you remember that there were also people in the air-raid shelter, and you run back … But it's too late. It was already too late the moment the bomb slipped through the hatch of the plane. Almost everyone has died. Only a few have survived. There are mangled, bloodied beings covered in dust and black soot, who just a moment ago were humans. And wandering about in the silence, you realize it was destiny. You did not get out of your own free will – it was your time left on earth that got you out. You feel somewhat aggrieved. But wait … If it was fate, then where did you find this burning desire to confront the pilot of the plane face to face? Where has that come from? No, it's not fury, not hatred: it's something cooler and more powerful. A feeling which even you find frightening. You realize that the pilot must have known full well who he was bombing. The scum at the controls of the plane knew there were no combatants here. He knew because the Médecins Sans Frontières staff had sent official notification to the Russian command that this complex held only the wounded. And, as a rule, most of the wounded are civilians. They asked that these buildings which held the wounded be protected from air strikes and artillery fire. Yet the Russians chose to strike those very buildings – turning the doctors into unwitting forward air controllers. And you're burning with a desire to find this pilot … And then what? You don't want to think of the aftermath of such an encounter. But haven't they bombed peaceful villages before? And anyway, aren't you a fatalist? Yes, they've bombed villages. But maybe they bombed them by mistake. Whereas this time it was no mistake. This silence, this continuous roar of water stirs a strange fear in you. No, not the fear of bombs and bullets – in the hell of Grozny you learnt not to be too frightened of those; rather a fear of something more terrible still than the horrific deaths in the air-raid shelter. But you don't know what is eliciting this fear. And then the fear gradually subsides and fades, though it will come back … Later it will return with more clarity … But you are a fatalist.

14

War is a strange phenomenon. Odd things happen during a war. If some souls who until then had been brothers-in-intellect find themselves plunged into long years of ardent hatred during a war, then other creatures, who could not possibly have been called kindred – at least in terms of species – become as close as brothers during the war and seek protection among each other. I remember how we found him wounded. A heavy 7.62 mm-calibre bullet from a Kalashnikov had pierced his wing, ripping out a small chunk of bone. He beat his wounded wing clumsily against the earth as my cousin and I gathered him up, wrapped him in a jacket and brought him home. He was a magnificent beauty of an eagle. He was badly injured and it was even suggested that we put him out of his misery, but my elder cousin Akhmed objected. The eagle wouldn't let anyone near him, only allowing Akhmed to examine and bandage him, and that only after first pecking him in the head. Realizing that the eagle needed qualified care, I approached some doctors from Médecins Sans Frontières, whose chief I was acquainted with, and arranged to have him examined. The doctors put him to sleep and operated on the wounded wing. They treated him to some meat, and a young doctor took one of his feathers as a keepsake. I nicknamed the eagle Earl, and he would respond, or rather react, to this name. My God, how he yearned for the sky! After long and vain attempts to take flight, he would clamber on to an empty fuel drum and sit for hours staring at the sky. In the first few days another eagle came and circled the sky with an alarming call. One day, though, the wounded bird jumped up on to the drum and answered his circling comrade with a long, forlorn, pining cry. From that moment his comrade stopped coming. The only thing that would make Earl draw close to unfamiliar people was the whine of the Russian aircraft. Upon hearing the roar of approaching fighter-bombers, he'd run for his life towards humans and shelter among them. Experiencing a fear that was baffling to him, he instinctively sought protection from the only creatures able to give it to him. But humans could not shield him. Soon after, he was killed by shrapnel from a cluster bomb. When the young Frenchman who headed the Médecins Sans Frontières brigade learnt from me after the war that Earl had died, he showed me the feather he had kept and said, 'This eagle too died defending the mountains in his own way.'

15

A few weeks later, the federal forces took Shatoy and Vedeno and the Chechen resistance retreated into the mountains, as their ancestors had done since time immemorial when outnumbered by the enemy. The fall of Grozny and the occupation of the Chechen plains hadn't seemed like a tragedy – it was what happened whenever the enemy was too powerful. And the Chechens had always returned to the plain. But when the enemy army entered the villages of Shatoy and Vedeno, in the heart of highland Chechnya, people became dispirited, and some of the less resolute were seized with panic. For the highlands are Chechnya's inner sanctuary, and while this sanctuary remains free of enemy soldiers, the Chechens are unconquered. Behind us we still had more mountains: Bamut, Yandi and Stary-Achkhoy were fighting on, and so the more tenacious kept up their spirits and prepared for new battles. But the Russian generals, rather than stepping up the assault, were celebrating their latest victory and doling out the awards and medals. They had, it is true, paid heavily for their victory. One Russian officer told me that after the fight for Shatoy they had to form an entire new motorized infantry regiment from a paratrooper brigade assigned to him. But who viewed these Russian Army casualties as a loss to the country? In response to the new situation, I joined a tactical intelligence team operating along this axis. I could, of course, be accused of flouting journalistic neutrality, but I had no reservations. I was fulfilling my civic and filial duty to the motherland, however grandiloquent that might sound. This war had stopped being 'somebody else's war' on the night of the New Year's Eve assault on Grozny. My starry-eyed excitement at the privilege of witnessing that first day of war had long ago given way to the cold cynicism of real combat. And that Chechen commander was a thousand times right when he smiled sadly in response to my self-assured words. A journalist can indeed take sides. And at certain moments in his life, he simply has a duty to act in the capacity of human being or citizen. Yet I never stopped being a journalist, neither then nor later. To observe impassively the destruction of your own nation is the lot of cowards, or outsiders with a homeland somewhere far away and at peace. But as subsequent events would show, I made a poor reconnaissance scout. Within just a few weeks I had committed a fateful blunder, in a clear demonstration of my reckless nature as a journalist.

News soon arrived of Shamil Basayev's daring operation in the Russian town of Budyonnovsk[26]. The psychological impact of this operation was tremendous. Chechen resistance fighters misread it as a signal from the command authorizing them to operate deep in Russia's vast heartland. And Russian society awoke to the reality that this was not a war waged in some faraway Chechnya; it was raging in Russia too. And the following day it could come to any town, bringing death and affliction in its wake, unless society could stop it. At that time Russian society still had the power to sway the government when it so desired. Boris Yeltsin, despite his nakedly imperialist agenda, was nevertheless deep down a greater democrat than any other ruler Russia had seen. Basayev's operation ended with a ceasefire and the start of negotiations, meaning respite for the combatants. But this pause was merely for those fighting: intelligence could not afford to ease off. Intelligence on both sides was hard at work, for where was the guarantee that negotiations would not break down tomorrow and hostilities resume? Within a short time, thanks to the brave agents who infiltrated the enemy, we managed to discover not just the quantity and type of our opponent's combat hardware, not just the troop strength and types of weaponry along this front, but also the enemy's plans to expand their offensive. We received confirmation of the accuracy of these reports a year later, when the enemy tried to prolong their assault. I was on my way back from a routine meeting with the commander of our intelligence task force when I committed my blunder. And this blunder would seal my fate. If, as they say, 'a bomb disposal specialist only ever makes one mistake,' then I believe in war any mistake is an unaffordable luxury. In war you need to use not just your five senses: you have to know how to listen to your heart, your sixth sense, your intuition, or whatever you want to call it. Failure to listen to your heart can lead to the direst of consequences. One of the many transformations that you undergo in war is the sharpening of your intuition, the ability to scent danger. And you must learn to exploit this truly priceless gift if you wish to survive the abnormal situation that is war.

II

From the Wheel of Time into the Circle of Pain

'How can you be enlightened if you are able to walk on past someone in pain?' the Sufi asked the dervish. 'The tree was suffering from the ants gnawing at its roots. And the ants were suffering from being forced to build a new nest in the roots of the tree. In their old nest they'd been disturbed by a gold ingot. Were you to feel the pain of another, you'd find reward in two realms: the gold ingot in this mortal world and blessing in the righteous world. You are not enlightened,' he told the dervish.

From a Sufi parable

1

The forest is nature's magnificent gift to man. It is the ancient cradle of humankind. The forest can feed you when you are hungry, it can warm you when you are frozen, it can shelter you when you have no roof, and the forest can also provide you with sanctuary in time of war. The great saint of the Chechen nation, Sheikh Kunta-Haji Kishiev,[27] taught his *murids* (disciples): 'When the forest sees a man with an axe, it starts grieving for its children the trees, who are still living, so hold your axe with your arm lowered. When you chop down a tree, explain to the forest that you act from necessity and ask for forgiveness, then the tree will be blessed. Respect the forest; respect the plant and animal world around you if you wish to respect God. True respect and honour for the Creator comes through respect for His creations. God does not need our Love; it is we who need the Love and Mercy of the Almighty. Remember that the condition, the purity, of our hearts is far more important than our outward demonstrations of faith.'

That great saint and humanist Sheikh Kunta-Haji alone achieved what the Russian Empire in over half a century could not manage – a cessation of hostilities on the part of the Chechen people. Yet for Russia he became the enemy. Or rather, he had been the Empire's enemy all along, for he had opposed the physical annihilation of his and your people. The Empire wanted your motherland, but free of the people who inhabited that ancient territory. The Empire only dared arrest the saint when, at his bidding, the people had entirely disarmed. And when his disciples then charged, with daggers drawn, into the cannons' grapeshot in an attempt to win back their Teacher, the great saint, Sufi and fatalist, with his feet now in shackles, stopped them. He did so because he had no desire, no right before God, to win freedom at the price of the lives of his disciples. The sage glimpsed far into the future and when he saw the tragic destiny that lay before his people, he became a martyr, sacrificing himself on the altar of spiritual freedom.

Your childhood was spent close to the forest. The woods began just a hundred metres from the edge of the village and stretched for kilometres. The forest harboured many wild beasts. Now and then they wandered into your village. But you would visit the forest more often than they would come to the village. From earliest childhood you used to listen to the forest. You used to converse with the forest and its inhabitants. The forest does not frighten you. Quite the reverse. You know the forest will protect you.

2

In the forest you have to become a shadow. You must melt away, merge with the forest. Particularly if there is a war on and you are a participant in that war. You must move without snapping one dry twig underfoot, without rustling last year's leaf fall, without disturbing the branches or grass. You need to be able to become any tree, bush, hollow or hill, you need to know how to stop smelling like a human if you are to trick the enemy. Your enemy is strong and wily. He too knows how to melt into the forest. He is dangerous. You know it, and that's why so far you have been lucky. Today you have been lucky. It is a sunny morning in July. You need to cover at least twenty kilometres of your journey before nightfall. You're carrying important intelligence given to you by your reconnaissance unit. And intelligence is valuable only while it is timely. You know that, and so you're hurrying. Besides, you also have intelligence of your own – you too are a scout, and no less able than the rest. After spending many hours merging into the shadows of the bushes and gazing through the remaining eyepiece of your binoculars, you've discovered the presence and location of two cleverly concealed Hurricane multiple rocket launchers. The firing range of these systems would allow the Russians to attack almost any rebel position on this axis. To do so they would, of course, need competent undercover agents working among the enemy, but they have no trouble recruiting agents. They have at their service large numbers of Armed Opposition soldiers, whose hands are stained with the blood of their own people. You've also managed to spot a hidden approach to the Hurricanes that is within range of an RPG-7 launcher. It is quite clear that the Hurricanes need to be taken out, and to this end you have devised a plan. At night, a small group of fighters is to creep up and fire at the Hurricanes with their RPG launchers. To do this there's no need to enter the mined zone around the Hurricanes, and the more distant approaches to them haven't been mined – that's already been verified. Then, without engaging the enemy, the group will escape under cover of fire from a couple of machine guns. There are two areas where there is a risk the escape routes might be blocked, so small ambush units could be left to safeguard the withdrawal of the main group. And, to be on the safe side, you've even managed to get the codes of the enemy light signals. You've encrypted all this information in a simple numerical code on some small slips of paper which you've rolled up and hidden in some antibiotic capsules emptied of powder. You've mixed them with genuine capsules and slipped them into the unbuttoned breast pocket of your shirt. You are wearing civilian clothes, which has its advantages. But the main thing compelling you to hurry is the intelligence, later discovered to be incorrect, that one of the delegates in the talks that began a week ago has arrived at headquarters. You urgently need to meet him for an interview. The truth is you are more journalist than scout.

You don't know the route through this forest. So you ask an old childhood friend to guide you. And, to his cost, he agrees. By setting off alone on this path, you are breaking orders. You were strictly forbidden to travel alone without an armed group. That doesn't mean you've been given your own guard of honour or personal security team, just that you are carrying important intelligence. But you cannot wait around for the group to arrive.

Your path runs two hundred metres from the militia base, so you and your friend are at ease and you chat as you calmly walk on.

Suddenly you are overcome by a burning wave of inexplicable fear, just like after the bombing in Shatoy. Your foreboding is so powerful that for a while you cannot take a step, while your friend walks on several metres ahead. You realize your intuition is alerting you to danger; you also know that you should trust your intuition – it has never let you down. Right now the most logical action would be to drop to the ground, keep low, and crawl ahead on all fours to find out the source of this sudden foreboding. But, overcoming your fear, you shut out your intuition through an effort of will and switch on your cold reason. And according to your reason there cannot be any danger; the enemy could not have come so close unobserved. So, feeling calmer, you continue on your way. All of a sudden your friend stops and says something quietly to you. You ask him to repeat it. Again you cannot hear him; you sweep your arm through the air and walk towards to him. You imagine he must have stepped on a mine and that's why he is acting relatively calmly. You've caught up with your friend, and you look over his shoulder to find a group of fighters who have stopped dead with their weapons aimed at you. They are about six or seven metres away. Bearing in mind that in the forest everyone keeps their weapons on the ready for encounters with strangers, you are not too alarmed. In any case, almost all of them are bearded, and some are wearing green headbands, the identifying mark of the resistance.

'Why have you stopped? They're friendlies,' you say, taking a step forward. You are armed. Rather nicely armed. Putting your right hand on the unfastened holster containing your loaded pistol, you walk towards them, saying, 'Don't point your guns! They could go off by accident. We're on your side.' At that moment the cold barrel of a VSS silent sniper rifle presses against your temple and you hear the quiet command: 'Hands on your head! Lie down on the ground!' Without waiting for you to obey, they whack you behind your knees with their rifle butts and bring you expertly to the ground, face down. They're not on your side. You realize that your war ends here. The blows from the rifle butts snap you out of the stupor of fear that in the first moments washed over you in a searing wave. Your first thought is to fight them. You wouldn't have a hope of surviving, but you would have a hope of taking at least one of the enemy with you … But just in time a sobering chill runs through you. If you attack, they'll take fright and gun you down. And once they've shot you, they'll kill your friend. And he's unarmed. They strip you of your weapons, tie your wrists with a belt, and one of them deals you some punches, asking how many of you there are. Then they gag you and lift you up. They go through the same process with your friend. They haven't yet searched you properly, merely taken your ID from your trouser pocket. While they are lifting you up, you deliberately lean forward and the capsules with the codes fall out of your breast pocket, unseen by the enemy. You are relieved. But the notes – they must have taken them along with your ID. Well, you could have acquired such information legitimately, as a journalist, and so you are not hugely worried. You're surprised at your ability to reason with such cool detachment at a moment like this, as though it was all happening to someone else.

They are now leading you some place, and you mentally run through your survival chances, concluding they are nil. What they have found on you ought to be more than enough for the firing squad. The only question is how long the torture will last. You know what awaits you there, and this knowledge doesn't make things any easier. Your best option would be to die before arriving. Then your death would be far swifter and easier. A wild, crazy idea comes into your head: you could charge into one of your captors with your shoulder and leap with him into the gorge. As luck would have it, you are on the edge of the gorge just now. Then, even if you should survive the fall, they'd be certain to finish you off. Having made up your mind to go through with this seemingly crazy plan, you suddenly pause. You cannot seek such a way out. You are a believer, which means you cannot commit suicide outright. Suicide is the most heinous of mortal sins. Besides, fatalists – and you count yourself one – do not run away from their rendezvous with destiny. Of course, your fatalism is grounded in realism. Yet none the less at this moment it has taken control. And so you walk on. You walk on towards your terrible meeting with destiny. There are thirteen of the enemy. They are a reconnaissance and sabotage group, professionals in their field. They operate boldly and skilfully. If they weren't courageous warriors, why would they have come so close to your base – and disguised as resistance fighters? One of them stares you in the eye and says, 'Look at him glaring like a wolf. I wouldn't want to meet him in a dark alley. If he'd realized who we were, he'd have killed us on the spot. I can see it in his eyes.'

Another answers, 'So let him look. That's all he can do now. His time is up.'

You listen to them and realize they don't intimidate you. Well, they don't really need to. They have already earned their reward. They are simply discussing the reality of what lies ahead for you. During a rest, as we get closer to their side, one of them gives you a second, more thorough search and finds a capsule which has got stuck in your pocket. He opens it. He finds the piece of paper with the numbers. He looks into your eyes. The commander asks, 'Well, what's he got there?' He winks at you, tearing the paper into little pieces with the words, 'Nothing.' You are grateful to your enemy for having understood you. For understanding that you are doomed. And as one warrior to another, he shows you respect in your ill fortune.

3

Before long you are delivered to the base of the 245th Motor Rifle Regiment near Shatoy. They tear the blindfold from your eyes and a colonel begins the interrogation. It is what is known as a 'high-speed interrogation', applied while you are still in shock. The colonel is holding your passport and press card in his hand; inside the passport is a photo of President Dudayev taken a month ago and dated. And he has your notes and some new poems written in your native Chechen and in Russian. The broad-shouldered, heavily built colonel looks you in the eyes and asks,

'Are you a combatant?'

'No. I'm a journalist.'

'Who is your commander?'

'I don't have a commander. I'm a journalist.'

'A journalist, carrying a weapon? If you're a journalist, then why are you armed?'

'There's a war on.'

'Where do you work?'

'You can see from my ID.'

'You're a combatant!' He's no longer asking but telling you.

'No.'

He steps forward and strikes your face twice with his elbow. In hand-to-hand combat, an elbow strike at close range is considered one of the most powerful blows. He knows this. You know it too. Your hands are tied behind your back. You sneer at him. That makes him see red. He grabs an assault rifle from one of the soldiers and fires a burst near your feet: 'Are you a rebel? Answer!'

Looking him straight in the eyes, you answer: 'No.'

Then he fires a single round into your right foot. The bullet goes straight through. Leaning slightly forward, you look silently at your foot, then look into his eyes. You do not feel intense pain yet. Just a smarting in your foot. You are still detached and contemplative: 'Have you had a good think?' you hear the officer's voice. 'Oh, I can shoot higher, you know … Do you have any idea of the agony?'

You notice the assault rifle is pointed at your groin and you shrug your shoulders. 'Well, that's it. I've lost,' you say, merely for the sake of replying. You are worried about the state of your guide and friend. He is still blindfolded, and he needs to hear your voice, otherwise he might think they've killed you and do something stupid.

'Want to die a hero, you bastard?' the colonel continues. His voice is creepily quiet. 'I can kill you and there'll be nothing to pay! "Attempted escape" …'

You notice the hand holding the assault rifle is trembling from barely constrained rage. For some reason you take in the fact that he is left-handed. 'Yes I know,' you say. 'But do I look like a hero to you?'

A brief silence fills the air. 'No. It would be too kind to kill you here. Your death will take place somewhere else. And it'll be a slow and painful death. Dress his wound and tie him to the post!' the colonel ends his monologue. They blindfold you and, striking you with their rifle butts, they lead you away. To be bandaged, as it turns out. After dressing your wound, they slip your hands, which are bound behind your back, over a post and leave you waiting in the hot summer sun for a helicopter. You have no shirt on – they stripped you of it upon arrival – plus your wound is bleeding, and as a result you are unbearably thirsty. Someone approaches and whispers quietly in your ear, 'If you want to avoid problems, keep quiet about some of the weapons you were caught with.'

This offer suits you fine, so you say, 'Agreed. What shouldn't I mention?'

'Don't mention anything except the RPG-18 and the hand grenades.'

'OK. Only don't blab,' you say, knowing full well it is one of the original thirteen who has decided to conceal some weapons and sell them back to your comrades. He leaves in silence. Hearing somebody's voice nearby, you ask for water. The reply comes: 'Want some water? Here!' And you're punched in the solar plexus.

Almost at once you hear the sound of a blow and a voice: 'You bastard! Beating a guy when he's tied up! If you're a real man, untie his hands; he'll rip your eyes out! Look pal' – addressing me – 'I'm sorry I couldn't shield you from the colonel, but that scumbag will leave you alone now.'

It is the voice of your unknown ally who hid the paper with the codes from his commander. You say, 'Thank you! For everything.'

'I'm afraid there's no water. If they bring any before the helicopters arrive, I'll make sure you get a drink,' he promises, walking away.

You realize that what's happening to you now is just a gentle limbering-up for what is to come. You know that you will die. And you'll die slowly and painfully. Nobody will be compassionate enough to release you with a blessed bullet. Everything you've done up till now ostensibly to save your skin – denying that you were a combatant, agreeing to keep quiet about the weapons – was done in pursuit of the one goal that matters to you: bringing closer the moment of death, so the torture will end quicker. Yet you also know the torture you'll undergo will purify you of all sins and you'll stand before God with a shining face. Perhaps the torture will even purify your torturers of their sins. You are a fatalist. You will have to travel through hell for an eternity in order to reach your paradise, your peace, that is so near at hand. That's what you are hoping. You are so tired. God is merciful, after all. He does not sentence people to serve their time in hell twice. So what now? Now there's nothing for it but to wait. Wait for the helicopters to come for you, bringing ... Not just your death. No, something more horrible still. So you wait. And standing in the fierce summer sun you quietly recite the verses from the holy Quran which you are capable of recalling. You recite mechanically, not really reflecting on the content. Here is the drone of the helicopter ... It is time. So they didn't bring you any water. They say that a dying man gets terribly thirsty. And how badly you'll yearn for that sip of water.

4

Come on now, remember. Remember everything you can. Everything you know about interrogation techniques: torture methods, psychological pressure designed to humiliate you and break your will. You don't know how it might help, but you desperately try to remember. In reality, you are simply fighting your fear. Yes, that's it. But what is there to be frightened of? After all, you've already realized your time left on earth will be brief. At least in the human dimension of time … Although it will stretch on endlessly in another dimension. And it is this other dimension that frightens you. Its inevitability frightens you. There is no alternative path. Perhaps you could have improved your lot by telling them everything. And perhaps that's what you'd have done, if you were an optimist. But you were never one to build castles in the air. Someone in your blood far stronger and wiser, some ancient, mighty voice in your blood begins to speak: *You are a warrior. And a warrior is dead from birth. His death is never seeking him: it is always there with him on his shoulders. So why did you get so frightened when you looked into the face of death? You knew you couldn't live for ever. Soon your ordeal will be over. No matter how eternal it may seem, it will not last long in time. You should know how to die in combat. If there's nothing left to fight for, then fight for your death. You're still at war. But now you face the most challenging battle of all on the warrior's path.* This ancient voice stirs some feeling in you … Is it pride, perhaps?

You may be lying wounded and beaten, face down on the dirty floor of a helicopter, but never in all your brief life has anybody shown you such honour as this. And what counts most of all: it is your oldest mortal foe showing you this honour. The Russians consider this tiny person so dangerous to their vast country that they have brought two helicopters especially for you. The reality is that helicopters always fly in pairs, but that does not matter, for this is the last mark of respect you will get in your life. So you cling to this false belief. In just twenty minutes or so, perhaps sooner, you will have to answer before God for all the sins of your ancestors. Meanwhile, you try to remember anything that might be of help in the battle to come. You feel the helicopter descending – it is over. You've arrived. This is your final stop. From here on you will start on a different journey, known but unknown, and thus terrifying. From here you will depart for eternity. This is a journey you'll have to make, one way or another. But how you make it is up to you.

The helicopter lands and you tumble out. They catch you below and slam your head against the tracks of an infantry fighting vehicle. Despite the blood gushing, you do not pass out. You hear them flinging your guide along with you on to the vehicle. All this time your eyes are blindfolded and your hands are tied, so you can only hear and feel. You feel not with your fingers but with the entire surface of your soon-to-be-tortured body. Before long you are thrown off the IFV and led away under further beatings. You are worried about your friend, he is not guilty of anything. They interrogate him first. You cannot hear the questions or his answers. Meanwhile, you're lying face down in the sun, and they are slowly and expertly beating you. You pray to God that your stories will match. And God hears your plea: they will match more or less. They lead you away to be interrogated. You are set in front of an unseen officer who asks you questions. You answer them. The story emerging from their questions and your answers goes more or less as follows.

'I'm a journalist. The guide is a guy I went to school with. He knew I was a journalist but he didn't realize I was armed. This morning I had a tip-off from someone that a delegate in the talks with the Russians had arrived at Chechen military headquarters, and so I was making my way there. I needed to interview him. It's my job. I'd left some weapons hidden in the forest, and when my guide saw that I was arming myself, he wanted to turn back. But I talked him into going a hundred metres further with me. Of course, I'm not on a salary, but there's a war going on. And it's my duty as a journalist to witness this tragedy at least, so I can write about it later. Yes, I think war is a tragedy. And I dream of it ending. It doesn't matter how, just so long as the killing stops. Why was I armed? Well, you can't work with them unless you're armed. They take the attitude that a man wandering around the positions without a weapon must be an enemy agent. I paid two hundred roubles for the RPG launcher out of my savings, and the hand grenades were a present from some rebels. No, I haven't killed anybody. I haven't fired at anybody. I've never been arrested. I served in the Soviet Army, then I studied at the Chechen State University. Before the war I never wrote about politics. I wrote only about culture and sometimes I wrote on science.'

They aren't happy with your answers. They suggest that you tell them the truth. You object: 'I've told you the truth. If you don't believe me, you can check with all the Russian, Chechen and foreign accredited journalists who are working here. They all know me.'

'Of course we believe that part of your story. You look too sophisticated to be a rebel. But we also know that you've lied to us. Now that is not in your interest. You'll tell us the truth anyway, in the end. Everyone always does. But it's in your interest to tell it sooner. Do you hear, your friend wants to tell you something'

– you hear your friend scream. 'He'd certainly advise you to tell the truth.'

'I have told the truth …'

'No! Not the whole truth. You haven't said anything about the number of rebels, the weapons they've got … You haven't given us the names of the rebels or their commanders.' As you discover later, your comrade's interrogation is following a different track. 'You haven't shown us the location of their headquarters and bases. You haven't told us who your notes on the sabotage attacks of a certain mid-ranking field commander were intended for and where you got them. It's a report with your findings meant for Dudayev or Maskhadov. Isn't it? And you're not a journalist at all. You're using your journalist ID as a cover. Who are you?'

'I got that information officially, as a journalist. And they're forever shifting their bases and headquarters about. As for names, no one thought to introduce themselves by name to me as I'm a journalist. They all have call signs, but I can't remember them. And I don't know the first thing about weaponry. I'm a civilian. And for my army service I was based at headquarters.'

'OK. You're under stress and we realize there's a lot you've forgotten. But we're here to help you remember it all. And the quicker you remember, the better for you. Now go and have a chat with our friend!' Once again you are led off for a 'chat', as blows from rifle butts are lavished upon you.

They run and slam your head against a pillar repeatedly, then they stomp on your wounded, bleeding foot. Dizzied from the blows to your head, you slump down in the guards' arms – but they won't let you fall to the ground yet, and dragging you further, they beat you even harder. Despite the many blows to your head, for some reason you've not passed out. Very soon you will desperately want to pass out, but you won't lose consciousness even for a second. They will not let you. They are experts. The guards hand you over.

5

Electricity is a blessing. It supplies mankind with heat and light, with communications; it has uses in medicine. Of course, if you are not careful, it can hurt you, kill you even, but these are accidents, and accidents happen in the course of day-to-day life. But it turns out electricity has one more application. It can be used for the methodical infliction of pain: for torture. You are no longer being roughed up any old how, with random blows from rifle butts and boots. No. You are being tortured. And the difference between the two is phenomenal. Beating is beating. It has no system: any old person can do it, using any old thing, in any old place. The soldiers beating you are unleashing all their fury, their dread of death, their sleep terrors and nightmares. They are blaming you personally for their grim, tented existence, for the cold and the hunger. To them the one person guilty of all their woes is you. And in any case, you are the enemy. All their hatred centres solely on you – because you are right here in front of them. They beat you because they're afraid; of you, of combat, of death. They punch and kick with fervour. The beatings in this place often result in disability and death and nearly always leave a permanent mark on your health. But the torture … Here everything is done slowly and meticulously; they strike each spot only for a matter of minutes, so the body cannot get used to the pain. The torture almost never leaves long-term outward marks. The torturer's task is not to cripple but to beat out of the victim the maximum possible information. And in the process, delivering the maximum degree of pain with the minimum possible consequences. No emotions are involved. That is if you're being tortured not by the sadistic OMON paramilitaries but by professionals. There are no feelings. There is only the cold calculation of professionals. Everything has been worked out down to the finest detail, and everything is done with a purpose. They are acting on a broad front here, working on body and mind simultaneously, trying to get through to you that you're nothing. There is nobody, nothing that can help you. Only you can help yourself, by giving them the truth. You need to take pity on yourself, and then your overlords will give the order for you to be pardoned; they'll let you eat and drink. They'll even arrange for your release. But you feel that they are lying. They cannot do anything. They are just torturers. They laugh … They sing an old pop song, 'Call Me Up',[28] as they wind the handle of an old-style telephone set. But this isn't sadism. It is their job. An ordinary job, which they do with skill and to their utmost ability. The longer and faster they wind the handle, the higher the voltage and stronger the current shooting through you. Naked wires are attached to your fingers and toes. To enhance the effect you are constantly doused with water. The current rips through your body like a thousand red-hot needles. Your body arches … You lie face down the whole time. The current is increased. The voltage is so high that your thumb nails are burning. But right now, of course, you're not aware of that. They continue to wind the handle, cheerfully singing, 'Call me up, oh, call me. For the love of God, call me …' You realize that they won't stop unless you scream. You let out a scream. This is the only torture to wrest a scream out of you. You're screaming more from impotent rage than from the pain. They stop. Only to start again five seconds later … They won't kill you until they believe that you have nothing left to tell them. Your task is to convince them of this as fast as you can. To do that you need to stick to your initial story, grit your teeth and not let a wrong word slip out.

Now somebody is feeling for a point along your spine. He pounds it with his rifle butt until you start gasping for air. Later you will need a long time in treatment for the slipped discs. One of them starts slicing off your ear, but he is stopped by someone else. Then your almost half-severed ear is kicked by someone in heavy army boots. You say nothing. When they stub out cigarettes on your naked body, it feels like a holiday. The pain from the cigarettes is so trivial after everything else that you rest. You rest and implore God: 'Either send me the Angel of Death or grant me the strength to bear this torture.' For the moment He grants you the strength. Of all your emotions, only two remain: hatred and fury. Hatred for your enemies and fury towards yourself. It does not even enter your head to feel self-pity. You are too furious over your mistake to feel sorry for yourself. You have nobody to blame. Nobody told you to take that track; quite the reverse, they tried to talk you out of it. You not only went, but you were even lulled into complacency, badly misreading the situation. And for the moment this anger is giving you the strength to endure the pain and humiliation. They know that the moment you start feeling sorry for yourself, you'll crack. That's why they keep on urging you: 'Come on, have pity on yourself. Surely a young guy like you wants to live? Think about your loved ones, your mother, they're all waiting for you, they love you. So why don't you take pity on yourself? Just tell us everything and the torture will stop. No one will lay a finger on you, and before you know it you'll be on your way home. You're a smart guy; why shield those gangsters who are trying to ruin our shared country? You're a sophisticated man, just look at that clean-shaven chin, now how on earth did you end up with those rebels?' From time to time they pause the torture and take you back to be interrogated. They ask you the same questions and you give them the same answers; then they start up the torture again. And so it goes on for hour after hour. They are getting tired. So it seems torturers do get tired, just like peasants at their honest labours. You lie in your position, face down. You are tremendously thirsty. It feels as if a drop of water could make you strong enough for a whole new life, like in the fairy tale. There is a damp strip hanging down from the blindfold on your eyes. You catch it with your lips and suck on it. With enormous pleasure. Its liquid is salty, but that doesn't worry you. It is moisture, after all. Someone speaks above your head: 'He's sucking from that rag all soaked in blood and water.' And the immediate command: 'Tuck in the strip! Let him die of thirst!'

When the naked wires are attached to your fingers and toes and the electric current shoots through you, the pain is extreme. But it can be tolerated. You have to strain every sinew, but you can bear it. The pain won't let you flag, it's sustaining the rage that you need so badly now. But there are parts of the body that are particularly sensitive to pain. When the current hits those parts, it becomes nearly impossible to bear the pain even briefly, and certainly impossible to bear it for long. And they know this. They are professionals; they know their field well. And that's why it is so horrifically painful. What can you do with this pain devouring you from within, like a sudden horrific affliction? You can oppose it with a weapon that is even stronger: love. You can love this pain. Understand that this is cathartic. Become a masochist for a while. This is your purgatory, but afterwards there will come eternal rest. You have no life left to fight for, but you still have your death. So fight for that! The right to die also needs to be fought for. All this pain ... The pain from all this torture you've endured here, it will last just a little longer. The day's not over yet. But it will be followed by eternal rest. Whether you cry or laugh, curse your enemies or beg them for mercy, they'll kill you all the same. So why not die without tears? No, not 'with a smile on your lips'. Just without tears. The only way to get revenge on your executioners is to frustrate them. They're expecting you to weep and beg for mercy; they're hoping to see your moral death before you die physically. For them you will only be defeated once you've died spiritually. But your spirit is not yet broken. Even if you once had the luxury of a choice, you don't any longer. You must die as their mortal foe. Even in death you must haunt their dreams and blight their lives. You died long ago, yet for some reason your soul is in no haste to abandon this miserable apology of a body. But you are persistent, you'll get what you want. You won't tell them anything more. Something's happened to your lower lip, but you haven't worked out what exactly. It seems to have split, and some skin is hanging from it. If your hands were free, you would rip off this skin. It's disturbing you.

'What's your rank in Dudayev's army?' they laugh. 'Well, it doesn't matter. We hereby promote you to the rank of general. Your president said that each one of you Chechens is a general, didn't he? Well, as you don't have the uniform, we'll give you the shoulder straps, direct to your shoulders. You don't mind, do you?' They say this as they do something to your shoulders. Of course, you don't answer back. And then you feel intense pain. This pain is nothing, though, compared to what you were feeling before, and you enjoy the brief rest it brings. You even ask yourself whether you're turning into a masochist in this place. But right now that can only be a good thing. In any case, it won't be for much longer.

6

You are tired. Your executioners are also tired. Once again they are taking you somewhere. You've come to a halt. They tear the blindfold from your eyes and shove you into a tiny room. It is dark inside. But your eyes adapt, and you see yourself and your guide sitting on the concrete floor of the anteroom to a bomb shelter. Rather, it is a huge rail tank car buried in the earth in case of war, and you are sitting in its 'lobby'. Your hands are still tied. A number of arrested soldiers are sitting here too. From the soldiers you find out that you are in Chechnya's main Russian military base, Khankala.[29] After questioning your friend, you are pleased to learn that your initial stories match up and you quickly smooth out with him some minor discrepancies. You also discover that despite the vicious beatings and torture including electric shocks, he has stuck to his initial story. You are grateful for this and proud of him. He has stayed the course, and you know you could go anywhere with this guy. Only you're not likely to be going anywhere soon – not with him nor with anyone. A quarter of an hour later, the heavy armour-plated door of the shelter opens up and you are led outside. It is evening. The sun has set. Some officers are standing in a circle, and you've been placed in the middle. You feel like Konstantin Balmont's scorpion: 'My enemies watch me from all sides. A tragic, haunting nightmare.'[30]

You read on the faces of all these officers nothing but icy enmity. They lob difficult questions at you from all directions. This is a psychological technique: if you force someone to answer a stream of rapidly fired questions, he will automatically start telling the truth. Because you cannot come up with lies at that speed, and nor can you stay silent. But you know about this technique and so far you've been coping. When you begin to feel yourself struggling to keep it up, you interrupt their questions to ask for some water. They toss a bucket of cold water over your head, suggesting you drink that.

At this point a tall lean officer with a grey crew cut walks up to you. 'Well, I don't know what you think …' he says to someone, 'but I'm removing him. He's a pulpy mess!' He orders them to untie your hands and he helps you up. You are wary. You know that in this place gentle words mean only more pain to come. He senses this. He tries to allay your fears. 'Don't worry, I won't be asking you questions,' he says, sitting you on a stool under a camouflage canopy. There's a truck with a red cross nearby. So you are in the field hospital. You look at your hands. They have turned into stumps of dark-violet. That's from the stagnant blood. The belt tied around the wrists was stopping the blood from circulating, and so they've swollen up and turned blue. All sensation is gone. If someone were to break a finger or chop one off, you wouldn't even feel it.

'You must be thirsty?' The officer's voice brings you back from your thoughts. You nod warily. 'Don't worry, I am a doctor,' he says by way of introduction. 'Sergeant, bring him some water! And I'll get everything ready in the meantime.' You are given an almost full three-litre canister of water and you drink the lot. Straightaway you start shivering violently. Seeing you shake, the doctor tells you that it's a normal response for the body to shiver if you drink water after what you've been through. He takes you into the back of a truck, lays you down on a bed and starts to busy himself with his medicines. You slowly drift off … But you

94

are brought back suddenly from your half-conscious state by the voices of some officers standing under the canopy: 'Cut his lip off, Doctor! He can be a harelip!' they shout.

You quickly raise yourself up on your elbows and say, 'Doctor, listen. Don't cut my lip off. They're going to kill me tomorrow anyway. Well, I'd like to die looking like myself …' You notice tears in the eyes of the grey-haired officer. 'I can't save your life, son. But I promise I'll save your foot and your lip. My God, how can they do this to a living person?' he adds quietly.

'Why waste your medicines on him, Doc!' someone shouts. 'Just leave him. He'll be dead by the morning.'

'Whoever he is, he's still a human being. I feel sorry for him, in any case,' the doctor replies. He fills a syringe for an injection, but you don't want one. You are afraid of being given a hypnotic such as barbitone. The doctor guesses your thoughts and says, 'It's novocaine, for pain relief.'

'No, I'll manage without. The pain surely can't get any worse.' He shakes his head and silently puts down the syringe. Once he has sewn up your lip – you later learn from him it was split in two and required thirteen stitches – and tended to your foot, the doctor gives you a shirt, a pair of trousers – yours are in shreds and resemble a grass skirt – and some old sandals of his. They are far too big for you, but in any case it's an improvement on being barefoot. And he also gives you a blanket to lie on, telling you, 'No matter what, you mustn't go to the lower end of the tank car. Lie on the concrete by the door. If you go in deeper, we'll need to amputate your foot. It's very damp down there. And the damp can bring on gangrene. It might be cramped at the door, but you'll be able to bear it. Use the blanket to lie on. It'll give some protection from the cold concrete.' The guard supports you as you hobble with difficulty to your dungeon. There you lie down on the blanket, near your friend, who has also been taken there. You are quite sure he'll be released. So you say goodbye to him now. In case they come for you tonight. He refuses to reconcile himself to the thought that you will be killed, but for you it is the logical end to this interminably long day.

Death is a leap over the threshold of existence into a better world. Only it's not like that for everyone. For some it means negotiating a soaring mountain pass rather than a threshold. Not everyone is lucky enough to take a little leap and find himself in the next world. You feel as if you've clambered to the peak of your pass. So you talk with your God. It is only when talking with Him that you can speak freely: He already knows everything, and He will understand you. And so you open up only to Him. You're rushing. You don't want to leave anything out. But your life has been brief, and so your speech does not in fact take long. You begin your conversation by forgiving all your friends and enemies. You forgive everyone who at some point might have harboured bad thoughts towards you, and in doing so has sinned. You even forgive your torturers and executioners. No, not out of neighbourly love, but in the name of God, who created each one of us. You beg the Creator to forgive them too, lest a single one of His creatures remain guilty before Him on account of you. You've thrown off the heavy weight of all worldly affairs and worries, all thoughts of life, and with a light soul, purified of love and hate, of joy and grief, you are ready for your meeting with God. There is only sadness, an endless, vast sadness. You slowly drift into a twilight zone between the two worlds. You are infinitely alone on your path to God and this loneliness will never quit your soul. You will remain lonely inside for evermore. You feel that you've reached the summit of the pass. And you are yearning to cross to the other, better world. But you cannot. A force stronger than your yearning will not allow you in. You struggle for an eternity for the right to depart from this life. And you give in, realizing that you haven't yet come to the end of your path here. You still have a little further to go. You still have to crawl your way through hell. And so you return.

You come to, lying on the concrete. Your head is on the lap of your brother-in-misfortune, and you hear him quietly shedding tears in mourning for you. You ask what he is crying for. He starts at the sound of your voice and, placing his hand on your chest, he replies that he wasn't crying. You are too calm, and this frightens him. The soldiers sitting there leave you in peace. You have to convince him of your sanity.

In the dark you hear the mumbling of the lieutenant (a contract soldier[31], as you learn later), who has been arrested along with two other officers and imprisoned here in the cellar with you. He is tirelessly addressing 'Comrade Colonel', who is sitting with him, and he's threatening to get mad, and accompanying this with an explanation of how scary he is when angry. You get fed up with hearing this and so you suggest he should go on and get mad or shut up. He asks, 'Who's that?'

The soldiers reply, 'A Chechen.'

'Is he violent?' he asks.

And despite the soldiers' assurances that 'He's mellow, he's taken a right clobbering', he decides to quit talking. A strip of light is showing through a small hole punched through the top of the tank car. It is dawn. But the dawn will bring with it new torture. For the first time in your life you are frightened of the dawn. You know they won't shoot you straightaway. You realized that during the night. You wait. Afraid. Afraid of not being able to take it. You don't trust your willpower and you don't trust your tongue. You're frightened of ceasing to be their enemy. You may have forgiven them, they may have stopped being the enemy to you, but you must be the enemy to them. They do not know how to forgive. They do not know the vast power hidden in forgiveness. They're revelling in their physical dominion over you. They are not free of hatred, and that is their curse. The door opens and you are led outside. You step into the morning sun and fresh air. Everyone is eating army porridge for breakfast – everyone except you. You are unable to. You can neither chew nor swallow. So you watch them in silence.

7

They've blindfolded you and are taking you for interrogation. As they bring you into the room, they remove the blindfold. Two men are in the room: a man just over forty with a black moustache who is in civilian clothes and a strapping guy in uniform without any rank insignia. You immediately work out who this second man is. He's a *praporshchik* – a warrant officer. In the Soviet Army, *praporshchik* was a rank for losers. For men who would never be officers but were no longer soldiers. The *praporshchik* usually serves in a position too demeaning for a professional officer but that cannot be entrusted to a sergeant. These are administrative roles and also what are tacitly regarded as valets to the generals and admirals (the Soviet Army didn't officially have valets). Of course, there were *praporshchiks* who were experts, but they were a tiny minority. When I served in the Soviet Army our platoon commander was a *praporshchik*. But I could never bring myself to call him one. And I wasn't alone – the other soldiers in the platoon felt the same. A first class professional, his intellect and skill inspired respect. Soldiers would nickname *praporshchiks* 'Swag-Baggers' or 'Dogs'. These *praporshchik* flunkies can always be spotted by their stunted intellectual development, the cowardly cruelty in their eyes and the permanently spiteful expression of a loser on their faces. 'I am a *praporshchik*,' he introduces himself, as though declaring that you've won a prize. 'I've been at war for the past twelve years, ever since Afghanistan, and the word "mercy" has been wiped clean from my memory. By the way, I've found out your call sign,' he tells you gleefully. It's "Dog", that right?'

'What, you've decided to name me that?' you ask.

'Ah, so he can speak!' he says, thumping you on the head with his fist, which is clenched around a pistol. This knocks you to the floor, along with the chair you'd been seated on. Getting up with effort, you sit back down. Next, the *praporshchik* comes up behind your back and whacks you round the head with the pistol butt. Your face strikes the table, and for a moment you lose consciousness. But a new blow to your kidneys brings you round, knocking the wind out of you. The *praporshchik* fires the pistol into the ground at your feet. The pistol has a silencer, and instead of shots, you hear pops.

'Now I'll smash your other foot up so bad it'll have to be lopped right off, you bleeding bastard!' he spits. But the seething *praporshchik* is stopped by the man in civilian clothing, who until now has remained silent. He's clearly an officer, although he is trying to play the part of a civilian.

'Are you an only son?' he asks. You nod in reply.

'And if you die, your line will end, yes?' You nod again, unable to speak from the pain. He is well-versed in your traditions. He understands the importance for Chechens of maintaining their genetic line, the blood of the clan. He's probably a native of the Caucasus himself.

'Look, we've thought things over and we've decided to give you a chance. You tell us all that you know. Show us on the map where the rebels have their base. Tell us the weapons they have, how many men are in Gelayev's special-forces unit, what their rank insignia is, the location of their positions, and we'll release you. If you refuse, then you'll be killed. And after they've killed you, they'll blow your head off with a grenade. And nobody will be able to identify the corpse.' Yet another demonstration of his knowledge of Chechen culture: corpses must never be abused or mutilated, it is an insult to the living members of the victim's clan; but what he doesn't know is that during war this rule takes on a different interpretation. 'But before they kill you, they'll make you speak anyway. We haven't yet tried our full range of techniques on you.'

'Look, I can't read maps. I don't know the first thing about weapons. I don't even know one end of that RPG you found on me from the other. I've never been to the bases – they never trusted me enough. And as for the number of men and the rank insignia of the special forces – I simply don't know.'

'But you're lying to us. You're on good terms with Dudayev. You had a photo of him, you had poems dedicated to him, you had a report intended for him, and you're trying to tell us that you and he aren't friends. You expect us to believe that? Why won't you look us in the eye when you answer?'

'First, tell me whose eyes to look into. You're both asking questions and you're both demanding I look you in the eyes. Well, I can only look at you one at a time. As for the poems … I'm a poet. And it's my right as a poet to dedicate my work to whoever I want. The photo of Dzhokhar was from a press conference. It's got the date on it, so you can go and check whether there really was a press conference that day. Those scrappy old notes of mine could hardly count as a report, they don't follow any system. And there's no intended recipient named anywhere.'

'You don't seem to understand what will happen to you,' says the colonel. You discover he's a colonel when an officer sticks his head round the door and addresses him by rank. 'Have you seen yourself in the mirror? Do you have any idea what you look like? Would you like a mirror?' You nod. 'Show him a mirror,' he says to the *praporshchik*.

'Maybe not … He might not be able to take it,' the *praporshchik* replies.

'Actually, I would like to look at myself,' you say, and they lead you to a mirror. From the mirror someone stares back at you. But it is clearly not a human. And it is certainly not you. There's a head swollen up to several times its size. Eyes that have no whites at all. Instead there are bloodied orbits with unnaturally narrow pupils peering out from their depths. Hair matted with blood from the numerous wounds and abrasions. The lower lip is almost split in two. Violet rings under the eyes. The lips are caked in blood. No, this freak does indeed have your eyes. Rather, the expression in the eyes is yours. Now you understand the stunned response of the officer who caught sight of you at breakfast as you sat apart from the other prisoners. You realize why he couldn't tear his eyes from you for several minutes in some sort of speechless stupor. And you understand why the wounded young Chechen they brought in during the night was asking for pardon: 'For the love of God, forgive me my weakness. I didn't realize the state you were in while I was groaning. I won't groan any more, please forgive me!' he said to you in the morning, as though he were in some way guilty before you. Meanwhile, the officer and the *praporshchik* wait for you to react. You are silent for several moments.

'Hmm! If only our girls could see me now, how they'd laugh …' you say quite sincerely, suddenly imagining yourself like this in your former life. The colonel's face turns white as chalk, and in a quiet voice he says to the *praporshchik*, 'Well, he has a keen sense of humour. He knows how to laugh at himself,' and he silently leaves.

Your hands are tied back up and you're blindfolded; then they set to work on you. The colonel was speaking the truth: they haven't yet put you through the full treatment. They tighten a noose around your neck, drawing it tighter and tighter until your tongue hangs out. Then they release it. They tighten it again … And they repeat this over and over. They lift your bound wrists above your head and suspend you by them. You feel as if your wrists are about to drop off. And you wait like that … At least if they dropped off the pain would subside a bit. You wish they would hurry up and drop off. Meanwhile, you barely notice the blows raining down on you. All your sensation is focused on your wrists. But these are professionals at work. They hold you in this pose fairly briefly. For just as long as is needed. To let you know what it would be like to stay that way a bit longer. They take great pleasure in vividly describing the effects of a similar torture technique which they call 'the rack'. They pull your hands behind your back and tie them back up again. 'Want to fly?' they jest. And again they hang you, but this time by your arms trussed behind your back. They slip nooses over your ankles and pull your legs apart until your hip bone clicks. And then they beat you. They beat you with the utmost skill. And they laugh: 'Look, you're a swallow. All you need now is to take to the air. But only if we let you. And one limb at a time.' This time they hold you a bit longer. Now you are suspended by your arms and legs and they can torture you for longer. But they measure out the time as precisely as jewellers measuring gold. If you can have professionals in such a craft, then these are true professionals.

Today the 'interrogation' hasn't gone on for long – just a few hours. By lunchtime they are bored and you're taken back to the cellar. But almost at once they bring you out for lunch. And once again the doctor comes for you. He examines your wounds and looks pleased. 'They're healing nicely. You don't drink or smoke, do you? Well, that's why they're healing so well. I specially left your ear, the "shoulder straps" and the other wounds untreated. I wanted to watch what your foot would do. It's a perforating wound, and that's good, but the bullet ricocheted and shattered the toe bone, so there was a danger of gangrene. But now I can see what a strong constitution you have. The foot will heal, only you need to keep it away from the damp,' he says as he tends to your wounds. When he has changed the bandage, you get up to leave but he stops you. 'Sit here for a bit, get some rest. You can't eat barley, well then, try some salad or tinned meat.' But you cannot eat those either. So he makes you some strong, very sweet tea. 'There's glucose in the sugar, it will keep you from wasting away.' For the next five days you'll be unable to eat anything, and throughout this period the doctor will give you sweet tea to drink, a glass a day, saving you from the ravages of hunger. His officer friends come in. And seeing your condition, they try to cheer you up with jokes and demonstrations of hand-to-hand combat moves. You look upon all this with detached tranquillity. If people knew they didn't have long to live, surely they would be so much more dignified. The doctor doesn't tell you his name. But you know that he's Ukrainian, he has a small house on the shore of the Black Sea and he's got six months left before he retires. For the rest of your life you'll nurture gratitude in your heart towards this man who did so much for you.

8

You were cruelly mistaken in thinking you had crawled to the top of your mountain. You'd thought this hell could not get any crueller. How wrong you were. Pain can be still more intense. Hell can be still more ferocious. The morning is fresh and sunny. You are led out of the cellar and, blindfolded as usual, you are taken for a 'talk'. The colonel will be 'talking' with you. Today he is livid. Raising his voice almost to a shout, he says, 'We've received intelligence about you from our people. You're a spy working for Dudayev! And you've been leading us by the nose pretending you're a journalist! If you aren't an agent, then why the hell did you look at our aerial photos and not show us anything?' He is referring to the time you asked them to show you first a map, then some aerial photographs, and after looking at them, you failed to show them the rebel base, claiming that you couldn't make anything out.

'Our source insists we mustn't believe a word you say. He says you're trying to infiltrate our intelligence. You've been given the task of being captured so you can infiltrate us? Is that right? Answer, you bastard!' the colonel shouts. 'You won't get out of here alive, I promise! Not a hope in hell! We'll release your friend, but not you. You won't see trial! Blindfold him and take him to be shot!' he orders. They blindfold you and lead you away.

'Don't worry, it won't hurt. One "bang" and you're dead,' a

soldier mockingly comforts you. You say nothing. What use are words, however brave and grandiloquent? And you don't even know what words would befit the occasion. They lead you somewhere and place you standing. From behind you hear the clicks of rifles being cocked. But suddenly there's a command:

'Wait, stop! We still have some questions for him. Bring him over!' And once again you are led away.

'So you're in luck, arsehole! But it won't last long. You can go on living just a little bit longer. And then you'll be winging your way to heaven … Promised you plenty of houris in paradise, have they? But here's the downer: you'll be arriving there one body part at a time!' he says, beating you relentlessly. They bring you to a room and sit you on a chair. An unseen person sitting opposite you begins the interrogation.

'Tell me your objective in trying to infiltrate our intelligence. Who assigned you to the mission?'

'I wasn't trying to infiltrate anyone. And nobody gave me any mission. I'm just a journalist, who was unlucky enough to be in the wrong place at the wrong time.'

'It all fits too neatly … What was your purpose in asking to look at the map and the aerial photos if you didn't know where the rebel base was?'

'I wanted to try and make things easier. I was sick of the torture.' In reality you'd simply wanted to appear willing to help so they'd decide you were a hopeless case: Look, I wanted to help you, but couldn't make anything out. It is only now that you realize what a hole you've dug yourself into. So you won't be enjoying a swift death after all.

'Ah, but we have detailed intelligence on you from our sources.' You realize that these sources are Chechens. And you can even guess who they are. But you say nothing. 'What's more, we've intercepted a radio signal where an order was given to get you released at any cost. You must admit, they'd hardly get so worked up over an ordinary journalist. This might sound to you like good news, but I wouldn't get your hopes up. We'll only release you after you tell us the truth. You're an intelligence officer, aren't you?' At that very moment, an FSB officer is spreading false information among your acquaintances that you've told your captors you're one of Dudayev's intelligence officers.

'No. I'm a journalist. If the rebels are worried about me I expect it's because they all know me. I was working among them.'

'Yet you don't know anything about them. I'm afraid that's not how it works. At least tell us their names.'

'They don't use their real names. They all have call signs.'

'What was your call sign?'

'I didn't have a call sign. Everyone called me by my name.'

'What call signs were the rebels using? What about Gelayev's special forces?'

'I can't remember.'

'What insignia do the special forces use? Do they have some kind of patches, distinctive headgear or something? How do they stand out from the other units?'

'I don't have a clue about patches or badges. They all look the same to me.'

'All right. We accept that you might have forgotten certain things. But here's where a little jab can come in handy. It's terribly effective at curing forgetfulness. Now the guys here will help you to remember, while I'll be on my way. As soon as you remember, you just call for me. Say the words, "Call him," and I'll be back. Careful not to overdo it,' he addresses someone. 'We still need him.'

'Sure, I'll sterilize the needle in a flame specially for him,' someone answers.

When you hear the word 'jab', your blood runs cold. So they've decided to administer a truth serum. At this point you don't know if they really exist, though much later you'll discover that this whole idea of an infallible truth drug is no more than a myth. But right now you're waiting for just such a jab. You're expecting to slip away gradually to a state where you'll lose control of your mind. They place your arms on the table. But why are they holding them down? And why both arms? The answer comes in an instant, when an insane pain shoots up like lightning from your fingertips … Shattering your brain into smithereens, it surges back down … And finding no escape route, it thrashes through your nerves, ripping and searing them … After the first wave, a second one strikes, still more raging. Red circles are dancing before your eyes. No, you don't scream. You cannot scream. You wheeze. The pain has paralysed your breathing and clenched your throat in a burning spasm. It slowly turns you inside out. And you drift off into darkness … But there's water. They always have water to hand. The cool, bracing liquid jerks you from your haven of darkness – back into the pain. But mercifully, such high intensity pain cannot endure for long. Were it to last just a little longer, you would die of shock. Your heart could not take it. And they know it. That is why they administer the pain in astonishingly precise doses. These are true professionals. And the source of this fiendish pain? Fine needles thrust under the nails of your index and middle fingers. Not too deep … Just a little beyond the white crescent. Perhaps there are people who could handle this particular pain more easily. But you nearly went permanently out of your mind. At least that's how it felt.

'So, do you remember?' Through a fog you hear the voice of your invisible acquaintance. 'You can go for now. Only try and remember. And when you do, call for me. You don't have much time left. It's better that you call for me, not the other way round. Take him to the cellar!' They lead you away, not forgetting to give you a good beating in their usual manner, but at the cellar entrance the doctor catches you.

'Come with me, my unfortunate friend!' you hear the voice of your saviour, and you try to smile. He pulls off your blindfold; peering into your pupils, he shakes his head dolefully and sits you on the familiar stool beneath the canopy.

107

9

Today, on day five of your stay in Khankala, the Russian Army's main base in Chechnya, they have stopped the torture. And you know that they won't restart it. Not because you've told them the truth, not because your torturers have suddenly acquired a conscience. No. They won't torture you for another reason. Because they mustn't allow you to die. At least not yet ... You find this more terrifying than the most sophisticated torture technique. Your journey so far may have been painful, but it was a known quantity. What comes next is a mystery. There's no chance of things improving, so that means they can only get worse. And you cannot imagine anything worse than what you've been through ... And so this lull terrifies you. The torture has almost killed you in any case. You couldn't have taken much more. The fact that they've decided to put you on trial, offering you a phantom chance to defend yourself in Russian law, is immaterial. You understand perfectly well that you won't live to see trial. It's just that something's clearly happened to make them change tactics. And you still don't know what it is. Later you will find out. But for now you are talking to a courteous lieutenant colonel. He is enquiring after your health, asking whether there is anything you need and so forth. You're not yet sure what to expect from this politeness and so you remain on your guard. Yes, you're

OK. You feel fine and there's nothing you need. Your eyes aren't blindfolded and the lieutenant colonel has introduced himself. It doesn't matter that the name is made up, all the same he has introduced himself. Aleksandr, as he calls himself, is interested in how you got caught up in the war, how you found yourself in the rebel camp.

'You see, I'm a journalist,' you say. 'It's not for me to judge who is right and who's wrong in this war.' You try to act the impartial journalist. And he tries to pretend he believes you. 'My aim was to witness the tragedy of my nation and then to write about what I'd watched. To tell people about the other side of war's romanticism. I don't want anything like this ever to be repeated, anywhere. History will judge whoever is guilty in this war, but nobody can bring back the dead. I was simply carrying out my job. And I was working in the rebel camp only because I was downright afraid of working with the Russians. Well, you can see for yourself how they've treated me.' You say 'they', in a conscious attempt to remove the officer from the category of your torturers.

'So you wanted to chronicle this tragedy. If I've understood you correctly?' the officer clarifies before continuing. 'We know that you're a journalist. We've read all your articles – you weren't lying to us. I found them interesting. You usually write on themes like …' He lists all the topics you write on. 'Listen, I believe you. Do you mind if we drop the formalities?' He shifts to a more confiding tone. 'It's just that they had to be convinced that you were telling the truth.' He has consented not to be one of them. 'I've come because I need your help. That's right. We need your help and I personally am quite sure that your humane values won't allow you to refuse. You are free to refuse, of course … But do you think that would be wise?'

'How can I help?'

'You can save a man's life. He's a good guy, a man worth saving. He's being held prisoner by your side. Here he is' – he shows a photo of a young man. 'He's a major. And an only son, like you.

We know that he's alive and we've a rough idea who's holding him. If you write a letter asking them to swap him for you, he could be saved.'

'Well, I can write a letter easily enough. But a letter doesn't mean that the rebels will want to hand over a major for me. I'm just a journalist to them, an outsider.'

'You're more than just a journalist to them. I think they'll hand over a major for you. Trust me, I know what I'm saying.'

'OK. But who should I address the letter to?'

'You just write it. We'll do the rest. OK?'

You write a brief letter, addressed to some unknown recipient, in which you ask them to swap you for Major So-and-So; then you are taken to the cellar. But soon you are summoned to your old friend the colonel. He is waiting for you outdoors, armed and in uniform.

'Do you have any close friends among the rebels?'

'Not as far as I know.'

'Who might be worried about your plight?'

'Anyone at all. I used to work with them, after all. And there weren't that many Chechen journalists working among them. So all the rebels knew us.'

'You're lying again! Why can't you tell us the truth?' he breaks into a shout. 'You want me to send you to the special forces for them to train on?"

'I don't understand what I've lied about. I was telling the truth.'

'The truth? You were telling the truth? The rebels have taken two of our soldiers and they're demanding we exchange you for them! Otherwise they will kill them! But don't get your hopes up! We won't swap you! We'll swap your guide for those two soldiers! And if the rebels don't agree, then you can kiss goodbye to your guide's home village! We'll raze it to the ground! And you personally will be responsible for the destruction of that village! You, and nobody else! You won't leave here alive, I'm telling you! You'll go to the filtration camp, and your guide will go home.

Your mission to infiltrate us has failed, and now they've decided to get you out? Take him!' he orders.

You don't believe him, thinking this must be just another ruse, but you are wrong. Your friend Adlan has indeed spent several days waiting in ambush with his group and they've captured two officers whom they want to exchange for you. And the colonel has done his utmost to see that the exchange does not take place, to see you join the ranks of those missing without a trace, but he has lost. They do not torture you again, although they continue leading you off to interrogations. But as both sides already know the questions and answers, the interrogations do not last long, usually around two or three hours. Now they have switched entirely to a war of nerves, and so far you are more or less coping. Although it is hard to say which of their tortures, the psychological or the physical, is the more barbaric.

One morning, the doctor comes for you earlier than usual. He lets you take a tepid shower – the first wash in your two weeks here. He carefully tends to your wounds. He removes the old stitches from your split lip and puts in new ones, using a special absorbable catgut suture. An officer friend of his brings you a new army shirt. You ask what all this fuss is about, and the doctor replies: 'Today they're taking you to a filtration camp. You're unlikely to get your dressing changed much there.'

You feel chilled by this news, but, trying to stay calm, you ask, 'Which filter camp are they taking me to? Do you know?'

'You'll be taken to PAP-1,'[32] the officer says. 'I managed to find that out. The situation there is rather worse than in the others, though you're not likely to find it much worse than here. The key to your survival is that you mustn't change your story, come what may. No matter what they do to you, stand firm. You can do it. You've already proved it here.'

'Thank you,' you say to these true friends. 'I'll never forget you.'

They feed you some salad, stewed meat and tea with biscuits.

'Andreyich, maybe you can find him a jacket?' the doctor asks the officer. 'He'll freeze if it's cold there.'

'Doc, there's no need …' You stop the officer who has already got up. 'You've done far too much for me as it is. Maybe I won't be needing any jackets there …'

They look at each other and silently shake their heads, lost for words.

'Thank you, for everything! Well, I'll be off. I want to say goodbye to my friend before they come for me,' you say, breaking the silence.

'Yes, of course. They'll be here for you soon. Go say goodbye to him,' the doctor says.

'And don't worry about your friend. We'll look out for him,' the officer promises.

You barely have time to say goodbye to your comrade before you're loaded into an armoured personnel carrier and the colonel drives you to the filter camp. The 'filtration centre', or, more accurately, concentration camp, scares both you and the officers, because there have been endless rumours about it, each more fantastical than the next. According to these rumours, what goes on there is enough to make Khankala and its torture seem like a holiday resort. And so you brace yourself for something still more terrible. You're met by the head of the filter camp, a dry, stubby little man of around fifty. They blindfold you and take you somewhere, then they place you face down on the concrete. And they start beating you. Several of them have surrounded you and are beating you. In silence. You too remain silent. Groaning and shouting would be pointless. In any case, this beating could be the prelude to something worse … Suddenly the beating stops. They help you up and carefully, warning you about obstacles so you don't bang your head, lead you to a cell.

10

As it goes, the filter camp, with all the brutality of its system, does not bring up such dreadful memories as the military base at Khankala. The filtration centre vaguely resembled a Russian prison, and life there was possible, if you could describe the prisoners' existence in even the best of Russia's prisons as 'life'. The only difference was that in a prison, you'd have a bare modicum of rights, if only in theory, whereas in the filter camp there weren't even token rights. There were zero rights; you were entirely dependent on the mercy of the team on duty and the investigator or operative allocated to you. In this system, the investigator did not play such a key role as in an ordinary non-military case. Here the most important work was done by the intelligence operative assigned to you. He decided how you lived, when you underwent torture and beatings and so forth. And thus he played an essential role in the prisoner's life. The operative assigned to me wasn't too bad. I met him around fifteen minutes after arriving in the cell. I'd been summoned for interrogation. There were three men in the room, and they were firing the same old wearisome questions. I answered on autopilot, without even thinking. By now I was as sick of the answers as of the questions. One of them broke from the monotony of question-and-answer by throwing me a new question about my reasons for remaining in the war zone – besides the journalistic work, which 'nobody would have asked you to account for; there's a war on, after all'.

'The number of times I've tried to explain. You wouldn't understand it, anyway,' I said wearily.

'I will understand. Try to explain it to me.'

And here I broke down and began speaking with enormous emotion about my desire 'to see everything with my own eyes and write a book about it'. The whole time he looked me intently in the eye. The other officer jumped to his feet and said, 'We're not interested in your fantasies. Just tell us the truth!' delivering a blow to my head. But the officer who asked the question stopped him from planting a second one.

'What do you want to hear from me? This is the only truth I know,' I told him.

'I believe you. You're a man burning with belief. My name's Nikolay,' he introduced himself, 'and I promise you: in this filter camp no one will lay a finger on you again. If you don't object, I'd like to have more contact with you. I'm interested in your views of the situation. It won't be an interrogation. We'll simply discuss things.'

At this point we were alone in the room, but that didn't change anything. I realized that these discussions would simply mean a new form of interrogation, but I didn't have much choice, in fact I had none at all. If we didn't have 'discussions', then we'd probably be having 'interrogations', and I was truly sick of them, so I said, 'I'd find it very interesting to discuss things. It could help me with my book.'

We were both well-mannered enough to keep a discrete silence about the fact that I stood little chance of writing any book, and he walked me back to the cell.

Nikolay kept his word: from that moment on nobody in the filter camp touched me. There was another officer, though – the one that hit me during the interrogation – who for some reason developed a ferocious hatred of me and did whatever he could to make my life even more miserable. But he concentrated his efforts on psychological torment. And, who knows, perhaps he was just playing the part of 'bad cop'. Nikolay, though, was the complete reverse: he always showed a sense of delicacy, and in our subsequent talks he never acted shabbily, nor did he try to catch me out with words or ask me trick questions. And our talks were interesting. It turned out he'd studied for a teaching degree and had a decent knowledge of world literature. Of course, I was aware of the technique of bonding with your subject by observing his habits, hobbies and interests. And so I was careful not to lower my guard. But in this case Nikolay did not have to change himself to fit in with his subject: he really was well-educated and knew about various trends in world literature. Mostly we talked about literature, but we would also discuss politics, both world and domestic. Of course, he would attempt to defend Moscow's policies and find justifications for the war in Chechnya; I would then counter with an argument no less compelling. At times our discussions made a scene worthy of some crazy artist. The filthy, beaten, stubbly prisoner, thin as a skeleton, and the clean-shaven pink-cheeked officer in his neat uniform sitting on old chairs at a rickety table in a room with scruffy walls, discussing world literature and politics animatedly, emotionally even, as if reaching a consensus between them might solve all the world's problems.

There was one other person who came for 'talks'. He wore a military uniform without rank insignia and he was notable for his exceptional politeness. His habitual and rather charming smile might have been thought sincere if it weren't for a sobering chill in the pit of my stomach, a telltale warning signal from my intuition. This time I wasn't about to ignore such a signal: I had paid far too dearly for ignoring it just the once. So while outwardly trying to appear calm and even rather friendly, I carefully watched my words. He also talked more generally about the Chechen war, about journalism and freedom of speech, but he did not have that fire which allowed Nikolay to argue heatedly in defence of his own views, while sometimes grudgingly conceding the points I made. Well, of course, he too would agree with me, only he'd agree with almost everything I said. And it was his readiness to agree with everything, his über-politeness, his knowledge of the topics in our discussions – except, of course, for the military and political – that felt learnt by rote, and this forced me to stay in constant danger mode. Eventually he revealed himself as an officer of the recently renamed FSB – until April 1995 known as the FSK, the Federal Counter-intelligence Service – and so my grounds for alarm were borne out.

A few days after my arrival, a noteworthy event occurred. The Red Cross visited the camp. They interviewed all the detainees privately and took letters for loved ones from those who wished to write them. They asked about the conditions in the camp – the torture, the food and so on; then they proposed that we each write a letter which they guaranteed to deliver to any address. They visited our cell first. After briefly outlining what they could do, they suggested we talk to them and write a letter to a loved one. They were particularly keen to encourage me; they must have been disturbed by my appearance. I turned them down, as I believed there was no way I'd ever get out of there alive, so why bother with letters. A letter would only bring more heartache to a loved one. A guy from our cell agreed to talk and they went off with him. Once they'd talked to the inmates of all the cells, the Red Cross workers returned to our cell and addressed me again.

'Young man, perhaps you'll decide to talk to us?'

'I have nothing to say to you,' I answered.

'Then maybe you'd like to write someone a letter?'

'I don't have anyone to write to ... There's no point.'

'Oh, go on, write a letter for them,' the guard interrupted. 'What's the problem in scribbling a few lines? They won't leave you in peace ...'

'All right,' I complied. 'Where do we go?'

We went to an empty cell with a table and two chairs. A Red

Cross worker who introduced himself as George gave me some paper and a pen and asked me to start writing. At this point the door swung open and my friend the polite FSB officer entered, accompanied by the guard. Not a trace of his politeness remained.

'You can only talk with this detainee in our presence,' he said.

'But we have an arrangement that we can talk to all the prisoners in private!' George objected. 'Up till now this arrangement has always been observed. What's the problem?'

'The arrangement does not apply to this person. Either speak to him in our presence or we take him away,' the officer snapped.

George began answering indignantly but I broke in: 'George, please, calm down. There's nothing I'd say in private that I wouldn't say in front of them. It's all OK ...'

It didn't even enter my head to complain about the detention conditions. In the first place, nobody's life had ever been made any easier by lodging complaints, and secondly, once I'd complained, they would leave, whereas I had to stay. Besides, in my situation, where each day of life felt more like an aberration than a logical consequence, it would have been absurd to complain about some 'conditions of custody' or other. After all, there was nothing holding me to this world, I'd settled my account with it. So my dialogue with George was rather odd.

'Do you think you're being held under acceptable conditions?' he asked, once he'd taken the letter for my relatives.

'Yes. If custodial detention can ever be called acceptable.'

'Are you fed well enough here?'

'We get fed three times a day. The food's OK.' In reality we were fed only twice a day, and we got some watery swill with a few peas floating in it that bore a vague resemblance to soup. We were hardly ever given bread, and bread was considered the most exquisite delicacy in the filter camp. Just plain old rye bread or white, stale or fresh.

'Do they beat you here?'

'In this filter camp they haven't been beating me.'

'What happened to your foot?'

'It's self-inflicted … I was careless with my weapon …'

'And when did you last have it bandaged?'

'Yesterday.'

'And what about your lip?'

'I fell …'

'Do you have any complaints?'

'None.'

George, of course, understood the extent of my sincerity, but he pretended to believe me. The unbearable smell of dirt wafting from me clearly undermined my words. He left and I went back to the cell. Around ten minutes later the guard commander came with some rice porridge and an entire loaf of bread.

'When did you last have your bandage changed?' he asked. 'Come on, be honest.'

'If I'm being honest, then three days ago …'

He said nothing and left, but he was back a few minutes later with the doctor. He called me into the medical room and ordered the doctor: 'Dress his wound properly!'

'I don't have any bandages,' the doctor replied.

'You can take one of my first-aid dressing packages. Only do a decent job.'

'To what do I owe the honour, Commander?' I asked in astonishment.

'See, you can always count on a decent guy no matter where he is. We know who said what. If there's anything you need, let me know, I'll do what I can.'

That evening I was transferred to a new, relatively comfortable cell. Its comfort consisted in the plank floor put in for the workers who'd fitted out the filter camp, and the curtain to screen off the corner where there was a milk churn for a toilet. The hardest psychological torment came in having to answer the call of nature in the same room you lived in. Almost in full view of the other cellmates. They would tactfully look the other way. The only way to reduce your psychological anguish was to eat less and go less often. Compared with concrete floors and uncurtained corners, this cell seemed a world apart.

A few days later my friend, whom I'd last seen in Khankala, joined me in the cell; other than that, life in the camp flowed on monotonously. I was convinced that they'd already released him and it came as a surprise when he appeared in our cell. I'd just returned from one of my 'talks' with the polite FSB officer. He told me that after I was transferred to the filter camp, they left him alone. In fact, they'd stopped using physical force on him after the first day of our stay in Khankala, but I'd been deeply worried they'd force him to 'fly' or give him a 'jab'. Fortunately, that was not what happened.

11

You met all sorts in the filter camp. From genuine supporters of Chechen independence, who had landed there through denunciations or during a 'cleansing op', to supporters of the pro-Moscow opposition, arrested for picnicking in a prohibited place or for some other such nonsense. There were also activists from the Japanese Hare Krishna humanitarian organization, and each day at a certain hour they would perform their prayers, loudly chanting their mantras. The Hare Krishna activists were released a week later. I'd shared my first cell with three Russian soldiers who'd been arrested for desertion and a young Chechen guy called Alvi, who'd been detained by the OMON at a checkpoint. Before his arrival at the filter camp, the OMON had put Alvi through the full works of torture in Assinovsky, a village in western Chechnya, but here in the filter camp they didn't beat him. What's more, a few days after my arrival they let him go. For money, of course. Once he'd been released from the filter camp, he went off to fight in the war, and six months later he fell defending the legendary Bamut[33]. He was released the night I moved to the new cell. In the new cell there was a Russian guy supposedly there for looting and a Chechen in his mid-twenties whose right-hand thumb was missing. They'd shot it off straight after arresting him. Both of my new cellmates had previous convictions and they'd done time before, which was responsible for some rather odd behaviour. They loved brewing *chifir* – ridiculously concentrated tea drunk in small sips. The camp regulations did not allow the making of *chifir*, but they somehow managed to light a fire with scraps of paper and rags and they brewed up their tea in an empty tin. Earlier, they hadn't a hope of making *chifir*, as tea was not issued to the prisoners. But when I appeared in the cell, everything changed.

The day after his release, Alvi posted a big parcel addressed to me. The camp allowed unlimited quantities of food to be sent to the inmates. And so Alvi sent an entire sack of goodies: bread, fruit, vegetables, sweets and several items of clothing for me. There was enough to share with all the prisoners in all the cells. At my request the guards distributed the food to everyone. Among these goodies was tea. And this tea served the noble and lofty purpose of *chifir*-brewing for the poor prisoners. A day later I was found by my relatives, who'd been searching for me all this time without success, and the problem of hunger was over.

Once a week the inmates were taken to wash. Strictly five minutes were allocated to bathing; if you managed to wash in time, all was well. If you didn't, then so much the worse for you. But I was denied even that privilege. The explanation offered was that my wounds needed to be protected from moisture. The constant sweating in the stuffy cell did not count: apparently that was not 'moisture'. The upshot was that in no time I had become the dirtiest prisoner in the filter camp. I realized that this was yet another method of psychological torture, but the knowledge did not make me feel any better or cleaner. All the detainees had lice. But the lice chose to give me a wide berth. I must have been too dirty even for those unsqueamish creatures. Before long our cell became crowded, as new prisoners arrived and old ones were transferred from other cells. Among the newcomers to the cell was the prefect of a highland area in Chechnya who had been denounced and arrested. We had known each other since before the war. So I immediately took him to a corner of the cell and instead of the usual story about how to survive in the filter camp, I had a different talk with him. We needed to sort out the details of what I'd tell them about him. They would be asking me about him, of that I was sure. Of course, in a situation where any newcomer to the cell, or even any of the old cellmates, could be a stool pigeon working for the enemy, you had to have a brave head on your shoulders to make contact like that. Only those who've been through a filter camp will understand. Distrust of your fellow sufferers was one of the rules of survival there. But things could hardly get worse for me than they already were. What's more, he didn't fall into the category of suspicious prisoner. He was completely beyond suspicion. We had barely started our talk when I was called out for an interrogation. A brilliant expert on the Quran and the son and grandson of peacemakers among blood-feud enemies, renowned throughout the land, he brought optimism and life into our cell. He banished everyone's sad thoughts about their fate, and their idle chat, and instead made them all recite holy surahs from the Quran by repeating after him. Strong in spirit and never despondent, he spent much of his time reciting surahs with us. And in doing so, he enabled the new prisoners to preserve a state of mental equilibrium in the face of their profound shock at what had befallen them. In the brief time he was with us, he taught the prisoners many surahs.

Unfortunately, a few days later they took him away – not to release him but to transfer him to another filter camp. He was released, or rather swapped, only a month later, by which time he'd been through the horrors of torture. The morale in our cell remained positive even after he'd left. Some of the prisoners, whose belief in God would normally have been confined to uttering the formula of faith, earnestly persisted in reciting the surahs he had taught them right till the end.

12

The physical and psychological techniques used in this filter camp in order to extract accurate intelligence are a topic that merits digression. As I've noted before, the rumours about torture at the filter camp were so dreadful that the doctor at Khankala had behaved as if he were seeing me off to the guillotine. Of course torture did take place. I had to share a cell with people who'd been imprisoned there since the filtration centres first opened in February 1995. Through long talks with these people, using classic journalistic detective work, I managed to find out that torture methods were used there, including electric shocks. And they used to hold night-time beatings. People were brought out one at a time and smashed up. The OMON paramilitaries were particularly vicious. It would seem that they only picked people with a sadistic bent to work for the OMON. Their torture methods included both the 'rack' and the 'swallow'. Attempted male rape and sexual abuse with objects were also used – indeed, perhaps there was actual rape – but such cases were extremely rare, and they tended to do this to prisoners who, according to some criteria of their own, they'd picked as falling into a specific category. Most likely, they degraded a man in this way when he elicited from them a reaction not of rage or hatred, both endemic in the camp, but of contempt. I happened to share a cell with a guy who came close to being raped. The system of raping prisoners – with the victim then becoming a pariah – was not invented in this filter camp; it was a practice common to all Soviet prisons and now to all Russian ones. But there were no crucifixions on the iron spikes nailed crosswise into the wall. Those spikes merely served for the structural support of the neighbouring cell wall. Nor did they hold prisoners for hours on end in the bus inspection pits filled with cold water. Those pits were simply left to pile up with rubbish. They were also mined in order to deter escape attempts. There were cases of prisoners being beaten to death; there were prisoners shot dead; there were mass burials. There were interrogations lasting many hours to wear down the subject to the point of exhaustion, where the prisoner was forced to watch other prisoners being tortured as a warning of what awaited him should he decide not to talk. They would cut prisoners' ears off – although not often – and break their bones. They would put a prisoner up against the wall and fire just above his head. A great number of atrocities were carried out, but there were also a lot of stories dreamt up by people with sick imaginations. At night you could often hear the horrific screams of prisoners being tortured. This made such an impression that some prisoners, even before the interrogation, were ready not only to tell everything, but also to invent things they thought their captors might want to hear. But the screams were not always evidence of someone being tortured at night – though they usually were. I knew that sometimes they would specially turn on a cassette player with recordings of screaming and groaning. It was a psychological torture technique.

During the Second Chechen War, too, similar tales circulated that were, mildly speaking, somewhat exaggerated. I managed to talk with some friends who had made the journey from the village of Komsomolskoye to the notorious White Swan prison[34], passing through the full programme of torture along the way, and who'd been left disabled. I have every reason to believe the stories told by these men. They knew me well and wouldn't have made anything up or hidden the truth, just as I wouldn't have hidden it from them. From their conversations it became clear that some people were getting carried away with their tales on the subject of torture. And the reason for such exaggeration was mundane enough. The Chechen command had consciously launched a rumour campaign, gently inflating the truth about the torture in the interests of propaganda, and the populace and the human-rights campaigners had eagerly taken up the cause. Here's an example. During the Second Chechen War, one human-rights organization put out information about the mass rape of a group of Chechen men by Russian Army soldiers during a 'cleansing operation'. When we investigated, however, we could find no evidence for the allegation and concluded that it was unfounded and the information disseminated by journalists had been erroneous. Such things often happen during war. I am certain that if this incident had been genuine, then a number of those men would have come and joined the resistance. Yet none of the supposed victims left for the forests. Looked at another way, it is plainly inconceivable for soldiers carrying out a 'cleansing operation' to sexually violate the men they were meant to be guarding. Rape did take place, but only in places of detention, whether temporary or permanent. And only against certain men, as has already been outlined. Perhaps someone in this organization had chosen to try to call the world's attention to the unfolding genocide in this bizarre manner. Yet if the world community had already turned a blind eye to the massacres of civilians; to the systematic destruction of Chechen youth, carriers of the nation's genetic stock; to the cultural, linguistic and physical destruction of a small nation that had been going on for many years, then that community was hardly likely to act upon such patently dubious allegations. Russia has powerful leverage over Europe: gas and oil reserves, a hefty portion of which comes from Chechen oil. And as long as Russia continues to possess such a persuasive argument, Europe will close its eyes to the 'war against international terrorism' taking place in Chechnya. But enough of my subjective views; let's return to the filter camp.

Beatings in the filter camp depended entirely on the whims of the soldiers on duty. If they were in good spirits, the prisoners would have a relatively quiet day or night. If they were in a foul mood or had been drinking, as was often the case, then you would wait for the fun to begin. The prisoners made splendid punch bags for the release of emotional tension. Those prisoners who wept and begged the guards not to beat them would get a particularly long and lusty punching. But if the detainee said nothing and didn't ask for mercy, they would quickly leave him alone. There were also plenty of methods of psychological torture. I'd already been through all the stages of psychological torture while in Khankala, so they didn't put the screws on me too intensely here, though nor did they ease up the psychological pressure entirely. Rather they applied new techniques that were unlike the ones I'd already undergone. Now there was less of the stick and more of the carrot – though so far without success. All their psychological techniques essentially revolved around making a person feel utterly worthless and impotent, and that it was futile to try to hide anything. The belief that you're entirely at the mercy of these men; that whether you live or die hangs solely on their whims and wishes; that if you do live, then it will be up to them what kind of life you have – all this will make any ordinary person feel doomed and that the only salvation lies in telling them everything he knows. The entire focus of their psychological assault was aimed at instilling such a belief in the subject. Psychological torture is one of the most brutal and barbaric forms of torment, because it assaults your most vulnerable point: your mind. The constant anticipation of something terrifying can drive a man insane, and while the prisoner is still deep in shock at his experience, such torture is all the more horrific. Fighters, after all, have good reason to be hugely nervous before a battle, and this is especially true of inexperienced ones. They can't wait for the fight to commence. Because there is nothing more dreadful than waiting for combat. The fight itself, no matter what the outcome, is never as awful for the fighter as the wait before the fight. That is why just before the battle begins, the fighters will be highly excitable, and the less experienced they are, the stronger the effect. When a prisoner is subjected to psychological torture – humiliation, insults, various techniques of verbal harassment and the like – he finds himself in a similar state. At that moment his will is at its weakest and you can extract almost anything from him. The aim is to crush the victim's will. And that is what makes it so truly barbaric.

13

There is one more aspect to the filter camp that poses a very real danger. Something more dreadful than any torture or beating. It is depression. Grim and gloomy, consuming you from within slowly and steadily like a venomous man-eating worm, the depression is horrific. It surrounds you on all sides like some stinking green swamp sludge, seeping into your being, into your heart and soul, eating you up. It drives you to the edge of the precipice of loneliness, beyond which lies nothing. Just endless icy loneliness. Depression paints in your mind's eye vivid images from your past – generally your happiest moments – to remind you that you'll never again experience such times. From now on you'll experience nothing at all. Neither life nor death. You'll have no soul, no body. Time will cease to exist; its endlessness and its fast flight are gone. All that exists is you. Like some vegetable life form. And you are completely at their mercy. You are beyond life, beyond death. But along comes depression with an alternative. A horrible alternative. It graciously offers you the chance to break out of the magic circle to which your terrible fate has sentenced you. Depression has come to your rescue; it shows you the path from which you can leap to eternity. Single-handedly, of your own volition. And here begins your tightrope journey across the precipice. Your dance between reason and insanity. Your desperate fight against the annihilator of reason for control of your mind. If you win this fight, you will stay human; even if you die, you'll die a human. But if you lose, you'll become nobody, even if you survive, you'll be nobody. Just another madman, with no life, no existence even – just an endless duration in wretchedness. But depression is offering you an alternative: death. Why not go to meet your death rather than wait for it to come and find you? In any case you are doomed. You have no chance of surviving. But if you go to meet your death … It takes a strong, brave person to do that. And surely you're not a weakling, are you? This alternative brings with it a whole range of options, the best being to attack the guards. They'll be only too glad to shoot you down. And at this point the question arises, Who granted you the right to end your life? Did God grant it? No. Did you grant it to yourself? Who are you to do such a thing? You're nobody. Nothing. Zero. Complete trash, as they like to remind you on a daily basis. Yet you are still a warrior. You are still at war. And this is your battle: a gruelling battle against yourself. Against your own weakness, your own cowardice, your own insignificance. And it is a battle you must win. And you do indeed win. Through long conversations with God. He will understand you – He's God, after all. You are learning to listen to your soul. You listen carefully to the voice in your blood. With a savage ferocity you rip away the cobweb of memories in which depression has entangled you and blot out all the idyllic images. In their place you paint ugly abstractionist pictures of your past. You look towards a future that you do not have. But what about rage? That impotent rage in your enemies' eyes is some kind of future, is it not? You have won against them. That must be the reason you could forgive them – you've already won against them. Or maybe you've just had very good luck … But do you really want to see their eyes glinting with the sweetness of victory rather than with impotent rage? Do you want to hand them victory over your soul? No. But you're no hero. You're just like plenty of other men – even among the enemy there are plenty just like you. Yet at the same time you are unique. You have fought your battle alone and you've been tremendously lucky. The realization dawns on you that you've won the struggle against the annihilator of reason. You've made it across the tightrope over the precipice. And the black monster of depression has lost its power over you.

14

Another practice that was common in the filter camp was the recruitment of prisoners as collaborators. This system had been developed to perfection in Soviet times and it continued to work smoothly now. People in the know, who had themselves worked a long time in the system, told me that no prisoner ever left the camp without signing an agreement to collaborate with the authorities. They told me the only time an exception was made was when they were exchanging prisoners for captured Russian soldiers, as they were to do with me and my guide. Yet I can disclose that we too were unable to escape that honour. My companion refused to put his signature to the form. He explained that before his detention in the filter camp he'd participated in the Russian-Chechen negotiations on the prevention of civilian deaths in the villages. The forthcoming prisoner exchange and the fact that he was telling the truth – he really had participated a few times in these negotiations, as was confirmed by their sources – meant they left him alone. But a similar approach was unlikely to work for me, bearing in mind my profession and the intelligence they had on me from their sources. So I needed to come up with something better. I knew that sooner or later they'd be making me a similar offer and I agonized over all the possible answers I might give. Needless to say, I wouldn't have dreamt of signing one of their forms. Our aims were too incompatible. And so, during one of our 'talks', the polite FSB officer said, 'If we were to release you, do you think you could carry on working as a journalist among the rebels?'

'Well, yes, of course. That's what I was doing before I came here.'

'But wouldn't they treat you with suspicion?'

'Why should they? No, it's out of the question. They'd have no reason to. I'm just a journalist, after all. I'm not interested in their military secrets, I never go asking too many questions. You have to know how to work with the fighters if you want to earn their trust. And I know how to work with them, that's why we've never had any misunderstandings.'

'That's good. And do you think you could work at persuading them to end the war? Explain to them just how pointless and futile the resistance is? Show them that Russia isn't really at war with them, she's not at war with the Chechen people; she's at war with a small group of criminals who've betrayed both Russia and the Chechen people. Tell them that the Russian Federation guarantees an amnesty for everyone who hands over their weapons, and we'll even pay them money for their weapons. We do realize that the vast majority of them are just ordinary guys who want to defend their homeland. That's their right, their duty even, you could say. But are they defending their homeland from the right people? We can offer the constitution, law and order instead of anarchy. We can offer social security, payment of pensions, instead of the enrichment of a small clique of criminals. We'll guarantee them employment, with salaries paid regularly. Now you, as an educated man, with a professional interest in politics, someone who has clout among the rebels and has won their trust, you could help bring about peace. The sooner we have peace in this place, the more lives we can save.'

So here it was, the very thing I'd been expecting and dreading. A rather thinly disguised attempt to recruit me. But at least I wasn't facing an ultimatum, as many others were. Not yet, at any rate ...

'Well, I wouldn't exactly say I have clout among them,' I said, trying to buy time. But my brain was not functioning well today. All my carefully prepared answers vanished from my mind. As it turned out, this was no bad thing. You simply cannot have a ready answer for a proposal like that. Unless, of course, you are an intelligence professional working for the enemy.

'Trust me, we know what we're talking about. You have enough clout in their eyes.'

'As you know, my home was destroyed. I don't have any paid work. I've got no end of everyday problems that only I can sort out. So my answer is yes, I agree to your plan. But on one condition. Issue me an official ID from your agency and pay me a salary. Take me on as an FSB officer. Then I'll go to the mountains and, openly working as an FSB agent, I'll try to talk the rebels into ending their resistance. There's no way I could work undercover. I just wouldn't know how.'

'But if you work openly, you could be killed.'

'No, they won't kill me. They all know me. I'll take care of my own safety.'

The officer looked at me long and hard, then sighed and said, 'You're too clever to be given an ID, a mission, and money into the bargain.'

'Then at least give me a document to say I've been through the filter camp.' These documents were given to everyone who'd passed through the camp.

'No. We only issue them to people whose innocence has been established. But we know perfectly well who you are. And don't forget we're not actually talking about releasing you without charges. We're just thinking over the different options.'

And that was the end of their attempt to induce me to cooperate. The polite FSB officer had no further 'talks' with me. I was to learn what had triggered this conversation a few days later.

15

I'd been unexpectedly brought out to the yard, where a man in civilian clothing asked me a number of meaningless questions. As the guard led me back to the cell, he leaned over me and whispered: 'You should pray, mate. They're deciding whether to release you. I genuinely hope you make it out of this hell.' Dazed by what he'd said, I completely forgot to thank him for this good news. My sensation was something like that of a man wounded in action as he's coming round from an anaesthetic. Hard on the heels of the awareness that you're alive comes a savage pain … And you don't know whether to rejoice at your revival. All hope of surviving had died in me and I felt released from all my debts to everyone, even to life itself, so the sudden promise of life came as such a powerful shock that my cellmates took fright when they saw me. They decided I must have been informed of the death sentence. The news was so surprising that it completely knocked me off my feet. I'd have handled the death sentence far more calmly, as it was the logical outcome I'd been expecting. So it seemed joyful news could also be upsetting. After thinking it over, I decided that it had to be the latest trick of the special-service agents and my old friend the colonel from Khankala: they were spreading disinformation. They were hoping to ruffle my composure with this shocking news. And once I'd lost control of my spiritual state, it would be all too easy to become putty in their hands. Having settled on this interpretation and extinguishing all hope again, I calmed down.

But a few days later the door of my cell opened and an officer called out my name and that of my friend. We stood facing the wall with our hands raised, as required by the regulations, and replied. 'Take your belongings and leave the cell!' he said. Such an order could mean a number of things: that we were simply being moved to another cell, or transferred to a prison, or perhaps we were even going to court for trial. I had no idea if condemned men take their belongings to their execution, but I decided that wasn't what was happening. So they had to be taking us some place for more interrogation. With some new masters of the torturer's art. Or else they were transferring us. And surely they wouldn't execute my friend. The cold truth was they could shoot people at whim, and they shot people for far less, but I managed to convince myself he was safe from execution. In the corridor we were joined by another prisoner; then they loaded us into an armoured personnel carrier and drove us towards our unknown destination.

In around twenty minutes the vehicle came to a stop. The noise from outside suggested we were in a town. There was a large crowd shouting. It sounded like some kind of rally. But why would they have driven us to a rally? My two fellow prisoners were watching spellbound through the slits in the armoured personnel carrier, and they joyously announced we were in the centre of a town and our relatives were among the protesters. I gave no response at all. Our unknown companion couldn't restrain himself and he called out from the vehicle to someone, but the soldiers shut him up. Irate, I turned on him, telling him to be a man and show some restraint. Rather sheepishly he went quiet. Well, if they were going to silence you anyway, then why not simply hold your tongue in the first place? To my mind it was more humiliating to shout and then be shut up by the soldiers than simply to stay quiet. Soon they took us from the APC and pointed out where we should go. I looked in that direction and saw my comrades, in full combat gear and armed. Trying to walk with a calm stride, though without much success, we went towards them – catching sight briefly of two officers walking past us – and we fell into their arms.

And only now did it hit me: we were free! I immediately began a mental conversation with the colonel who'd promised me death. 'It's all over, Colonel. You lost. You cannot kill me now. Even if you set up an ambush on the road, you wouldn't be killing me. Even if I die this very minute, it won't be you who's killing me, Colonel. You didn't keep your word. I got out alive. For you, Colonel, I'll live for ever. You lost. You were weaker.' My conversation was cut short by a barrage of questions from our friends about our physical and psychological state.

We drove from the town to our freedom in a convoy of cars carrying delegates from peace talks with the Russians. We came to a village in western Chechnya, but we had to travel further. The Chechen command had carefully chosen a route into the mountains that was more roundabout but less risky. They said they'd received intelligence about an ambush set up by Russian special forces in the Argun ravine along the route they'd initially planned. In the company of loyal friends, we set off on horseback into the mountains, riding along remote forest paths towards our comrades. At first after my release, the joy at feeling free – not at being saved, because they could still kill me now, but specifically at feeling free – was so powerful that I feared for my sanity. I was afraid that my heart might not be able to take the strain. Although why should I fear for my heart and mind now, when they had survived the strain of the torture at the filter camp? After we'd been riding for about an hour, the first signs that the torture had taken its toll appeared. My entire body began to ache; gradually the dull, nagging tenderness turned into a pain as fierce as during the torture. And slowly the feeling of joy was supplanted by a pain that for a long while continued to plague us, especially at night, along with the dreams of the filter camp.

16

When the Chechen singer sang, 'There's nothing more terrifying than the courage of a man who's doomed,' you never really reflected deeply on the meaning of those words. No doubt the singer did not truly understand the words he'd penned. Yet this song expresses the essence of a man whose spirit is at its zenith. Man is a predator. If in this dog-eat-dog world he hadn't been a predator, man, who is quite feeble if you take away his intellect, could never have survived as a species. When our distant ancestor, armed with a stone axe or wooden club, came face to face with the mighty cave bear, he'd have been fully aware of how puny he was compared to this giant. But he would also have realized that the bear was free to leave without hurting him, whereas he did not have that luxury. If he let the bear go, he would encounter an enemy still more powerful and ruthless, an enemy he'd be condemned to lose against: hunger. And so this greater fear in the face of a more potent opponent forced our ancestor to attack his formidable enemy and win. Win for the sake of life. Or else die. Modern man would call the taking of such a decision – the decision to submit in such circumstances to one's predatory instincts – strength of spirit. And often the outcome of a confrontation between warring parties or individuals comes down to which side has more strength of spirit.

In early August 1996, such a situation arose in Grozny. On 6 August the armed forces of the Chechen Republic entered the city and in a matter of hours effectively took control of it. And it was not the first time that year they'd taken Grozny. In March, Chechen units had seized and held it for an entire week. This time round, the Chechens were so successful in sealing in the Russian Army units based in the city that the slightest activity on the part of the Russian artillery and air force would have inevitably involved friendly fire. And without backup from artillery and air strikes, they were powerless and vulnerable. The Chechen resistance fighters were positioned just a few dozen metres from the Russian units. And this prompted the famous forty-eight-hour ultimatum[35] delivered by General Pulikovsky, which finally forced both sides into an impasse. Neither side could withdraw without losing Grozny and thereafter the republic. And indeed, nor could they leave unless there was a decisive battle where the massive loss of life would justify giving up the city. Before the countdown began, most of Grozny's residents fled the city. And the 'poseur fighters', as the Chechen people scathingly referred to the fighters who were empty show-offs, fled with them. A small group remained – around 850 men; with the resolve of the doomed, they took up their positions and waited.

You were in excellent spirits, despite the highly tense situation. It often happens as you wait for close combat to begin. And though you weren't taking up arms yourself, the reason for your good mood was clear: you were among your own. You'd spent the past year in the occupied city and your links with the resistance were plain to everyone except those who'd rather not know. One day you even managed to go to the mountains with a group of Japanese journalists, posing as their translator at the checkpoints. They spoke fluent Russian and you didn't speak a word of Japanese, but the soldiers at the checkpoints didn't know that. Your semi-underground life, in constant expectation of a second – and final – arrest, had taught you to weigh up situations soberly as they arose. If the worst came to the worst, you could always put up a fight.

Not long before, in mid-July, at the military commandant's office in Grozny, you'd faced the chillingly real prospect of arrest, and you were hugely grateful to your Creator for your narrow escape. You'd gone to the commandant's office to pick up some passes for yourself and some colleagues at the literary anthology *Orga*, which you were working for at the time. These passes were simply pieces of paper issued to local journalists along with press registration so that they could go about their work without hindrance. You'd got a lift in a military truck – civilian vehicles, unless they had a special pass, were stopped a few kilometres from the commandant's office, based in Grozny Airport. Arriving without a hitch, you found the right room on the first floor and asked for the passes. The major enquired which publication you were from, looked through the paperwork and said, 'The FSB has refused one of you a permit. But the others will be ready tomorrow.'

'Who was refused?'

Silently, the major showed you the list: you saw your name with a line through it. Perhaps it would have been best to leave quietly, but the chances of being let out without them checking your ID were slim. People were checked on their way out too. They must have waved you through on your way in because you'd arrived in a military truck. If they spotted somebody whose name had been crossed out on an FSB list, they were bound to take a closer interest; for you that was tantamount to death. In a matter of seconds all the arguments for and against flashed through your mind.

'Why did they refuse his permit? He's a good guy,' you resumed.

'Well, if they refused it, there's got to be a reason. He might be a "good guy" to you, but clearly the FSB think differently. Not the sort of journalist to be trusted. Wait a minute, who are you? And why are you so keen to defend him? Your name?'

'Aliyev,' you blurted out, the first name you remembered.

'Did you show your ID?'

'No. I wasn't asked for it.'

'Well, I'm asking. Where is it?'

'I left it downstairs. In the car.' This was, of course, a lie. You had your documents on you. And there was no car downstairs. But you'd realized that if they checked your papers now, there would be no way out of here. Attempting to deceive an official was grounds enough for arrest. Yet even without deceiving them, your chances of arrest were high. Fully aware of what you were doing, you decided to play this out to the end.

'Let's go and get it, then,' the major said, clearly deciding something was up.

'No, you wait here, Major. I'll bring it up for you. After all, you don't think I could escape from this place, do you?' you said wryly, half-asking, half-reassuring him.

'Certainly not. Go on, then, let's see it! Quick!'

You walked out of the building and, racking your brains frantically, you headed towards the checkpoint. You had no plan at all; your only hope was luck. Maybe you could find a military truck and persuade them to give you a lift. If it came to it, you could always lunge at the soldier at the checkpoint and die swiftly. But you had no intention of repeating your journey to hell. In the meantime you could act as if you were waiting to be picked up by some vehicle. And at that moment you saw a yellow minibus driving away from the checkpoint. You ran after it and flagged it down. There was a young guy at the wheel and two old men were in the back.

'I'm in trouble. I need to get out of here urgently,' you told the driver. It must have been plain that you were in trouble from the deathly pallor of your face. 'But if they check my papers, then you'll be in trouble too,' you added. 'If you drive off, I'll understand.'

'Jump in!' the driver said abruptly. 'Don't show them your papers unless I say so,' he added, pulling off.

We had barely gone a hundred and fifty metres when we were stopped at the next checkpoint. Your new friend fished out a pass and thrust it through the window, addressing the men rather gruffly.

'And who's in the bus?' one of them asked.

'Can't you see? They're with me,' the driver cut him short and drove off. Fortunately, at the rest of the checkpoints nobody moved to flag him down and you safely made it to the centre of Grozny. Neither of you said a word for the entire journey. You both realized that questions were inappropriate. It was only as you were leaving the minibus that you thanked him and he wished you luck.

And now, observing the Chechen fighters' grim determination to make Russia pay for this city ten times more dearly than during the New Year's assault, you saw parallels with your state of mind on that occasion. Then you were faced with a choice between being arrested and disappearing for ever and trying to find your chance and grab it. As a last resort, you'd had the option of attacking the soldiers and dying before they could arrest you. Moved by your fear of a greater calamity, a greater anguish than the fear of death, you acted boldly and you won.

The resistance fighters holding the capital also faced a choice: withdraw from the city they'd regained with such vast losses and allow the enemy to occupy the small amount of remaining free land in their motherland, or fight and force the enemy to withdraw, or, if it came to it, make them pay dearly for the city. They chose the second option and they too were victorious. Among the General Staff of the Russian Army, prudence won out over ambition and they rescinded the ultimatum a couple of hours before the deadline. The Russian command had understood that the only men left in the city were the brave, and, as the song says, the courage of a doomed man is terrifying. Terrifying in its ferocious desire not to live, but to die. In battle against the enemy, like the ancient Vikings died. Here was the song's hidden message.

17

And then? Then came life, with all its delights and monstrosities. The long, arduous return to life and to trust in people. The slow realization that the entire world is not your enemy and not everyone is a beast. The occasional, and thus all the more harrowing, dreams from that hell. There was the post-war euphoria, and the gradual sobering up. And work – this time as press attaché to the Minister for Industry in the Chechen government, where we would wait for months on end, along with many others, for our wages to be paid. Russia's economic blockade had catastrophically widened the social rift between the small layer of rich people and the great swathes that made up the rest of the Chechen population. And against the backdrop of this artificially engineered slump in the economy of the region's wealthiest republic, the now compliant Russian media, along with the agents among the local population working for the Russian secret service, did everything they could to stir up resentment against the democratically elected government. The incursion into neighbouring Dagestan by volunteers led by Shamil Basayev[36] to go to the aid of our 'insurgent brothers' became the official *casus belli* for the start of the Second Chechen War. But when the Russian politicians and military men speak about 'the invasion of Dagestan by Basayev's gang', they knowingly lie. The entire staff of top-level

Russian agents spent a long time working on luring Basayev into Dagestan. And eventually they succeeded. Among these agents were some fairly well-known people. It is for the historians to judge who prepared the Dagestan operation, how they did it and why. But here is one small episode by way of evidence. In May 2005, during a current-affairs programme on television, Russia's former Prime Minister Sergey Stepashin said, 'Our troops were pulled out of Botlikh[37] a month in advance, clearing the way for Basayev's entry into Dagestan. Now that is something the Military Prosecutor should have looked into.' He was referring to a period when Basayev was flatly refusing to go to Dagestan. It was only later that he agreed to it. The preparations for this war were laid a long time earlier, in the summer of 1995. That was when Moscow realized they had lost the first war. And at that point they decided to make preparations for revenge. Everything else – the apartments that were blown up, the terrorist incidents, the luring of Basayev to Dagestan – these were all merely stages on the journey towards the bigger goal. But a proper investigation into that, along with dates and names, is a job for the historians. This book does not attempt to chronicle the history.

III

Autumn Shot Dead

Towards evening, a peasant approached them carrying a heavy burden and he asked the way to the nearest town. The Sufi immediately stood up, took the load on to his back and walked with him part of the way to show him the path. Then he returned to the crossroads.

'You spent all day sitting in meditation and never answered the people who came to you with questions or seeking your advice. Yet you helped that poor peasant. Was he a secret saint?' the youth asked.

'He was the only one truly searching for what he named as the object of his desire,' the Sufi replied.

From a Sufi parable

1

The most beautiful time of year in Chechnya is not spring. Despite the tumult of the greenery, the delirium of all the rivers and streams, the heady scent of the flowers, despite the cheery sun spilling out laughter, spring is not the most beautiful time of year. Spring has plenty of rain, vital for nurturing all this hectic, moisture-hungry life. The rivers and streams turn murky and turbulent from the abundant rain, and from the melted snow gushing down from the mountain tops. The clean, dewy, silvery air quivers and chimes; it sings a million different songs in a million voices and when you breathe in this resonant air, you inhale all of these songs. And they insistently, brazenly continue to resound within you, taking over your mind, spawning bold dreams and desires. In spring, life's egotism comes to the fore. All life forms, from the smallest insect to a human being, from a slim blade of grass to the trees, the mighty giants of the forest; all are consumed by a thirst for life. All are absorbed in themselves. Busy clinging to this life, trying to prolong it through their offspring, their flowers, their labours. Only the snowy mountain peaks gaze upon all this crazy tumult with wise serenity. As if they knew that ephemeral spring, tipsy on sunshine, was frolicking like a young girl just for them, infusing nature with life just so that, during the long winter, to the sad songs of the blizzards, they could admire a different world, contemplative and unhurried, twinkling far below at their feet in a million fiery stars. Spring is too impetuous.

And summer is not the most beautiful time of year. Summer is too seductive and passionate. It harbours many sacred and sinful secrets. In the summertime, the soul is poised on a fine filament between heaven and hell. Summer is too emotional.

And it is not winter. Winter is a time of forlorn and wistful waiting for the playful young girl of spring. Winter is too serious.

The most beautiful time of year in Chechnya is autumn. Autumn heralds a brief period of harmony between life and death, between light and dark, between the mind and the soul. Autumn is a time of placidity, where every living thing cannot but help get a little closer to the God that created it. Rivers and streams become crystal clear, as if washed of the sins of men; the sky becomes deeper. Lakes become limpid blue and bottomless. They enshrine within their waters some sacred mystery. The sun does not laugh: it smiles. Warmly and sincerely, like a young mother smiling at her first-born son. The entire world arrays itself in gold and crimson. And the air isn't intoxicating: it is honey-sweet. And the world doesn't go wild with a million chiming songs. There is only the plaintive chirping of the wintering birds bidding goodbye to the summer and the sad honking of cranes flying in formation. And the rain does not pour down. No, it cries teardrops. Mournfully, quietly. It is silently crying for the immensely sad and beautiful autumn. And when the snow-capped mountains erupt in gold at dawn, they look like a fine queen preening herself and gazing into the polished shield of her beloved knight. Early autumn in Chechnya is warm, fertile and pure. No wonder the Chechens popularly call it 'orphan's summer'. Autumn is a sacred time of year for the Nakh. It is the time of year for concluding important business, for weddings and housewarming ceremonies, for forgiving your enemies and ending vendettas. Autumn is a time for making peace and helping each other. It is selflessly generous. It is magnanimous and sad. And this sadness holds the knowledge of the innermost mysteries of life and death.

And so it was that autumn. The autumn of 1999 was remarkably beautiful, warm and fertile. The colours were exuberant; Chechnya's lakes were blue, her rivers clear, the sky was deep. And the cranes, those sad angels of the earth, when they left their homeland, did not fly in their usual clean, confident 'V' formation. That autumn they circled and circled the sky, honking plaintively, and only then did they spread out into a long 'V' as they left for the south. It was as if they were bidding farewell to the people who would not be there to meet them in the spring with excited cheers or quiet prayers of thanks. As though they were giving those people a last chance to hear their sad song. Their wailing lament. They knew. They could sense it. They are angels of the earth, after all. Calamity was closing in on Chechnya. A brutal calamity, terrifying in its barbarism. A huge dragon with many heads had departed from the snowy northern steppes for our warm, fertile land. It was heading south again, with its glittering scales of steel. And the whole world, which declared its highest values to be human life and liberty, was to watch the latest murder of a small nation and secretly rejoice. Rejoice that the dragon thirsting for human blood had gone to a small nation somewhere down south, and not to them. If the dragon had to be fed, then why not sacrifice the weakest – the people with nothing to lose but life itself. So the first victims appeared. The first brooklets of blood, which would soon turn into furious torrents.

That's why the cranes are circling. Many of those now alive are seeing them for the last time. The whirling of the cranes is a gift to them, to the doomed, before their meeting with destiny. A reminder to them that they aren't leaving because they are superfluous: they are the chosen ones. Their chosenness will bring them hell on earth and martyrdom, and through their suffering they'll purify all of their nation's generations of sin. To them befalls the cruel honour of burning in the flame of forgiveness. Farewell chosen ones. Goodbye motherland. And that is why autumn is raging. It will not be allowed to fade away quietly to the gentle whisper of the dying leaves and the sad song of the cranes. For this autumn is to be crucified and shot dead. And the snowy winter blizzards will grieve for the autumn with their horrible howl.

2

On 29 September 1999, Russian forces – up to 80,000 according to the official Russian Ministry of Defence records, although independent sources, which have traditionally been more trustworthy, claim it was 150,000, meaning two armies – crossed into Chechnya on three axes. In fact the first Russian troops crossed the Chechen border on 19 September, but the full-scale invasion began on 29 September. Just as they'd done five years earlier, the army entered the republic from Dagestan, Ossetia and the Stavropol territory. The Russian Empire, spread over an eighth of the earth, flung its entire military and economic might at tiny Chechnya, whose entire population barely amounted to the population of the average Russian city.

This time Chechnya was significantly weaker than in 1994. Bled dry by the previous war, which had claimed the lives of at least 10 per cent of the population; sapped by the devastation and the economic blockade that had followed the war; crippled by domestic turmoil; lacking a regular army – this time the Defence Ministry existed merely on paper, and the entire standing army did not even make up a regiment – Chechnya for the second time in just five years met in mortal combat with the Russian ogre. The Chechen field commanders were, with a few noble exceptions, drunk on victory, and they forgot they were dealing with Russia, for whom peace had been merely a preparation for war. Indeed a significant portion of these 'war-hero commanders' had emerged only after the first war ended. The Chechen people, who'd suffered such heavy losses, suddenly discovered a suspiciously large number of unknown heroes and generals, many of whom had their sights set on nothing less than stardom. Meanwhile the true hero of the conflict, the Chechen people, who had won that gruesome battle through the blood and lives of their finest children, found themselves in severe economic, political and legal crisis.

It may be fashionable to blame all of Chechnya's woes on Russia, but what was to be expected from an enemy state, and one that had suffered so humiliating a defeat? Russia saw Chechnya as a hostile territory, with all that entailed. And so Russia's intelligence agencies operated to further the interests of the state. But could her army and intelligence services have achieved even this hollow success if it weren't for the many people in Chechnya willing to sell themselves, to be traitors, willing to be faithful servants of the enemy in exchange for a chimerical profit, willing to perpetrate the most barbaric crimes against innocent people and to mire their political opponents, yesterday's brothers-in-arms, in slander? It was they, these 'new generals', the 'politicians-cum-warriors', along with the Mammon worshippers desperate to prove themselves and ambitious for power at any price, who wittingly or unwittingly became Russia's most faithful allies, actively assisting her secret services. When they slung mud at their former comrades in the election campaign, they were trashing the ideals for which the people had laid down their lives in the war. The very fact that these field commanders were fighting for the presidential throne spoke of their ambition for personal gain, rather than for unity, when faced with a far more severe and complex challenge than the war itself had been: how to rebuild the country's shattered economy and infrastructure. Instead of shedding sweat and tears, our new 'brigadier generals' were busy revelling in victory and flaunting their pact with Russia at every opportunity. The Chechens' naïve belief that Russia would stick to the peace treaty served them poorly. For as Chechnya grappled with profound economic and political crisis and struggled for survival, Russia was preparing for war.

And the preparations were wide-ranging. First they carried out – very skilfully, too – an information blockade of Chechnya. After this they rolled out a sweeping programme to destabilize the country and stoke volatility in Chechnya. To this end they deployed their network of agents that had infiltrated all levels of Chechen society; they also mobilized their propaganda resources to create a negative image of Chechens in the eyes of the world. Fully aware that they'd lost the last war not because of any military weakness, but because they'd failed to shore up support for their operations at home and abroad, the Russian government concentrated their efforts on accomplishing this task. And as subsequent events clearly showed, they achieved a resounding success.

When the first war ended, the pro-Moscow opposition grew particularly active. A large number of undercover agents, left in Chechnya when the Russians withdrew and supplied with communications equipment, were regularly providing the Russian secret services with reliable intelligence on the situation in the republic. They acted with such confidence – or perhaps it was incompetence – that they were more or less openly recruiting among the unemployed Chechen youth and sending them to training camps near Moscow and Volgograd, where they created special-forces units made up entirely of Chechens. Over the last hundred years there has probably been no country in the world where enemy intelligence agencies have felt so free and confident as the Russians did in Chechnya at the time. For example, in a hundred-strong Chechen militia unit based in the town of Urus-Martan at the start of the second war, fifteen secret agents working for the Russian special services were uncovered! They were Russian Christians, most of whom had recently converted to Islam, claiming to be attracted by the idea of a 'pure' Islam. That is, before infiltrating the unit they had 'embraced Islam', which further illustrates how seriously the Russian secret services took their preparations. They were discovered by chance: one of them lost his nerve and confessed. And not only did he confess, but he also turned in the others. It is not normal practice for the secret services to use planted agents who know each other, but it seems this was a case of a special-forces unit (which usually operate as groups of thirteen to fifteen men) that went under cover for a specific goal – sabotage, say. This interpretation is supported by the fact that all of the agents had the same commander. Yet how many such agents went undiscovered? And there was no one to fight this rising tide of spies. Chechnya did, of course, have her own secret services. Indeed she had far too many for such a small country. But they were all busy fighting for influence over the President and for their own survival. And as part of their struggle for survival, they were fighting for control of the oil, the only source of real revenue.

Today, when all manner of experts attribute the Second Chechen War to Vladimir Putin, they are either simply wrong or they are being disingenuous. These experts have overrated Putin's rather modest intellect and they flatter his vanity by crediting him with the planning and orchestration of the Second Chechen War. The fact is that preparations for the war were afoot before Putin appeared on the scene. As any member of the military knows, in the short period Putin was in office prior to the war it would have been impossible to prepare a military campaign of this magnitude.[38] Even if we go back to his appointment as head of the FSB, 25 July 1998, before which no one had heard of him, Putin would not have had time to plan the campaign. The entire territory of Chechnya had been reconnoitred and charted, right down to the finest detail, including footpaths and animal tracks, ruins and springs. Command-post exercises had been held where the fictional scenario was an imaginary enemy in Dagestan and Chechnya. Large sums were being lavished on destabilizing the republic. A huge number of agents had been planted throughout the entire Chechen infrastructure. This war was handed as a gift to Putin, to allow this unknown FSB colonel to ensconce himself in the Kremlin. Confirmation for this can be found in the careless slip – or perhaps it was a deliberate remark – in a television programme by the man who, until 9 August 1999, was Prime Minister of Russia, Sergey Stepashin. Referring to the war that had already begun, he said, 'Of course we were a bit hasty with sending our troops into Chechnya. The operation had been planned for March 2000.' That moment with Stepashin was only shown once; when the programme was rebroadcast the section had been cut by the censors.

For the Chechen people, who had ended the previous war close to breaking point, the second war came as a genuine national disaster. With her economic footing far too shaky for a war that in its degree of violence and number of civilian casualties would far outstrip even the 1994–6 war, the Chechen people, isolated and friendless, found themselves face to face in mortal combat with an ogre gone berserk. And against the backdrop of the grisly rampage in Chechnya, the leaders of the democratic world held friendly meetings with Putin, invested their capital in the Russian economy and took a sympathetic view of Russia's 'war on international terror' taking place in Chechnya. The world community's contribution to Russia's so-called 'war against international terrorism in the North Caucasus' will be judged by history, as will the 'danger of Russian territories being annexed with the aim of creating a united Islamic caliphate' – what a joke! – by 'international terrorists entrenched in the Chechen Republic'. But let's not get too lost in the wilderness of politics.

3

That autumn, despite the desperate resistance put up by the militia-men, the Russian Army stubbornly pushed on towards the capital. Armed with massive manpower, vastly superior military hardware and total air dominance, and with the advantage of the element of surprise, the Russian command spared neither money nor men (and their men were suffering heavy losses, despite Chechnya's apparent weakness) in their bid to advance. The Chechens were not ready for war, and they did not have time to organize a proper defence at the border. They were forced to retreat, fighting a rearguard action. Their lack of preparation was compounded by Maskhadov's diplomatic efforts to avert the outbreak of war and the belief that there would be no invasion. Nevertheless, by 15 October, I was setting out for the Tersky Ridge, around forty-five kilometres north of the capital, as part of the Almaz assault unit, 80 per cent of whom were veterans of the last war. That's not to say I was a fighter in the unit; I was still doing the job of a journalist, but now in a military setting. The situation required that all journalists be embedded in a unit, where they came under the responsibility of a specific commander. Most of the men in this unit were people I'd known or been friends with since the first war. On the very next day we were withdrawn from these positions and sent back to base; another unit then dug in at this sector.

At the start of the war, the Defence Committee had held a meeting at general headquarters and decided to mount defences in the major towns such as Grozny, Gudermes and Urus-Martan. The strategic thinking behind this approach is a separate topic, but the key point was that the large towns should become the main hubs of the resistance. Yet despite the skilfully mounted defence, the only place that truly became an epicentre of resistance was the capital.

The Russian Army, of course, chose Grozny for their major assault, deploying vast numbers of forces there. According to the official Russian records, up to 25,000 soldiers advanced on Grozny against 7,000 defending the capital. This figure of 7,000 defenders includes all the logistical support, as well as the hidden pockets of 'poseur fighters', who, unbeknownst to the command, were trapped in the encirclement and sat out the entire battle holed up in basements, only emerging into the daylight to join the breakout from the city. In truth, there were never more than 3,000 Chechen defenders fighting on the front line. The figure of 25,000 attacking forces is also doubtful, if only because in one narrow defensive sector, where forty militiamen were dug in, an entire battalion of motorized infantry was advancing with all its attached forces – tanks, artillery and the like. It seems the Russians did not count their numerous logistical units, an essential component of any offensive or defence, and they conveniently forgot about the attached forces, which included both Interior Ministry and internal troops, as well as the Chechen Armed Opposition units, along with many others, to say nothing of the total dominance of the airspace and the stark superiority of their hardware. Generally, when the authorities announce that 'such and such a battalion seized and held such and such a town', the uninitiated will believe them. However, people who saw with their own eyes at least two battalions being used in the attack will at once think it's a deliberate lie. In reality, though, the authorities are not lying; they're simply not taking into account the number of units attached to a particular battalion. This system allows the Russian Army command to speak 'truthfully' about the modest number of troops involved in an operation, and also their modest combat losses (officers don't get much stick for losses in the attached units), against a backdrop of enemy numbers expanding pro rata. And that's just what they did with Grozny in the autumn of 1999.

Be that as it may, the Defence Committee's plan to create hotspots of resistance in the major towns – Urus-Martan on the western front, Gudermes and Argun on the eastern front, and Grozny on the northern front – failed. Instead of several large hubs of resistance, with constant harassment by mobile units at the enemy's rear, we ended up with only one. This failure was caused by two major developments. Firstly, in November 1999 a large, well-armed resistance group abandoned Urus-Martan when the threat of encirclement forced them to retreat to the mountains. Secondly, at the end of November 1999 the Yamadayev brothers[39] surrendered Gudermes to the Russians without a fight. To be fair, it should be noted that the majority of the town's inhabitants had insisted on Gudermes being surrendered. On the other hand, you cannot defend your homeland from an aggressor without exposing the civilian population to harm. Ferocious fighting continued in many villages, especially in the foothills and mountains. By 2 December 1999 the Russian Army had fully encircled the Chechen capital.

4

The Russian soldiers in this new war were a different breed. The officer corps was more experienced; they had benefitted from the lessons learnt from their mistakes in 1994–6. In the first war the Russian soldiers and officers had retained a certain spirit of romance, a respect for the right of the Chechens to be masters of their own destiny. After all, both sides had emerged from the same school of patriotic rhetoric, believing the Soviet Army to be the 'defender of peace and friend of liberty'. At that time the principles of democracy weren't just an empty phrase. This time round, though, the Russians made no secret of their determination to wreak vengeance at any price. Neo-totalitarianism, which began in 1993, when Boris Yeltsin ordered the attack on the Russian parliament building,[40] had established a strong enough footing in Russia by the end of 1999 to parade nakedly, unashamed before everyone, even God Himself. The three interwar years had been spent kindling the soldiers' and officers' animosity towards the Chechen people, desensitizing and brutalizing them. All manner of methods were utilized for this, ranging from the falsification of history, whereby the Chechens were presented as savages who would only respect violence (an old trick used over the centuries by the Russian tsars in the Caucasian wars), to the video screenings of the executions of captured contract soldiers and

Russian secret agents (the Chechens hadn't executed conscripts in the first war) carried out by fighters bereaved of their loved ones. And, of course, there were the public executions of criminals who had been sentenced by a court, which so shocked the world. The Russian butchers could shoot innocent Chechens without trial by the thousands in their torture chambers scattered across Russia; they could wipe out tens of thousands with precision bombing and in their 'cleansing operations' in Chechnya itself; none of that, of course, shocked the world. All that was merely 'human-rights violations'.

Here is a wonderful example of soldier training techniques. In February 2004, long after the declared end of the 'military phase of the counter-terrorist operation' and the start of the rebuilding of post-war life in the republic, the pro-Kremlin newspaper *Komsomolskaya Pravda* ran an article on the instruction of new contract soldiers in the Russian Army's 42nd Division, stationed in Chechnya. 'The colonel explained to the contract soldiers in simple and accessible language that a long time ago the Chechens had descended from the mountains, and they'd adopted the custom of blood revenge from the Kumyks.' The article also reported how the colonel emphasized that 'the Chechens only respect power and violence', and they live 'on land that since time immemorial had been Russian'! The journalist penned this piece without a hint of reproach; quite the reverse, this was meant to be a worthy example of soldier education. It was plain that with training like this, the soldiers' incentive to fight would rocket and they would consider all Chechens the enemy. Hatred, after all, is one of the strongest of human emotions.

So the new war followed new rules. But it was in Grozny that the Russians met their match. The vast majority of the defenders of the capital were veterans of the previous war and masters at urban combat. All the famous Chechen field commanders had remained in Grozny with their units.

5

And so there began a long, mutually exhausting siege, with frequent assaults against certain sectors, which the defenders would nevertheless repel fairly successfully. In the protracted battles of modern siege warfare, what counts is not which side has greater amounts of troops and equipment but which side has fighters who are stronger in spirit. It takes great strength to endure the nervous exhaustion of a stand-off. The chief preparations were tactical and psychological. Every fighter who chose to stay in the city knew what he was signing up to and went into it with his eyes open.

The defence of Grozny was planned in the finest traditions of military science and with an expectation of sustained fighting under siege. The command had neither the time nor the machinery to build fortifications. Instead, they swiftly turned the natural terrain and the city's buildings into a line of defence. The initial jagged line was designed to gradually draw the attackers into the city, engage them in urban combat, then massacre them. Indeed, this tactic met with some success in the south-east, north and north-western outskirts of the city. It was in those areas that the enemy suffered their heaviest losses. But the Chechens never managed to provoke the Russians into a full-scale storming of the city. Either the enemy saw through our scheme or they learnt about our plans through their undercover agents, but around January 2000 the offensive suddenly slackened. Instead, equipped with an admirably accurate map of Grozny that broke the city down into grid squares, the Russian artillery and tank crews found it easy enough to pound the city relentlessly, one square at a time, from under cover. And the air force, enjoying total impunity, carpet bombed entire neighbourhoods into rubble, wantonly destroying the roads with bunker-busters, despite the fact that the militiamen weren't using them, as they had no armoured vehicles. Yet, despite all the attempts to break their spirit of resistance, Grozny's defenders, the finest of warriors, who had willingly united to do mortal combat with their age-old enemy, continued to hold the capital.

After capturing some of the commanding heights around the city, the enemy stepped up their bombardment. They fired on virtually every street and alley, especially in the south, south-west and south-east districts. They deployed chemical weapons, in particular hydrogen cyanide, whose bitter-almond smell is unmistakeable. The Russians had plenty of undercover agents among the defenders of Grozny, who provided them with information on the situation in the city. And yet they could not close down the channels through which the militiamen were getting their food and ammunition. And the militiamen were even acquiring weapons and ammunition from the Russian side: from Russian Army officers; from the Russians' loyal allies, the Chechen special forces; and from the OMON paramilitaries. Only one hospital was functioning in the city, and its staff were performing daily acts of heroism, saving the lives of wounded fighters and of the few civilians whose misfortune it was to remain in the city. In brutal conditions, under the constant shelling and aerial bombardment, doctors performed the most complex neurosurgical operations; there were many whom they effectively brought back from the dead. The presence of these health professionals in the besieged city, heroes every one of them, from the nursing assistants to the Minister of Health, who had remained in the capital with his doctors, saved a great many lives.

In the three months of fighting, for two of which Grozny was fully encircled, the Russian Army and their Chechen allies failed to achieve any tangible results in a single sector defended by the militiamen. What's more, they could not stop the evacuation of the severely wounded and the sick from the besieged city, nor the entry into the capital of small numbers of fresh groups, composed almost entirely of 'old school' warriors. While these groups could not influence the outcome of the battle, they were badly needed to lift the morale of the besieged. The fact that the resistance could sneak in new groups and remove the wounded meant that the blockade was porous.

Here's an illustration. In January 2000, an ad hoc group headed by a commander whose call sign was 'Abu Huraira', armed to the teeth and with a full cadre, carrying no ID whatsoever (as you'd expect for a special-forces unit), passed all the many roadblocks and entered Grozny in a minibus. They had come from a Chechen border checkpoint, where they'd carried out a special assignment for the command. I met them and talked to their commander.

'How did you manage to cross through all the enemy check-points without any problems? You were driving through enemy-controlled territory, after all.'

'It was easy. We armed ourselves, got in the minibus, put at the wheel one of our men who's infiltrated the enemy and has a Russian pass, and set off.'

'And why did he need ID if none of you had any?'

'Well, of course he needed it! If you have a full crew who are meant to be sneaking behind enemy lines for sabotage attacks, you can easily arouse suspicion. If you ran into a top pro at one of the checkpoints, he could ask all sorts of questions. So your story is that the driver's taking you to your destination, linking you up with your contacts and driving back so he can return later to pick you up again.'

'Did you come to Grozny on orders from the command?'

'No. After we'd completed our mission, our orders were to stay at the base awaiting further instruction. But our comrades were being killed here in the siege. And we managed to persuade Angel[41] to allow us to join our brothers-in-arms.'

'Your unit was among those involved in the legendary defence of Bamut in the last war. Tell me, is this war different from the first war? And if so, in what way?'

'Oh, there's a huge difference, especially in the type of warfare. In the first war, most of the civilian casualties were from the airstrikes and shelling; this time round there are far more victims from the deliberate destruction of peaceful villages, the killing of civilians. And then there are the 'cleansing operations'. This time the villagers cannot talk the Russians out of destroying the villages visited by the resistance. Yes, and Russia has prepared much more thoroughly and seriously for this war.'

'Do you think they'll take the capital?'

'They'll only take Grozny if we decide to abandon it.'

'How do you think the war will end?'

'It can only go one way. At some point Russia will leave our homeland. This war is the beginning of the end for Russia. It's producing thousands of Russian killing machines whose minds are unbalanced, and the ones who survive this slaughterhouse will take back home to Russia ideas about the value of human life they picked up here. Russia is not just at war with us, Russia's at war with its own citizens. They are preparing butchers for their own people.'

'And does that make you happy?'

'No. It pains us. The Russian people have suffered enormously under all sorts of rulers as it is, and now they're preparing a new set of death squads to use against them. On the other hand, who's to say? Maybe the Russian people somehow deserve their fate? Nothing ever happens by chance in this world. It's all the will of God.'

'And do our people deserve this war?'

'Perhaps they do to a certain degree. We let this clique of Kremlin crooks and all the undercover Russian agents give our nation a bad image all over the world; we let them drag us into this war. Unfortunately, both the innocent and the guilty are now paying the price. Just like in the story about the Prophet Moses.'

'Do you think the incursion into Dagestan was a betrayal of the Chechen national interest?'

'No. We're certain that Shamil[42] and his men were tricked into it, just as they tricked our entire people.'

'What about the current situation? Do you see this as a religious war?'

'It's a war for freedom. You can be a believer without the need for a war. If you believe, then no one can take that faith away from you. For us, the war will end when the Russian Army leaves Chechnya.'

And this was how the majority of fighters defending the capital felt, even if some individuals, and some groups too, stubbornly insisted this was a war of religion. It is telling that the ranks of the resistance included many Russians. They were Christians, yet they fought valiantly 'not against Russia but against the Federal Army'. Each had volunteered. There wasn't a single prisoner forced to fight against the Russians among them. Such a tactic would have been far too risky in a war like this.

As much as the defenders wanted them to, this time the Russians did not pluck up the nerve to storm Grozny. And so Grozny – meaning 'terrible' in Russian and named by General Yermolov in the nineteenth century to strike terror into the Chechens – did indeed become a symbol of terror for Yermolov's Russian heirs in the twentieth and twenty-first centuries.

The Russian Army stubbornly continued to pound the city. And the encircled militiamen just as stubbornly continued to hold on to their capital. The city had long ago ceased to have any strategic importance, but for the warring sides possession of Grozny had a psychological importance. They were like two tarantulas locked in mortal combat, unable to back down. Yet victory in this battle would be pyrrhic. Siege warfare is essentially a war of nerves, a battle of the spirit. And from this battle of the spirit Grozny's defenders emerged victorious.

6

Encirclement, blockade, siege. These synonyms, used exclusively in the context of war, have struck fear in me since childhood. Like some impending doom, from which you could only escape with help from outside. In the Soviet films and history textbooks, war always meant combat action: there was a front and a rear, and the fighters had freedom of manoeuvre. If the enemy became trapped, the outcome was clear. When the enemy were encircled, they were doomed. They could never break free. All they could do was surrender unconditionally. And nobody ever came to their rescue; our valiant Soviet Army wouldn't allow that. Whereas our men would always break out of an encirclement or blockade, and with minimal losses to boot. Because our side was fighting for the beloved Soviet system, the motherland and the Party. Meaning we'd fight on ferociously, and help was sure to come. The command would never give up on trapped soldiers. No matter what, our comrades would break through the blockade to come to our aid. That's what we were taught in our textbooks.

However, history also tells of other battles, in earlier times, when a fortress could withstand a siege for a long period, sometimes even for years. But these were mighty forts, specially designed for prolonged siege warfare. They had thick walls of stone, deep moats, tall ramparts, strong garrisons and ample supplies of food and ammunition. Yet by the start of the twentieth century, even the mightiest of forts had become irrelevant to modern warfare. And what of the twenty-first century? There are no tall stone walls, no mighty cannons, no deep moats in modern siege warfare. There are none of the essentials for a fort under siege.

What your fortress does have, though, is a modestly sized garrison equipped only with small arms; narrow rifle pits and trenches dug by hand; the fragile walls of buildings perforated by shells from infantry fighting vehicles, to say nothing of tanks and artillery. Your fortress does not have mighty defences with fortified gun posts. But aren't you on your own land? Aren't you fighting for your people's very right to exist? So you don't have machinery for digging trenches? No problem. We'll dig them by hand. Besides, our enemies have plenty of machinery. Combat machinery. And they're eager to help you out ... How does the law of ballistics go again? Two shells never hit the same place twice? Well, that's perfect. The bomb and shell craters will become our hideouts. They're hitting the same place again? That's because they're firing thick and fast. It's not the rule, just a one-off. You know that any populated area, no matter how frail its buildings, can be transformed into a sturdy fortress, given the will. And our will is strong enough – oh, yes. And that is what gives you a very important edge over your enemies.

That is the reason the city's defenders are stronger in spirit. It's why the enemy cannot smash the resistance and take this fortress. And it's why this lethal battle has endured for many long days and nights. It is dragging on relentlessly. The enemy are not tiring. They have plenty of soldiers; the weary ones are relieved by fresh forces. But nor do you tire. You cannot afford the luxury of growing weary. For there is no one to take your place. You swap positions, but the positions are everywhere. Shrapnel litters the entire city. The one place where you can snatch some rest is the forward line of own troops. There the enemy are simply too close. They cannot use their artillery or aircraft for fear of friendly fire. All they can do is shoot. But can their shooting stop you from sleeping like a baby? No. Even the roar of the guns mixed with the bombs acts as the perfect lullaby. The thing is to adapt to it. And you are adapting to it. Slowly you begin to realize that fighting from inside an encirclement is not the end; it's merely combat in four directions. And the combat going on for month after month has its advantages. It won't let you slacken or relax. It teaches you to treasure each moment of life. To understand the inevitability of death. The closeness of death makes a philosopher of you. Well, perhaps your philosophy is strange and unintelligible to the vast majority of people. But who are these people? They're God's creatures, just like you, and they are mortal too. If your philosophy is alien to them, that's nothing to worry about. You can understand them easily enough. But you cannot demand understanding from them. You're wiser than that. You realize that death is not terrifying. Death is wonderful if you know what it is you're dying for. You've learnt to live in combat. No, not to exist in the constant expectation of death. But to live a full-blooded, unforgettable life while embracing your death. To savour each moment.

And you realize that you will never again sense life so fully as now. Even if you survive. There will be long, painful memories. They'll bring an endless pining for comrades who can never again smile; they'll bring a quiet, bitter-sweet nostalgia for this fullness of life, already lost for ever. Suddenly you realize that no matter how long your life continues after this, you'll die agonizingly long and live maddeningly briefly. Yes, even if you live to a hundred, your life will be briefer than just a few minutes of life spent here. 'Normal life' will take its course and it won't stop to notice you dying each day over and over in your memories. You will never again love life as you love it now, when it is so palpably brief.

All that will come later, assuming this stupid body of yours isn't left to lie in the rubble and it journeys on further with you. In the meantime, live! While life goes on. Don't think of death.

It doesn't matter that almost every day you see people departing from this mortal world. No, do think of death. But don't think of the life you had or the one you could have had beyond this kingdom of death. Let your past life remain as memories. They will hold you back from the edge of the abyss when the present becomes too terrible.

And so you live in the present moment. You sever yourself from the past and reject the future, instinctively realizing it's the only way to cope with the pressures of war. You think about the past only as something utterly strange and unreal, as if those events didn't happen to you. The past is a dream, and not always a happy one. What of the future? The best future you could hope for would be instant death. That's how things seem if you judge by the reality of the situation. But if you judge by the state of your soul, you have to survive. Your principle, 'I want, I can, I must,' won't let you give in and depart from this world so quickly and easily. You are interested in observing yourself. You are interested in seeing what awaits you. You write poetry. For some reason your finest poems emerge during the most difficult and dangerous times of your life. Or perhaps they seem the finest to you because they're written at moments like these? Beyond the city there is nothing. There is no one. Nobody needs you there. All the living have already buried you mentally. Yes, your body is functioning, but you yourself are dead. You are a warrior. Have you forgotten? And a warrior is dead from birth. His soul never belongs to this mortal world. But this realization will make you strong and won't let you give in. You will survive because you've already been buried.

7

The most horrific image in war is that of refugees. Not the destruction of once-flourishing towns and villages, not the death before your eyes of dozens of people – friends and strangers, civilians and combatants. Not the bestial cruelty. No, that's not fair. Beasts aren't cruel: they're hungry. Whereas the enemy, the soldiers of the Russian Army, are cruel. They're not hungry, they're cruel. Senselessly cruel. Without any objective. No reason – just for kicks. And death is not terrible. Death is the natural and inevitable end of the path, the end of everything bad which you cling to because you know no better. You witnessed how thirty women were buried in the cellar of a three-storey building that had taken a direct hit from a bomb. All of them were women. They'd come from the neighbouring houses and gathered in the cellar, thinking it the safest refuge. It was a bomb shelter which they'd known of since Soviet times. What they didn't know was that during the Soviet era such bomb shelters were built not to protect the population from nuclear bombs but as mass graves for the easy burial of corpses. Military engineers in the Soviet Army could hardly be suspected of being short on intellect: they understood perfectly well the sheer folly of such shelters in these wars, when your capital, as a major industrial centre, was likely to be among the first hit in a nuclear attack. But the women weren't experts on nuclear blasts, just as you weren't (you found this out from a retired major who'd served in the Strategic Rocket Forces), and they hid in the Soviet bomb shelter, hoping for protection from the Russian bombs.

The explosion blew away half the building. Of the thirty women, thirteen were dead. The city had no rescue service; there were only the resistance fighters defending the city. It was they who pulled out the victims from the wreckage of the building. They hauled them all out but one. They couldn't free her. A heavy reinforced-concrete slab had come crashing down on to her and smashed her hips. And three storeys of the building had collapsed on to the slab. To raise this slab they'd need lifting equipment. Or time, plenty of time. But they had neither. Trying to alleviate her agony, they give her some sips of water and wipe her face with a damp cloth. She is young, maybe thirty-five, pretty. She begs them to finish her off, she can't take this horrific pain any more. The pain-killing injections do not help. There is no hope of pulling her out alive: she'll die before they manage to dig through the rubble by hand. But she'll die in terrible agony. And then a fighter pulls the trigger. And he weeps. Loudly, unashamed of his tears. You realize this fighter won't survive the war; he won't be able to live after this. And he does indeed die soon after. Need I add, heroically?

As for you? You're grateful to the fighter. You appreciate what pain is. You still haven't forgotten when it was you dreaming of relief from a bullet. He brought her a swift death rather than letting her perish in agony. He released her soul from the burden of torture and for this she forgave him. But what were these women doing in a city under siege? Did they have nowhere else to go? Surely they have some place they could go. All the rest of the city's residents have gone somewhere. Perhaps they saw the columns of refugees abandoning the doomed city and decided to remain true to these ruins till the end. Perhaps they realized that the most horrific image born of war is refugees.

172

You saw the refugees leaving the almost dead city and felt a strange, bitter mix of shame and fury, humiliation and hatred. Gazing at these people driven by the fear of death to face the untold humiliations and insults of drunken, louse-infested enemy soldiers, you shuddered as though discovering something chilling. You saw drivers in private cars scavenging the roads for passengers. These were Chechens charging fantastically high prices, a month's earnings for cab drivers in peacetime, to drive their fellow countrymen out of the zone of fire. You saw people, the most dangerous species on the planet, omnivorous predators, meekly paying these vultures their money to save their pitiful lives and you understood: the enemy has won against them.

People striving to reach enemy territory, where they'll face endless humiliation just so they can rejoice over a can of rotten stew and a packet of pasta while looking to the enemy for protection – an enemy who has come to destroy, to 'filter' all the males 'between the ages of ten and sixty'. The enemy has not conquered them, as there was no fight: he has defeated them. Perhaps those who meet the enemy with weapons in their hands will lose the battle and the enemy will conquer them, but the enemy can never defeat them. Because their spirit is invincible. These refugees do not equal the entire nation, in whose name its finest sons have doomed themselves to a fiery hell. That nation is fighting by their side, it is dying from bombs and shells, it is starving and freezing, disappearing without trace and looking its executioners in the eye, silently falling from the bursts of automatic gunfire upon the tormented earth of its desolate motherland. This nation is invincible. Just as its spirit is invincible. But perhaps you are too harsh on these people saving themselves and their children from a senseless, cruel death beneath the rubble of houses and from the shrapnel of bombs and shells? Don't people have a right to save their lives by any available means? Of course they do. You are far too harsh on them. You cannot blame people for choosing humiliation over death. For fleeing from hell, hoping for proper

173

remains and a proper resting place after death. And can you judge those drivers growing rich on the nation's disaster? Why bother? One cannot judge these vultures; God will be their judge. Everyone can be understood. And should be understood. Then why does it seem as if the enemy has humiliated your motherland not through war and devastation, not through starvation and killing, not through violence against civilians, but through the swarms of refugees, with their desperately pitiful look, turning to their centuries-old enemy for protection from death? Why are you haunted by a sense of shame and hate, humiliation and fury? Why do you not want to live, you desperately don't want to, after the terrible image of faces distorted with fear, of people driven into the unknown – into the known – by the instinct for self-preservation? Why is there such gloom in your soul that you start to hate life even more than you hate the enemy? God will be the judge of us all. May He forgive us.

8

The world's best composers are Edvard Grieg and James Last. So different in style. They are the best because they have been granted that title here, by you, inside the flaming ring that encircles the besieged city. You already knew these composers before, and many others besides, but only now have you recognized them as the finest.

You were wandering as usual through the city's ruins, filming after the latest bombardment. You saw a half-ruined house, an old building from the seventies. For the Chechens that is relatively old. After all, not a single Chechen house has stood for longer than fifty years. Ever since Civilized Russia arrived in the Wild Caucasus … The house is a good one. Clearly built with money earned by seasonal work in Kazakhstan, Siberia or central Russia. In Chechnya among those of a certain age you'd be hard-pressed to find anyone who hasn't travelled for seasonal work at least once. In our beloved republic, despite enjoying vast natural resources, efficient agriculture with fine pasture for animal husbandry, and being industrially developed, unemployment among the indigenous population reached disastrous levels. The Chechens, no matter how highly qualified, could only dream of finding work, even a rank-and-file job, in many sectors in their home republic during the reign of the 'most just and humane system on Earth'. Jobs in those sectors were available only to members of other ethnic groups living in Chechnya, first and foremost the Russians. And that was why the natives left each spring for the construction sites of Russia. They had to survive somehow.

Under the battered canopy are quite a few scattered cassettes. There's a whole range of styles and genres of music. You grab the first two that come to hand: Edvard Grieg and James Last. You're a bit peeved not to have found any more of your favourites. But never mind, you don't get to pick and choose in war. You take both the cassettes with you. You could imagine the original owner putting on Grieg's music and drifting into a deep reverie … This brilliant music cleanses his soul, making his thoughts purer. But that would be too trite. A tired old literary cliché. So you imagine nothing, just silently leave with the cassettes. Besides, in this strange, drawn-out war you've become something of an egotist. Or rather you were an egotist from the outset, along with all your fellow human beings, but until now you've managed to mask your personal ethics. In this place, though, such pleasantries are meaningless and your egotism shines through more clearly. There is somewhere for you to listen to the tapes: you have an old car, a Lada, with a young fighter at the wheel. The commander of the Almaz unit has seen to that. In this car you travel the city, filming its death on a video camera. You have naïve hopes of preserving at least some of this footage. You also drive to the firing positions in this car. It has a stereo with the usual selection of pop-music cassettes. But from now on you will listen to these composers and be carried away for a time into the mysterious, fantastical world of classical music. This music will accompany you on all your trips across the city. The sound of this mysterious music will remind you that you are vastly alone in this unjust world. And James Last's 'Lonely Shepherd' will accentuate and deepen your loneliness and longing, seeking and finding an ally in you. The music of Edvard Grieg and James Last will ring out to the roar of guns, and the rumble of bombs, and the whirr of shrapnel.

And it will stop ringing out on the snowy, blazing night when the abandoned car catches fire …

Tonight you are at the radio communications post. You often sit here, and you've witnessed many events from this post. You witnessed the entire battle of the Black Wolf unit against the attacking enemy forces. You heard how, with several men lost and nearly all of them wounded, including the unit's commander – only three fighters were unharmed – they were forced to retreat slowly, fighting their way out in ferocious hand-to-hand combat. And nobody broke rank, not even the wounded. While the enemy, stunned by such obstinacy, did not dare push the assault further. The fighting went on the entire day. That day the enemy launched five assaults on Black Wolf's positions. It was mainly the infantry delivering the attack, supported by artillery, mortar and tank fire. By evening, all that remained at the unit's positions were half a dozen burning enemy tanks and infantry fighting vehicles and almost an entire company of dead enemy soldiers. Such battles were flaring up with astonishing frequency all around the city's circular front line. And often they would end with the Russian Army denied even token success.

Today is one of those rare nights when, in the chill air, a disquieting lull freezes over the city like a black shroud. The city seems rapt in prayer, withdrawn into itself, like an ancient old man. In the sky around the city hangs a fiery necklace of illumination rounds, fired by the enemy who have come to kill it. Occasionally you hear long bursts of automatic gunfire in the distance: a sure sign of the clash of hostile reconnaissance teams, those aristocrats of war. It's the lulls in combat you find difficult. You cannot get used to them. Lulls mean danger. And so you listen especially attentively to the night. The night is silent. Almost angelically peaceful … But you know this is just an illusion: the night is not peaceful at all. A night like this is particularly dangerous. It is like a boa constrictor, playing dead as it waits in ambush for its victim, only to spring to life at the right moment in a dappled, lethal strike. Only the radios, those remarkable surrogates for living people, attest with their crackle that this city, in which you're listening to the night, is still alive. It is mauled, mortally wounded, but still alive. And it will stay alive for as long as its living defenders remain there. Motionless in the glacial darkness, the city reminds you of a lion, mighty king of the animals, mortally wounded yet still dangerous to the pack of hyenas encircling it with burning eyes, patiently waiting for its death.

The familiar call signs and the usual talk on the airwaves do not distract you from your contemplation. But suddenly you hear an unknown voice in the enemy tongue. It is a Russian radio operator who has hacked into your radio channel. You, too, often hack into their channel, so this is nothing unusual. The operator is making random calls to the defenders of the capital. One of them responds. The bored radio men fill the airwaves with insults and curses, threats and challenges to fight. The other militiamen, who are used to such scenes, do not react to the dialogue between the nervous comrade and the enemy radio operator. But as passions reach boiling point, you decide to intervene.

No – you don't utter a word; you simply bring the live microphone of the radio set to the speaker, from which quietly flows the magical music of James Last. You could of course have given them Edvard Grieg, but you decided not to. You thought Grieg is better understood when listened to in solitude. The spirit of his music is too independent to be confined to a collective audience. And so you let them listen to the wonderful, sad music of James Last. The airwaves instantly fall quiet, with only the bewildered voice of the Russian radio operator softly saying, 'Who's that?' You reply, 'James Last, "The Lonely Shepherd".' You are perfectly aware that using the airwaves for music is categorically forbidden – radio communications have an altogether different function – but this is a special case.

The sad, enchanting music fills the airwaves, rising to the dark frosty sky like the doomed city's final prayer. The city prays not for its own salvation: it prays for the salvation of the souls of those destroying it. And it knows that thousands of human souls, both destroyers and defenders, are praying alongside it. Each soul prays for something secret of its own. In this twilight silence, the city softly weeps tears of smoke, flowing straight to the sky, to God. It weeps for itself as it will never be again. Weeps for its inhabitants whom it will never see again. Weeps for its defenders, those who've fallen among the bones of the ruined buildings, and those still alive, still defending the city's mournful shadow with a sacred tenacity. The city weeps for an island of love and life in a sea of hate and death. It knows, it senses, that it will drown in the sea of death and hate; it will choke under the terrible wave of cruelty. Left without its defenders, it will call to the Sky for a long time yet, in the thin voices of crying women and children led to their execution, the mute moans of dying old men, the infinite hatred and scorn for their executioners in the eyes of its gunned-down and tortured inhabitants. And the Sky in response will weep fire. Its fiery tears will fall on the remains of the city, burning up the last souls in the dying city. The Sky will wail with a bloodcurdling howl, like an outcast angel. Again and again the Sky will cast down fiery tears upon those who left without protecting the city to the end. To the last soul. The streets of the city, where once, long ago, happiness smiled, will now for a long time, for endlessly long, be colonized by horror, hate, fear and betrayal. For a long time Grozny will frighten the world with the appalling sight of its ghost.

And so the city prays. Through the rare silence. Through the sad music. Through the black tears of the smouldering ruins. Through the whispered prayers of its defenders. And not a single person dares commit the sacrilege of interrupting the prayer of the great city sentenced to death. After this fantastical music, after the tenuous panpipe, whose trembling sound has faded from the airwaves like the dying moans of a wounded bird, you listen along with the others for several moments to the silence. Then you hear a quiet, almost whispered, 'Thank you' – and the psychological battle between deadly enemies ceases for this one extraordinary night. The Sky grants the city respite until dawn. And at dawn, as if ashamed of the night of silence, it will cover the city in a cloak of fire.

9

From time to time the city would experience a lull, if you can call the soft banter between the mortar men and gunners a lull. The defenders would try to make the most of this time. They'd go about their day-to-day business: replacing the tired fighters in the trenches at the first line of defence, washing and mending their clothes and boots, stocking up on food and ammunition. Despite the winter, the city was full of mud. The smog from the blazing industrial plants, the dust from the bombed houses and buildings, the streets and roads ripped up by bombs: all were a source of mud, and there had always been mud in the trenches and dugouts. Under such conditions, the problem of personal hygiene soon arose. For a while I would simply warm up some water on the wood-burning stove which I used for cooking, and I would wash in some secluded spot. This was hardly the same as a bath or shower, but it allowed me to maintain basic hygiene. But one day a comrade came and invited me to go for a wash. When we got to the place, I was quite astonished to find a long terrace hung with rows of hoses and pipes gushing with hot water. Under this improvised communal shower the fighters were washing themselves and laundering their clothes. It turned out that since Soviet times, water from a hot mineral spring located right in the city centre had been routed here through a pipe for drainage, and the fighters had adapted it to their needs. The salts in the water made it unfit for drinking, but for washing it was perfect. The high mineral content made the water an excellent disinfectant. It was piping hot – around 80°C as it emerged from the conduit – so the showers had been set dozens of metres beneath the pipe. This ensured it cooled to the desired temperature. On almost any given day, even under the most horrific of bombardments, you would see fighters washing there. And they would carry on doing so right until the breakout from the besieged city.

The streets of the city painted a terrible picture, worse than the scenes of even the wildest sci-fi movie. One street had a vast cavity from a bunker-buster, and at the bottom of the cavity sat a UAZ jeep. It had fallen in during the night; the driver hadn't noticed the hole. At night-time, the few cars moving about the city would drive with their lights off because of the blackout. On another street in the city centre, a tall sewer pipe was jutting into the air; a bomb had ripped it out of the earth and left it upright. And from the top of the pipe swung the corpse of a man hanged for his activities as an FSB agent. How they managed to hang him from such a height was not clear; there were certainly no cranes in the city. When you moved about the city, it looked dead; even the stray dogs had dwindled. The occasional resident and the military patrols were the only reminders that the city still contained life and was continuing to fight.

Sometimes it was possible to visit old friends from before the war who'd chosen the difficult path of the warrior and had stayed to defend the capital. One unit was led by a poet famed throughout Chechnya; among its men were a scholar and a singer-songwriter. It was a cultural unit, and their small headquarters became a kind of cultural and intellectual centre for besieged Grozny. We often gathered there. We'd discuss the situation, talk about the way out of the war crisis. We would analyse what was happening and debate which path Chechnya should take in human history. And of course, more often than not, we would simply recite poems, listen to the singer playing his songs, and we'd talk about world literature. And yet no one released them from combat duties. In addition to their frequent visits to the positions across the city for cultural activities, they had to freeze in the icy trenches alongside all the defenders of the capital and repulse the enemy attack in their defensive sector. Like everyone else, they too lost comrades. The time spent with them, the recollections of peaceful pre-war life, the talks we had in our circle about poetry, music and art would help you to forget, if only for a short time, where you were. It was a kind of psychological escape. They were luckier than I: all of them were in the same unit. I only got to visit them from time to time. But for me, under those conditions, that was already quite something.

10

By mid January 2000, it became clear that soon either the attackers would storm the city or the defenders would break out of the capital. Both sides were in a strategic stalemate. In military and political terms, continuing to hang on to the city had long ago ceased to make sense. The capital no longer had any symbolic, strategic, political or propaganda value. Besides, the resistance forces outside the capital were clearly not sufficient to counter the Russian troops' slow but stubborn encroachment into the mountains. The Russian command was making active use of its airborne troops, attacking the rear of the resistance and seizing the commanding heights. It was clear that the fighters outside the Grozny ring did not have the capacity to fight effectively both the advancing troops and the airborne paratroopers. This left the far more battleworthy group in Grozny in considerable danger. So the command of the resistance made the decision to withdraw them from the encirclement.

The main problem was that after the breakout – assuming all went according to plan – the group would have to traverse many kilometres of enemy-controlled territory to get to the mountains. The shortest route to the unoccupied zone was twenty-five kilometres as the crow flies. But that route would have been suicidal: it was open fields all the way, and tightly controlled by enemy troops. The Russian aviation and artillery would be certain to massacre the entire group. So they chose a route that was longer and trickier but offered a better chance of crossing without exorbitant losses.

For the enemy command, a breakout was only to be expected, but nevertheless it came as a surprise. That is, they were waiting for it to happen, they knew we had little choice but to try to escape the encirclement, and there was not much time left – if we'd waited just a bit longer, there'd have been nowhere for us to go. That's why they were in no hurry to storm Grozny, fully aware of how such a bold move on their part would play out, while they waited for the breakout to happen some time soon. It was just that they didn't know when; the command of Grozny's defence maintained absolute secrecy as they prepared the breakout.

At the end of January the rank-and-file defenders of the capital discovered they'd be leaving the city. They only learnt which sector had been chosen for the breakout just before beginning the journey. And so on 30 January through to 1 February 2000, the 7,000 strong Grozny force, divided into three groups, began their escape from the city that they had successfully defended for several months.[43] Fighters from the commandant's office were in charge of the route reconnaissance and the breakout itself, and they were the last to flee the city. When they left Grozny, enemy forces were already in the capital and going on the rampage.[44] The first column contained 2,500 fighters. They had strict orders not to engage with the enemy and not to return fire. This order may at first seem strange, but it was given for a sound reason. If we had answered fire with fire, as the first group to leave, we would not only have betrayed our locations and given away our true numbers, but we'd have become bogged down in battle and held up the breakout, thus condemning to a 'heroic death' our comrades who were still stuck in the city. And there were 4,500 of them, including many of our very finest warriors. If the Russians had discovered how few of us there were in the besieged city and how many were breaking out on the first night, their troops would have been able to prevent the rest from leaving.

Contrary to popular belief, the Russian secret services did not have accurate information about the size of the group defending the city. Astonishingly enough, even some of our fighters were taken in: they thought that the Russian security services knew not just how many of them there were, but also the name of every one of Grozny's defenders. This was, of course, no more than a myth, and one that had been deliberately spread by the Russian side as part of their psy-ops. The objective was to induce feelings of helplessness in the resistance fighters, give them a sense of the inevitability of punishment and get them to crack. The intelligence gathered through the Russians' network of agents was based primarily on information from the first days of the war. And at that point there was a huge deluge of men willing to take up arms for the defence of freedom. Yet most of them couldn't withstand even a five-minute artillery attack, let alone close combat, without panicking. This great wave of volunteers joining the ranks of the resistance had not suddenly been overcome by the spirit of liberty, nor were they compelled by their sense of dignity to choose life in death's shadow over a life of humiliation; no, they were motivated by greed. Plain old greed. Believing that sooner or later the Russians would pull out of Chechnya and those who'd fought against them would be showered with perks and privileges, these men had swelled the ranks of the resistance for their own self-promotion, simply wanting to show their faces. These were the men whom the Chechen people contemptuously referred to as the 'poseur fighters'. After enlisting in the units and hanging around for a week or two among the militiamen, these guys then vanished. Thus they documented their participation in the war, hoping to turn up later and claim their 'hard-earned' perks. And since there were quite a few of these 'fighters', the Russians' figures for the number of defenders in the capital were hugely inflated, and this worked to our advantage.

The Russians didn't summon the courage to attack us even while we were on the road, when fighting columns are particularly vulnerable, despite their overwhelming superiority in troop strength (even going by their figures), and there wasn't time for them to mass more troops and hardware along our route.[45] We would halt at each stopping place for only as long as was needed for any straggling groups to catch up with us – generally it was from dawn to dusk. The enemy could not ascertain where the group would stop next. Only the group's top command had this information – even the junior and intermediate commanders learnt about it only at the last minute. They did, however, manage to mine our already reconnoitred route out of the city. The explanation for this was quite simple: a covert observation post set up by the Russians had noticed the Chechen scouts walking along the route, and, just to be safe, as the rules of war dictated, they had mined it. And although it came as a complete shock to find ourselves stepping into a minefield on land that had been reconnoitred earlier – and we lost comrades there, including commanders – the fighters kept their wits in this unforeseen situation and they performed their mission honourably. Throughout pretty much the entire two-week journey from Grozny to the mountains of Shatoy, this minefield at the exit from the city was the only surprise from the Russians that the group encountered.

From then on, the Russians' actions would follow the same pattern: they'd quickly cut off the village where the group had halted for the day, using the considerable forces they had available, but they would not dare enter into close combat, instead keeping to heavy artillery shelling and air strikes. And while they waited for reinforcements, the resistance fighters, who'd spent the past months fighting while fully encircled, found it easy to battle their way out of the blockade and go on their way. Another thing that worked to our advantage was the fact that the Russian officers, whether consciously or not, were reluctant to come to the aid of other units. It meant operating virtually in the dark, without proper reconnaissance, and against a seasoned opponent. And it was they who'd face the blame for any losses, rather than the units they were rescuing.

People met us in a variety of ways. In the vast majority of villages all the inhabitants would come out to the edge of the village and welcome the groups of fighters as heroes. They put them up in their homes, fed them and let them dry their clothes. In one village some locals (thankfully not many) wouldn't allow the fighters into their houses, not even to perform their obligatory prayers. The idea of using or threatening to use force against these people was unthinkable. None of the fighters would have stooped so low.

The men had no need to carry more than the minimum of provisions, as we were travelling most of the way through populated areas. At the expense of field rations, they carried as much ammunition as possible. Unlike food, that was something you could not pick up anywhere, and supplies were being continually spent. Now and then you might manage to seize some trophy weapons, but if you ran short of ammunition, they were nothing but trophies. In the villages where we stopped, the group would be replenished with new recruits. These were volunteers joining our ranks to fight in the war. And though we had no weapons to spare for them, nobody had the right to prevent them from defending their homeland. That was, after all, the key principle of a people's war, of partisan warfare: the only men fighting were those willing and able to fight, and, unlike the army, there was no compulsion. That's why partisan forces are traditionally stronger in spirit.

I remember some young lads who joined up with us on the road. They came from different villages. The youngest was fifteen and the eldest nineteen. At first I thought they were attracted by the romance of war: all the fighters in white camouflage smocks and bristling with weapons did indeed make an impressive picture. But after talking with them I realized that romance wasn't the main factor behind their decision. I asked them, 'Why have you chosen this difficult and thankless path? You're so young!'

They replied, 'Have you ever witnessed a "cleansing op"?'

I answered truthfully that I hadn't yet done so. They continued: 'Well, when you see one, that'll put an end to your questions. You have no idea what it's like to stand to attention in front of a grungy, louse-infested soldier, who in normal circumstances wouldn't even dare look you in the eye. To see his revolting grin and listen to his insults and taunts … And knowing that you've got to take all this not from some strong warrior who's defeated you in battle, but from this vile, barely human scum, who gets all his strength from numbers and weapons. You start loathing not just him, but also yourself, for meekly taking this humiliation. Well, from now on we're not going to take it any more.'

I didn't ask them any more questions. They died very soon after, no doubt due to their inexperience. One of them lived barely twenty-four hours; the second a little longer – two days. The third survived this trek, but he was killed later.

It came as quite a shock for the defenders of the capital to find out how much moral support they enjoyed among the population. After so many days and nights besieged by our mortal enemies, we'd begun to forget that beyond our fiery encirclement there was a life to which we were connected and there were people who hadn't forgotten us. We'd begun to forget there was a Chechen people, who identified with us and admired our glorious battle. Glorious not through its heroism, but glorious simply for being. And as for the stereotypical heroism where the hero sacrifices himself in the name of victory – whether that is in fact heroism at all is open to debate.

11

In the last days of January, plenty of snow was piling up in the city. This fluffy white heavenly grace concealed all traces of the fierce fighting. The snow fell in big soft flakes and the world became a wonderful fairy-tale blur. And no matter how much the Devil rejoiced in the war, filling every alley with the hum of shrapnel, lavishing blasts upon every courtyard and street, he was powerless against the snow. He could not take away the good spirits this clean, soft snow brought us. The most important thing in war is not the past, not the future, but the present moment. And if in the present something delightful is happening, even if it's nothing exceptional, why not be happy? Teetering between life and death, you were always living in the present. Not glancing over your shoulder at the past or peering into the future. That made things easier.

But the snowfall doesn't know and doesn't care about what is easier for you. It simply jerks you out of your diabolical present and for a brief time leads you by the hand – like when you were a child and your mother led you back home from the streets after you'd become lost in play – to a distant, joyous past. This past is an illusion. What you so bombastically refer to as your past is in fact the life of some other guy, someone you thought of as yourself. But he is not you. You and he are two different people;

as unalike as a crystal and a stone. He was a young romantic. You are a mature cynic. He trusts people. You do not trust even yourself. He loves to laugh and dream. You like to think and analyse. He is in love and sure of himself. You are lonely and doubt yourself. The only thing you have in common is your faith in God. But here too you're not quite the same: he just believes unthinkingly, whereas you believe consciously.

Here he is in a beautiful park in the now ruined city. There is the same unearthly, fairy-tale snowfall. With him are two girls. One of them is his sweetheart. She's no sylph, no queen, no angel. Just an ordinary girl. But with an extraordinary heart. Because she is in love. The thick snowfall turning the city ghostly, the empty park the city has offered up to you, the sweet, loving girl at your side are all making you deliriously happy. This happiness is enough to supply the whole world. You love the world because she is living in it. You want to make this world happy for her and you believe that you can. The three of you are throwing snowballs. For a long time, enraptured. At this moment there are no happier persons in the world than you.

Wait ... Did that happen to you? Was that really you? No, it can't have been you. It was that other guy, whom you persist in identifying as you. But does it matter? Surely he won't mind if you return for a moment and become him? If you become, for an instant, as happy as he was back then? No, of course not. He'll understand. After all, he is your reflection in the unshattered mirror of the past. Now he is gone. He's dead. Or rather, you're dead, and he is alive. And he will live as long as the planet spins around the wheel of time. Now the city is gone. It was killed, callously, cynically, and you took part in this murder. You contributed to the death of the city. Even though you were trying to defend it. These ruins today, for an instant, must be feeling happier, like you are, through becoming their reflection in the unshattered mirror of the past. And the park is gone: in its place lies a cemetery. The broken and scorched tree trunks have become gravestones for your fallen comrades. The ghosts of mothers mourning for their sons, raising their dark, dry branches to the white, snowy sky. And you'll never be able to throw snowballs again in that park. You will never be the way you were. When you were little, you used to fight the children who went nesting. You felt the pain of the unhatched, unformed chicks and their parents. Whereas now you see pain, but cannot feel it. Not even your own. And if you cannot feel pain, you won't be able to feel happiness.

On this strange, snowy, fiery night you hand over the city, along with the graves of your comrades, and your memories, to the wild barbarians and you leave. You leave for the mountains, along with the thousands of your comrades who are still alive. Just as over the centuries your ancestors escaped the countless enemy hordes. They left intending to return. And return they did. Perhaps it's no coincidence that you are visited by memories today. The dying city foretells the cruel fate awaiting its ruins, which are to be blown up over and over again by the barbarians in a wild frenzy of fury, in vengeance for its rebelliousness, until the ruins become riddled with craters. It foretells your fate, and it bids goodbye to you, its defender and executioner. And in parting, as a sign of forgiveness, for a brief moment it whirls you into the past, it lets you glance into the unbroken mirror of the past. You are grateful and silently receive its forgiveness. But can you forgive yourself?

12

Over the white snow stretches a long chain of silent white ghosts leaving behind the blazing ruins. It is us in camouflage smocks. The unearthly snowfall has just stopped. Behind us is the ghost of the city, mourning for us. We are silent. Our silence is an answer to all the countless questions that we've asked ourselves and that anybody could ever ask. Our silence is more painful than the agony of torture. The narrow path across the minefield that our sappers had cleared has been mined again. And from the right the enemy are firing on us. They're firing randomly, it's true. But why are we silent, Commander, when we're clutching weapons in our hands? Let us off the leash, Commander, and we'll silence them. We'll silence plenty of them for good. All their tanks and artillery, aircraft and hardware are powerless against us in the night. Night is for warriors whose spirit is stronger. Our enemy isn't cowardly or weak. But we are angrier. We'll fight with no regard for losses. Not for our country, not for freedom. Not for our religion, not for some lofty cause. We will fight for the silence. For our painful, bitter silence on this frosty, burning night! But we cannot reply. We cannot condemn to death our comrades who will break out tomorrow. And the day after.

You're near the head of the column but not one of the first. It is the first men who blow up on the mines. You hear the explosions and see their bloodied bodies. A mine inflicts the most horrific of injuries. Many survivors of mines would be better off not surviving. But it is God who determines our life spans, just as He grants us life itself. Your video camera is in your rucksack. It doesn't have a night-vision mode, and without that it is useless by night. You watch three young men run into the minefield, shouting, 'In the name of God, we'll clear a path for our brothers!' But they don't manage to clear a path. All three are blown up by mines after just ten paces. Dawn is breaking. Dawn is not our ally: we are knights of the dark. We won't have time to reach the village and take control of it.

The commander of the Almaz unit asks his fighters, 'Are you willing to engage the enemy to provide covering fire while your comrades enter the village?' He asks, fully aware of what the answer will be. He could order them and the order would be carried out. But in this war, asking your men is not shameful: it is an honour. Having obtained their unconditional consent, he quickly deploys his unit, and they take up their fighting positions. You run with them towards the positions, pulling the camera out of the bag as you go. Now it is light and you can film. The enemy know that now they'll be coming under fire from light machine guns, powerful flamethrowers and grenade launchers, their fire will be met with a storm of fire, and they cease their attack on the column. The enemy know all too well how adept their opponents are at shooting. And they have no desire to become their targets. While their comrades are covering them, the fighters take the village, but now some of them have to return to the city. They will break out with the rest of the fighters over the next two nights. Under still heavier fire. And once they've rejoined the first group, they will continue to cut through the enemy forces for many more nights.

13

Night. Dark, starless night. Silent white shadows have flocked into the yard of the town hospital. Mutely they fall into formation. In low voices the commanders call out the names of the survivors, while the survivors remember the fallen. You have gathered to start the journey across the snowy fields to your destiny. You are leaving your wounded comrades in the hospital, which is why you are departing from here, from the hospital yard, bidding them farewell before the march. Your comrades await different fates. Some of them will be hidden by the locals; others will be taken prisoner by the enemy, who will enter the town in the morning. Some of them will be tortured to death; some will be imprisoned with long sentences, while others will be released for a ransom paid by you and their relatives. And everyone who falls into the hands of the enemy will undergo torture. But now neither you nor they have a choice. You realize this perfectly well. The men staying behind realize it, they can see what awaits them, yet they remain in the town of their own free will. So as not to burden their comrades, who must make their way through the enemy hordes for an unknown time. And those of you who are departing silently accept their sacrifice. There's a chance, however tenuous, that at least a few of them may survive. You know, just as they do: if you take them with you, they're sure not to survive.

You'd simply be condemning them to a harrowing death before your eyes. Your war has grim rules.

You go into the hospital to take leave of your wounded friend and to give him a shot of pain-relief from your supplies. As you are saying goodbye to him, you intuitively feel someone staring at you. Turning round, you meet the gaze of large black eyes – infinitely deep, like lakes at night, far too beautiful for war. And these eyes meeting yours suddenly glint with an inner lustre. Or perhaps it's the glimmer of a tear? Her gaze continues to plunge into your eyes as her lips whisper, 'It's you? You're alive?'

'Strangely enough, yes. As you can see,' you reply, not quite sure what this question signals – joy or annoyance.

But the owner of the astonishing eyes, a slender, youthful, beautiful dark-haired girl of eighteen or nineteen, dispels your doubts: 'My God! How glad I am to see you alive! You're not wounded?' And receiving a reply in the negative she continues, 'I need to talk to you. Wait for me in the street.' You nod and leave.

Of course you remember her. You happened to meet a few times in the encircled city. A native of Grozny, she'd stayed behind along with her brother, bandaging the wounded on the front line and cooking food for the defenders of the capital. The Chechen women have always stirred your admiration: mothers, sisters, daughters, wives. In these troubled times, many of them have found the strength to be with their men, to protect their children from the wild enemy soldiers, to die from the rounds of automatic gunfire. And, through it all, to remain beautiful and feminine. You often recall the speech of a Russian officer in the First Chechen War, given at a checkpoint where his unit was on duty. Addressing the three of you who made up the international group of journalists, he said, 'You see, they will always remain Chechens. No matter how much we go on the rampage here, we cannot win against them. They lived for seventy years in the same country as us, yet they never became "Soviet people". I've seen what their women are like. They have so much courage and grit that I take my hat off to them. These fragile creatures defend their men so bravely at the checkpoints that there's no shame in standing down in the face of such powerful love. And I would never take their men away from them. It's hard to conquer a nation whose women find the strength to defend and remain true to their men. I respect this nation and I'm grateful to their women for having such hearts. You cannot take their men away from them. It is a terrible sin.' In the pale light of the hospital streetlamp you watch the girl approaching and you take a step towards her. You see that she is agitated.

'Please don't think badly of me, but I have to tell you ...' she begins. 'It's just I don't know if I'll survive, that's why I've decided to talk. No matter what happens, I want you to know that I love you. Since the first day we met. I don't know why, but from the moment I saw you I felt sure of my love for you, and as time has passed this feeling has only grown stronger. I don't need you to search in your heart right now to answer whether you love me. I know you had no idea of my feelings. I need only one thing: promise that you'll find me when you are able to. If I'm alive, then find me alive, but if not, find my grave and make sure it's mine. I promise you will come to love me. I feel it. I'm sure that you will love me. It will all work out for us – my intuition has never let me down. Do you promise you'll find me?'

'I promise. No matter what, I'll find you. Even if it takes me the rest of my life. I'll find you and ask if you still love me, and if you answer "yes", I'll take you with me straight away. If I make it out of here alive ...'

'You will survive. Nothing bad is going to happen to you. I feel it. Believe me, I know, without you I can never be happy. But now we have to part. You're going with the advance guard, they're waiting for you. I'm sure we'll be together. Stay alive ... Stay alive and find me ...' she whispers, disappearing into the snowy darkness.

Neither of you is aware that you are seeing each other for the last time. Yet her intuition didn't deceive her. You survived. So did she. Several years later you kept your promise. You found her. Or rather, you found her mother ... She hadn't mentioned you to anyone, she left you no letters. But you knew she waited for you. And now she was married. Her unsuspecting mother told you her address and let you know she'd been married against her will. You went to find her. But you didn't meet her. There was no point. You couldn't have asked her the key question, and without that question the meeting would have brought her nothing but pain. You merely saw her one last time, silently bade her farewell and left without being seen. She probably never found out that she also kept her promise; you fell in love with her ... You managed to fall in love with her in the brief moment her hurried whispering lasted in the snowy night. With her astonishing confession of love as she stood facing the Angel of Death, she will remain in your memory for ever. For the rest of your life you will love perhaps not her, the actual woman, but that mysterious night and that beautiful confession. You will love a woman capable of declaring her love while gripping an assault rifle and standing between two worlds. And perhaps you owe your strange survival on so many occasions after that night to her confession and your promise? Or perhaps, intuitively sensing that you couldn't survive any other way, she deliberately gave you a straw of life to cling to? Who knows? But all the same you will believe in the sincerity of her love for you. And this belief will preserve in your memory one of your warmest recollections.

14

These days and nights are so alike and so unlike each other. You greet each dawn to the rumble of guns and the whine of aircraft, and, having set up a watch, you sleep like a log to this Satanic music. And each night you fight your way across the white fields, while in the sky above fiery flowers burst into bloom. Only these bouquets are offered not to you but to the Angel of Death. Each day flourishing towns are turned into ruins merely because your path cuts through them. A profound sense of guilt and grief haunts you as you see houses so lovingly built turn to dust before your eyes. The dull, gnawing sensation that you are almost as dangerous to your own people as your deadly enemies expels from your heart all other emotions – fear, pain, desire for life – filling your heart with one great indelible feeling: hate. This hatred and rage, born of the despicable guile of the adversary, who can only destroy towns but dares not enter them until after you've left, makes your spirit invincible.

You leave your wounded comrades to be hidden by locals,[46] who understand perfectly well what will become of them if they are found by the enemy. The mortally wounded are given hand grenades. They know what to do with them. And you go on your way. If the enemy crosses your path, you simply wipe them out. But you do not seek encounters with them, and the enemy tries not to cross your path. They prefer to fight you from a safe distance, and then to enter the village you've left and fight its civilian population. Your enemy has always been mindlessly cruel to those who are weakest. The master of world literature, Leo Tolstoy, who served as an officer in the Russian Army and fought against your people in the nineteenth century, drew attention to this trait in his brilliant tale *Hadji Murat*. Yet he was perhaps alone among the enemy camp in grasping the essence of your people's fierce resistance to the Russian invaders. And once he'd understood it, he was the first man brave enough to glance into the inner world of his former foes. He was the first to create faithful translations of selections of Chechen folklore. It was he who acknowledged the mindless cruelty of Russian soldiers towards the defenceless and the weak. Such are their rules of war. But you need to walk on. Straight ahead.

15

The forest. The winter forest is extraordinarily beautiful. And sad. It is like an enchanted realm, punished with silence for the polyphonic frenzy of spring and summer's feathered songsters. Only the whisper of the wind and the savage whistling of blizzards disturb the silence. On the long winter nights you can listen to the bewitching, majestic howl of the wolf – luring you on a reckless journey, as the Pied Piper's flute lured the children of Hamelin –which immediately makes the piteous, cowardly yelp of the jackal break off. Amid the deep black of the treetops, the scarlet berries of the bitter guelder rose flash like the bright flames of a bonfire in the gloom of night. The guelder rose is a symbol of life. Such is the winter forest from afar. Once you find yourself within the forest, you understand the quiet is merely soundlessness. The winter forest lives a life that, though not as noisy as in spring and summer, is nevertheless intense. The life of the winter forest is the wisdom of an old man who has realized the vanity of bustle. Wisdom loves quiet and contemplation. The soundlessness of the winter forest is not silence; it is the hush of wisdom contemplating. That is how you remember your forest. The one you grew up close to, time and again returning to its mysterious world. You loved your magical forest. Loved its noise and soundlessness, the songs of its feathery residents and the howl of the wolf. It was truly beautiful. But this forest is not like that. It is terribly uncomfortable and gloomy. And scarlet fires of bitter guelder rose do not burn here.

This winter and this forest will leave you with a shiver in your heart, which will appear whenever you see a winter forest, even in pictures. You have already been in the forest for two days. The snow is waist deep. It is a mountain forest, which means that, besides the snow, you will have to tackle the ascent of many mountain passes. There is no food. A trek meant to last a day goes on for ever. Your guides have lost their way. You cannot sleep. Sleep means death. Those who fall asleep in this forest will never wake up. You can rest for no more than three minutes. The risk of falling asleep is great. You cannot light a fire. They serve as excellent targets for enemy gunners and pilots. You have to wade through countless rivers and streams. That's why your feet are wet. It's pointless drying them.

You have walked without rest for two nights and a day. The second night is ending. You are very tired. While you were idle in the encirclement, like all your comrades, you grew unused to long treks without rest. The brief nocturnal battle-march, fighting your way out of the city, over the past few days has not done much to return you to form. You are racked with hunger. But you are tormented still more by lack of sleep and rest. So far you have refrained from eating snow, realizing what dangers that brings, but you're not sure how much longer you can hold out. You have stopped to rest. Along with the commander of the Almaz unit and several other commanders, you seek out all the fighters who have fallen asleep in the forest and round them up. Here is a good place. It is a small hunting lodge. You lay down the wounded in it. You can also light fires briefly. In front of a fire your chances of not freezing rise sharply. At last your comrades set about lighting a fire and you go off to sit down and rest. For precisely two minutes. You cannot risk any longer. But you fall asleep almost at once … You come to your senses with somebody shaking you hard. Opening your eyes, you see the face of your friend leaning over you. You try to get up. But your arms and legs do not obey you. It's as though they have gone. In their place is a heavy, unfeeling weight. You realize they are frozen, yet for some reason you accept this fact calmly. It seems fatigue has blunted your survival instinct – a dangerous symptom. But even with your survival instinct functioning, what can you do if your body has failed?

'I think I've had it. You'll have to walk on without me,' you suggest to your comrade. 'I can't move my arms or legs. They've given up on me.'

'I can't leave without you! Up!' he orders. Then he grabs you and puts you on your feet.

'Everything's all right now … In an upright position I won't die of frostbite … I've got to move … Look, I have nine lives like a cat …' you try to joke, making clumsy attempts at movement. With the help of your rescuer at last you start moving and for a long time you walk round the fire, until you are satisfied that the blood has started flowing to all your organs. You survive not because you are strong. You've simply decided not to fight your survival instinct. It is prompting you about what to do. There are times when the only correct answer is to surrender to the power of this mighty instinct, although for most of your life it has to be kept under control. And this is just such a situation. Then you manage to get half an hour's sleep in front of the fire. At dawn, when the campfires have been smothered, you set out once more. Your camera batteries have almost run out, yet you manage to film a little of the trek. On the third night your resolve breaks and, along with the others, you start to eat snow. Many of the fighters have been having visions since the second night. Some see food, some see a freshly made bed, some see horrifying chimeras and wild beasts. Everyone who sees hallucinations reacts vividly to them, but happily there are always others on hand who do not see them at that moment, and they bring the raving back to their senses with shakes and slaps.

Time behaves oddly. Sometimes it freezes for several years, sometimes it rushes at the speed of light … A moment ago you were walking surrounded by beech forest up to your waist in snow. But now you are in a city! This city is astonishingly beautiful! You have never seen anything like it, not in pictures, not at the cinema. Nowhere, ever. The city has no people, no cars, no factory chimneys or advertising billboards in sight. It is empty, but so clean and beautiful that somewhere deep within your heart arises a dim unease and anguish. Your mind tries to answer the question of how you came to be in this warm spring city bathed in sunlight. *Have I really been out of it for so long that I failed to notice how we got here?* you ask yourself. Have we taken this city? But where's it located? There isn't any place like this anywhere, is there? You cannot find any answers. You would dearly love to stay in this city, but an unknown force is pushing you away from it. 'What city are we in?' you shout to your comrades.

'We aren't in a city, we're in the forest. It's a hallucination. Wake up!' They shake you. While you saw the city, your eyes weren't closed, you are absolutely sure of this. But now the city vanishes and in its place appears a winter forest. You are distressed at losing it, but you have to keep moving so as not to be left here. The city will appear before you often, very often, enticing you again and again. And often you will ask about it. This heavenly city will never leave your memory. Later you will ask all those who survived the trek about their visions, hoping to find at least someone who saw your city. You will search subconsciously for a witness with whom you can talk about the city. You will search for a friend among the living and you will find none. You will turn out to be the only person who saw this strange and beautiful city.

The fourth, last and most trying day of the trek through the mountain forests. You are enfeebled not by hunger; war has taught you to endure hunger. You are enfeebled by lack of sleep. And you are still eating plenty of snow. This saps your energy more than the hunger and physical exhaustion. The bland, distilled snow water goes straight through your body, washing away any minerals that remain. As a result, you become dehydrated and lose energy more rapidly. But a weakened body is no reason to give up the struggle for life. And so you obstinately walk on ahead. Sometimes shots from grenade launchers and assault rifles are heard: these are the men firing at the enemy seen in their hallucinations. You are on the mountain pass. The nearest water is a fair way off. You see a fighter lying in the snow; he is raving.

'Brothers, let me have a sip of water ... I will make it, I'm alive ...' he murmurs. Some of his comrades are motionless nearby. You lean over him with your flask.

'It won't help – we've given him water. He's frozen. He doesn't need water. Well, he doesn't need anything now,' they say.

'Do you know him? Can you inform his family?' you ask.

'Yes, if we survive ourselves. He's from our unit. Thank you.' The strangers show you gratitude, although it is unclear what for. And the fighter, a mere kid, dies before your eyes.

Your comrade, having spotted more passes beyond this one, has given up. He sits down in the snow and says, 'That's it! I can't go any further. I'm staying here. I don't have the energy to move – you go on ahead.' You look at his face; it is as white as a corpse. From experience you know a face like that tells of extreme wasting of the body. You read in his eyes a strange remoteness. As though he is no longer here, but not yet there ... On his face is the stamp of a person on the path to eternity. You cannot allow him to die so easily. He is your close and loyal friend, who time after time has rescued you from certain death. You look him in the eyes. You hold his gaze so that he cannot glance at eternity: 'Look at my eyes! Can you see me and hear me?' Receiving an affirmative answer, you continue: 'You know I don't have the strength to carry you. I'm on my last legs myself ...' He nods.

'I cannot stay here and die with you. I am a warrior, not a suicide case.' In vain you try to provoke a reaction with this taunt. 'I won't leave you to die here. I've left behind more than a lifetime's worth of fatally wounded men. The only way I'm leaving is if I'm certain of your death. I will only leave here if I'm sure that I'm leaving behind my friend's corpse, not a man who's alive and will slowly die while watching me walk away. So if you cannot walk on right now by yourself, I'll kill you and go. At least you'll have fallen as a warrior. I won't allow you to die like some starving dog. If I know that you've fallen as a warrior, even if by my own hands, I'll leave at peace with myself. If you get up and walk on, have no doubt we'll make it out of here alive, even if it is against your will. I give you my word I'll keep one of these promises, whichever you decide on.' With this you load a cartridge into the chamber and point the barrel of your assault rifle at him. He knows you would never say anything like this unless you meant it. You have known each other for too long. Looking you in the eye intently for several moments, he gets up silently and walks ahead. And you will not leave his side until you arrive, alive, at your destination.

You wearily drag yourself along an old road leading towards a village. You see a fire. It is your comrades: they have lit a campfire under cover. To warm themselves and boil some water. Hot water warms your insides so well. They invite you to the fire and offer some boiled water. You reach into the pocket of your jacket for something and come across a little sachet. It is a seasoning sachet from a packet of instant noodles which served as your ration on the night you broke out of the encirclement. At the time you put two sachets (one with oil and one with spices) in your pocket and forgot about them. The sachet with the oil burst but the one with the seasoning has survived. You pour the contents into the mug and stir. Never in your life, neither before nor afterwards, have you ever drunk anything more delicious. Even the same drink specially prepared by you later will not possess a fraction of the flavour.

Your commanders do all they can to get you out of there alive.

They deliberately spread information that you are awaited ahead by people who have come to your aid with food, dry socks and so on. This instils hope and the desperate desire to make it in the hearts of men who are by now ready to give up. Who are tired of battling against death and ready to submit to it. Due to the 'honourable lie' of the commanders and these elite warriors' personal qualities, you emerge from the forest with far fewer losses than might have been expected. Especially considering that for the first two days you had to exchange fire with enemy forces on the commanding heights. Finally you come to a small mountain village where you are awaited by fighters and locals who have driven from many villages with food and transport.

It is deep, dark night. Or you think it's dark. You can no longer trust your eyes. Transport is here, and men who aren't from your column. These people smell different. The smell of food. You are put in a minibus. Your comrades are sitting there. Someone runs up to the car and calls out to you. Having assured himself that you are in the vehicle, he walks off. The minibus is moving. You are offered some cold boiled meat brought by the people who met you. You take it and try to eat. But you cannot swallow it. You have eaten too much snow, and when you try to swallow you get a terrible pain in your throat. The hard, grainy snow, swallowed without waiting for it to thaw, has grated your throat like sandpaper. You give up your vain attempts to swallow the piece of meat and fall asleep.

You are woken by someone calling to you. You get off the minibus. A pale dawn is breaking and you recognize the house of your aunt and your cousin who came to meet you. It was he who called out to you in the minibus. They do not recognize you straightaway. Neither your relatives nor your comrades. It seems your appearance has changed dramatically. You must have lost weight. You take off your sodden boots and slip your feet straight into icy water. Your toes have gone dead and this is what you must do to restore them to life. The toenails are black, whereas the toes are very white. Later these nails will fall off and new ones will grow. But you have been lucky. After a while the sensitivity returns to your toes. They start hurting horribly. But you welcome this pain. No, you have not gone crazy; it's just this pain is a good sign. It means your attempts to preserve your toes (throughout the entire journey you kept trying to wriggle your toes, whether walking or resting) have been successful. Strangely, now you do not feel hungry. Even sleep does not come. You must have slept your fill in the minibus. You tried falling asleep, but you dreamed your comrades were walking across a minefield, you began calling to them and then awoke.

You ought now to relish this indefinite period of rest. But it seems you have grown completely wild in this war. You simply don't know how to occupy yourself. You cannot write yet. In this situation you couldn't hope to preserve even a fragment of your writing. You do not yet know that soon (a week after your arrival) you will set off with a group of fighters to take up new positions at the top of a mountain, and for a long time you will be stuck there, in the winter forest, encircled. Then when you finally leave – still alive – you will hear the terrible news of the tragedy in the village of Komsomolskoye. And you'll long regret the fact that you survived, and feel your guilt before those who perished. As if, had you been there with them, it could have changed something. But that will come later. Now you need to rest. Yet for some reason rest does not come. Your soul is troubled. You feel people are tired of the war. And that is the most disastrous thing that could happen. That is bad.

16

The group that had broken out of the sealed city and for two weeks fought their way across occupied territory to reach Shatoy district in the mountains met a depressing state of affairs. Almost all of the commanding heights had been captured by the enemy. The vast majority had been brought under control as the breakout from Grozny was underway. That is, over the past two weeks. The Russian Army command, realizing how the situation might escalate if the Grozny group joined the fighters in the mountains, took urgent action to seize the commanding heights, creating for this purpose the special Army Group Centre. This force operated from the south, moving up from the border with Georgia and dropping airborne troops to capture the heights as they met up with troops advancing from the plain. As ever, the Russians paid scant regard to losses among their own soldiers. And their pre-emptive tactic worked.

Our group arrived in the mountains to find itself effectively locked in. The key feature of mountain combat is that the side which controls the heights over the roads and tracks, over everything essential to life, controls the entire situation. And here the situation clearly favoured the enemy. What's more, we were facing a food crisis. The local population, a potential supplier of provisions to the fighters, was suffering acute shortages. The

Russian political and military leadership had been enforcing a blockade of the mountainous districts, barring humanitarian organizations from travelling to the area with food aid. They knew that the fighters would be powerless if they lost the support of the population. And this could only be achieved by pushing the people themselves to the brink of survival.

Some time later, when the resistance had withdrawn from the mountain districts and the Russian troops entered them, it was discovered that certain unscrupulous Chechens had been making a lot of money out of this human disaster. They had gone to the people and told them, 'I've struck a deal with some Russian Army men. They'll give us an armed escort for the trip to buy food at the market in Shali.[47] But they need a hundred dollars from each person.' Being completely trapped, the people agreed to pay from the last of their savings what was at the time a huge sum so they could survive. It later emerged that the Russians had not demanded any payment at all. One woman could not come up with the full sum. All her appeals via the Chechen middleman for the price to be reduced fell on deaf ears. In desperation the woman decided to go straight to the Russian officer. When he heard her plea for him to accept 'a little short of one hundred dollars', he was astonished. And when he learnt who had been collecting such sums, allegedly on his behalf, the officer confronted the Chechen in front of everyone: 'When did I ever ask you for a hundred dollars? I just asked for some cash for booze and fags, and only if you could spare it and didn't mind. I'm not offering to take you for money; I'm doing it because I want to remain human.' The most interesting detail in this story is that the Chechen middleman was a well-known and respected religious figure in the mountains. Or at least he was until that day.

It was not possible to procure food from outside the republic. The only road connecting Chechnya and Georgia had been held by the Russians since December. And the resistance fighters, armed only with small-arms fire and coming under bombardment from the air, could not attack the well-fortified enemy positions, defended with mortar batteries, mountain guns, anti-tank guided missile launchers and the like, on the commanding heights above the road. Of course, they began fighting fiercely to recover the heights from the enemy and they even enjoyed some success in this. But they could not turn back the tide on a larger scale. The command of the Chechen resistance was clearly faced with the task of switching to the tactics of guerrilla warfare. And guerrilla warfare follows entirely different rules: it is a war to grind down the enemy.

17

The snow falls thickly. The February snow is damp and malleable. The moisture soaks right through your clothes and you freeze even more than in the biting cold of January. The February frost gradually chills you to the bone, and it doesn't abate for a long time. Today you've withdrawn from the heights you were holding, and you're hiding in a remote ravine in the forest. Your small unit has split up into four groups and fanned out. You have one night to dig a dugout by hand and go underground. You have to disappear before the enemy do an air reconnaissance. Sodden with sweat and snow, together you dig into the frozen ground. Only the top layer is frozen: beneath there is ordinary soil, full of stones and tree roots. The soil in the mountains is always stony. But you'll be underground by dawn regardless. You're no stranger to this task. 'Work your hardest, then work harder.' Before dawn you have finished the dugout. You cover it with a double layer of logs, disguise it with snow and the freeze begins. Your sweat is cooling down and your clothes are soaked through. With you is a wounded comrade. You cannot light fires in the forest – enemy troops are all around and close by; they are based in the village just a kilometre and a half away. The dugout has no stove, so there's no flue. The hole in the roof does not draw the smoke up. This is not the steppe, where the winds roam free

– it's a mountain forest. You light a small fire on the floor of the dugout and try to keep warm. But you merely poison yourselves with pungent smoke. Luckily, it is getting light and you need to extinguish the fire. The next evening some of your comrades make their way from the village to you. They bring a little food and a milk churn with a chimney pipe. You adapt the churn to make a perfect stove, and you no longer freeze at night. But during the day it is still cold. You cannot use the stove during the day: the smoke would be visible for miles.

There is plenty of water. A small brook runs along the floor of the ravine. True, it is icy cold, but it's excellent for maintaining hygiene. You couldn't, of course, wash clothes in it – there's nowhere to dry them, but you can certainly wash yourself. You quickly get used to it. On the road to the ravine there's a Russian checkpoint. The only path to your camp goes along the floor of the ravine. Once every two or three days your comrades take this path to bring you some food. But to reach you, they must hoodwink the soldiers on duty. One of them heats the bath-house, prepares a good spread, and invites the frozen, half-starved soldiers and their officer: 'Come and take a steam bath, have a break from the war with some home cooking.' And while the soldiers relax, your friends have time to bring you provisions. Your enemies know that you are somewhere in the forest; you heard them say so on their radios. But without knowing which grid square you are in, they cannot blanket it with artillery fire and air strikes. And they don't have the appetite for entering the forest and combing it – the losses would be unjustifiably high. So they prefer to block all the paths from the forest and wait. Wait for the snow to melt. The brief period between the snow and the spring foliage is when you are most vulnerable. In the meantime, what matters for them is not to let you out and not to let food in to you. At night, while you use the stove, the snow on the dugout melts and unmasks you, so each dawn you have to recoat it in snow. A few days later, though, your friends deliver some white sheets and you arrange them over the dugout. No matter how difficult the conditions, the camp requires round-the-clock guarding. You take turns at keeping watch in half-hour shifts. Standing any longer would be difficult – the frost is merciless. But there are only a few of you, and you have to relieve each other too frequently. You don't get time to rest and catch up on your sleep. So you propose having longer shifts and thus longer breaks for resting. This helps. Now you're standing on guard for longer and you also get longer to rest. Whoever is on duty has to keep watch over the entire camp, not just cover one direction. That means he has to keep moving about. And a man who is continually moving has less chance of freezing.

In March, the command decides to withdraw you from the forest. Your small unit has been unable to take on political propaganda or tactical missions. When your unit was dispersing through the forest, there was one task you were to carry out urgently, should the need arise, and without waiting for orders. If the Russian troops in the village went on the rampage – killing civilians, stealing from their homes and so on – you were to break out of the encirclement immediately, join up with your brothers-in-arms who were still in the village and attack the enemy. Breaking out of the forest encirclement would have posed no problem: you could take out the checkpoint in the ravine in one minute flat. What's more, lately you've become quite experienced at breaking out of encirclements and you've honed your skills. Had it happened, the enemy would have seen a fight to remember, yet you'd most likely have been killed to a man. But as the Chechen proverb goes, 'The brave man throws caution to the wind when he's doing battle.'

The enemy forces, though, have been particularly calm and quiet, and you've managed to avoid a hero's death. And that means your unit currently has no mission to carry out in its present form. So the decision to withdraw from the encirclement makes sense. By now some of the resistance forces have disappeared to legalize, to varying degrees, their situation, while others are falling in the unequal battle against the enemy hordes in the village of Komsomolskoye.[48] By the rules of guerrilla warfare, you too ought to legalize yourselves – some of you partially, others completely. You've pulled out of the forest following the usual pattern: by passing the ravine checkpoint in twos and threes. The new village administration installed by the Russians is doing everything it can to save your skins: they help you escape from the district to a place where, so long as nobody talks, you can safely get your passports registered.[49] Those who are carrying their passports get help from the village administration to register them. And for those who don't have one, they issue refugee certificates. Indeed, the Russian police themselves know perfectly well who they're dealing with: one said as much when you were registering as a refugee. He said they'd simply rather not 'have somebody's soul on their conscience. No matter who that man might be.' These were ordinary policemen who hadn't been through the Russian propaganda mill. You all make it out of the forest encirclement without losses. For a few weeks you live with relatives in the same village and quietly go out of your mind. It's as if these people have drunk of some poisoned water and they've all gone mad together, like in one Sufi parable. They positively savour every detail of the deaths of your comrades drawn into the cul-de-sac of fire in Komsomolskoye. They are crying and grieving for the fallen youngsters, admiring their heroism and endurance, yet … You just cannot listen to the detailed descriptions of the deaths of men who only yesterday were sharing their last crust of bread with you. And you have nowhere to go and hide. There are many refugees; you are surrounded by people. And all of them, everywhere, are talking about this tragedy. But fortune saves you from sinking irrevocably into hatred for them. You manage to get a lift in a car going higher into the mountains, to a small village. There you find dozens in the same situation and you live there for many months. These villagers are tactful enough not to mention the tragedy in front of you and your comrades. They take care of you as best they can: warning you in time about 'cleansing ops', hiding you in their homes and feeding you. Not one resident of this little village, no adult or child, has informed on any of you to the enemy. Indeed, neither did any of the villagers near the forest camp where you were encircled for over a month. Quite the opposite: thanks to their help and efforts you all managed to break out alive and unwounded. Over the course of some months, you all gradually get yourselves legalized, later to rejoin your comrades.

18

Today is quite a momentous occasion. It is remarkable for two reasons. Firstly, I'm travelling to a temporary police station. On my own initiative. Voluntarily. Not, of course, to repent of my terrible sins and ask the occupying police for forgiveness – for amnesty, in other words. It's just I need to go legal, and that requires registering my passport at the police station. According to certain sources, whom I'm inclined to trust, the police have put out an all-points warning for me – that is, I'm on the wanted list. So I've finally made myself an enemy. That was just what I'd hoped to avoid while living for several months in the small mountain village and fleeing into the forest every time a 'cleansing op' began. But today I've been informed that my friends on the other side of the barricades have managed to get me off the wanted list. And so I'm on my way to register. There are no guarantees that it will all go smoothly. My friends might even be drawing me into a trap. But I have to try. And so I'm going.

The second reason this day is notable is that for the first time after a long break (it's been over ten months, since October last year) I am going out into the world. Well, this 'world' is actually just a small district centre, hidden in the highlands. Never mind that I'm wearing old, faded jeans that were once black, soft-soled canvas shoes donated to me by a kind-hearted mountain villager (wearing boots is out of the question – they'd arouse suspicion), and an extra-baggy denim sleeveless shirt over a T-shirt, a gift from a relative. But then there is life in that world. Proper life. Civilian life. Even if it's surrounded by checkpoints and army units. You can buy things; there's a real market. It may be small, but it's real. And you can ask the traders who've travelled to the market about the situation in the capital and on the roads. Get news straight from the horse's mouth. The information you obtain from official sources, with the help of a small transistor, has no claim whatsoever to truth. And so the only reliable news source left is word-of-mouth. I quickly obtain the coveted registration stamp in my passport before heading for the centre of the village. To get the stamp I have to endure several minutes of feeling horribly impotent. They lead me through the back door, bypassing the queue; an officer stares at me for a whole minute before smiling and saying, 'OK, lad. You can live.' Without a single question, not even a routine one, he stamps the passport.

The village centre, where the market is held, is the hub of social life. I approach some women traders who at a glance realize where I've come from and willingly provide me with the news I am after. Then a friend and I go to a kebab house and sit at an outdoor table. Soon we are joined by two soldiers and an officer, a major according to his shoulder straps. As our table is the only one with empty seats, they ask if they can sit there. Little by little we strike up a conversation. The officer is in the engineering corps and the contract soldiers are in the motorized infantry. When they hear my profession, they take an interest.

'Were you working in the national media?'

'You mean the Russian government media? No. God forbid that I'd ever do that.'

'Why's that? You mean because …' the officer says with a knowing look.

'No, not "because". It's just they do an awful lot of shameless lying. And I don't like lying.'

'OK, I understand. They're as good at lying as the government are. But that's no concern of mine. My concern is building. I didn't come here to fight but to build. I'm not here to shoot people. In fact you're more likely to shoot me, but I'm not planning on any shooting. I have my own approach to this war. I want to build.'

'I'm not interested in shooting anybody either. I'm a man of peace too,' I say.

'I can well believe it,' the officer says before departing.

'And why did you sign up for this war? Doesn't it weigh on your conscience?' I ask the soldiers.

One of them opens up. 'Everyone thinks that contract soldiers like nothing better than to go to war and kill innocent people. Take me, for example. I came here purely for practical reasons. I have two children who live with my wife. We got divorced and I pay her alimony. There weren't any regular jobs going. Here they were offering good money and so I took the job. The money I get here is way more than I could ever earn back home. The vast majority of contract soldiers have a home, a family, kids. What makes us come here isn't bloodlust but necessity. If someone shoots at me, of course I'll shoot back, but I've never opened fire first, and I don't ever intend to. You get all sorts among us – there are scumbags too. But, trust me, the lads hate them and try to get rid of them. I'm not just making a song and dance for you because you're a journalist, to paint a positive image of Russian contract soldiers. I know you're not at work right now and you can't write about this. And when you can, you won't bother. I'm just trying to explain that not all contract soldiers, not even most of them, are monsters and murderers. Although you come across all sorts … The Internal Troops are bastards. It's them who go around committing all sorts of horrors against people, giving all the soldiers a bad name …'

'Do they feed you well?' I interrupt his monologue.

'Huh, if only! There's tinned meat, condensed milk, cans of one kind or other and crushed oats. Every single day. That's why we've come here, for some fresh meat. We need some vitamins. The body wants at least a bit of variety. Our living conditions are worse than for cattle. They probably do it on purpose, to make us get angry and take it out on the civilians. But we haven't gone completely barmy from this war. We talk with the locals, we can see that the only thing these people are guilty of is living on this land. And they're not guilty before mankind. They're only guilty before the monsters on both sides.' As he speaks, his friend is nodding in agreement. They say goodbye and leave. And we leave too. I can't be sure whether he was putting on a special act with this monologue or whether he was speaking from the heart, but my feeling is that these men were talking sincerely. I realize that they are the enemy – only yesterday we might have met on the battlefield – but after all, the enemy are human too; they have feelings and thoughts. And they had no reason to hide anything from me or to lie. Well, I'm the enemy to them. They're not stupid; it's as obvious to them who I am as it was to the women in the market. They weren't bothered about what I thought of them. And why should they care what an enemy thinks? We're not obliged to be polite or high-minded with our adversaries. We have to be ruthless with them. Well, then, there's no need to make an effort to look good in front of them. That is how I see it. And so I decided they were being sincere with me.

19

One hot day in August 2000, I returned to the city that I'd left burning in the snow more than six months earlier. Finding yourself back at the site of past battles that you've fought in or witnessed brings up strong emotions. That's what happened to me. At first they wouldn't allow me into Grozny, telling me it was closed to non-residents. But then fortune came to my rescue. While I was standing at the checkpoint, trying to persuade the OMON officer (who clearly expected some cash for his services, cash I didn't have) to let me pass, a bus arrived. Ignoring the officer's signal to drive on, the bus braked sharply and out poured several women. Without a word, they grabbed me by the arm and bundled me into the bus. Quite stunned, I didn't have time even to murmur before I found myself on board. The officer, who was just as surprised, merely managed to shout, 'Hey! He's not allowed in the city!' To which the lady ticket collector replied, 'You'll get a case of beer from me!' And the bus drove on. I discovered what was behind this incomprehensible action a little later. It turned out that two sisters of a comrade of mine who'd fallen in battle were sitting on the bus; recognizing me, they decided I was about to be arrested and promptly shared this news with the passengers. And then these women, these brave and courageous Chechen women, decided to rescue a complete stranger from torture and death, fully aware of the risk to themselves. Of course, I told them that they'd arrived in the nick of time and had they come even half a minute later, I'd have been locked up at the checkpoint and soon sent onward. It didn't matter that this was not the case. Here were somebody's mother, somebody's wife, somebody's sister, acting on just such an assumption. So for me, this act might as well have been saving my life. I offered to buy the ticket conductor the case of beer which she'd promised the officer, but she wouldn't hear of it. Then the bus drove down the street where six months earlier we'd had our base and headquarters, and this stirred up a storm of memories. No matter how much I tried, I couldn't hide my emotion. The streets where there had been huge yawning pits from the bunker-busters were now filled in and resurfaced. Many of the roads, squares and avenues were blocked to traffic. Most of the bridges over the river Sunzha had been destroyed. Almost all the high-rise buildings had been blown up when the Russian troops took the city. These buildings were destroyed intentionally, supposedly because snipers were shooting at the soldiers from them. And this was while the city was suffering a catastrophic shortage of housing and thousands of refugees were sheltering in tents in the neighbouring Russian regions. But this reproach should be addressed to the Chechen administration, not the occupying forces. The remaining buildings and private houses were bereaved and desolate – it was a heart-wrenching sight. The dark holes of blown-out windows were staring at the world like blind eyes. The blind eyes of the world. Men blinded by hatred were blinding the land. The amount of dirt in the city was unbearable: a layer of dust had coated everything, from food at the market to people and cars.

Among the colourful and noisy crowd you could clearly pick out the officials working for the new pro-Russian administration. As a rule the senior government officials only ever appeared in a suit with a white shirt and tie; they had government-issue cars and they'd wear their suits even in the heat. For some reason they always wore the top two buttons of their jackets done up and the bottom one left undone. Clearly it was a nod to fashion. But it looked ridiculous among the ruins. The more minor officials and clerks wore pale shirts and ties. And they all carried the obligatory portfolios or briefcases. On subsequent trips to the capital I often made use of this costume – a suit and tie, with a folder under my arm which I'd stuff with some newspapers and blank sheets – and not once was I asked for my documents, not even during a 'cleansing op'. Female officials and all the secretaries were dressed as if for a fashion show. Chechen women on the whole like to dress prettily, regardless of the situation, but this was straight off the catwalk. To my delight, the majority (though not all) of my friends from the artistic community did not look like the crowd of officials: they'd managed to retain their individuality in dress and behaviour. But the most important hallmark by which you could pick out these new officers was the expression on their faces. They primarily showed two emotions: fear and greed. If among the Russian soldiers, fear was generally expressed through their behaviour – verbal mockery of those who were unable to respond in kind, wanton cruelty during the arrests, moving about the city only in highly armed groups – then in this case fear was quite visibly written on their faces. Fear of their Russian masters and fear of their implacable enemy, the resistance fighters. This was despite the fact that the guerrillas only went after officials (leaving aside servicemen) who collaborated with the enemy secret services and informed on the fighters' comrades and supporters. But for some reason all of the officials were frightened. Against the backdrop of widespread financial hardship, their relative affluence also stood out. Yet this did not satisfy them; they expected still more for their loyal service. All the officials, the local ones and those posted from Russia, were busy embezzling Russian government funds. Many of them went on to build themselves rather grand houses that clearly had not been paid for out of their salaries, while others bought property in various regions of Russia in case they had to drop everything and flee.

And amid all this ostensibly peaceful life, right in the city centre, where I'd just arrived, a unit consisting of Chechens and Russians was conducting a 'targeted special operation'. Alarmed, ashen-faced mothers were carrying out their own counter-operation, leading their menfolk – sons, brothers, husbands, who had been buying or selling goods – away from the market and standing in for them. Many of the kiosks and shops closed as though a wand had been waved. They did so in response to the appearance of the 'anti-terrorists', who would regularly fleece the traders. Of course, fleeing the market was unlikely to save any man who was already marked out for arrest. Realizing this, the men tried in vain to resist their women's efforts. But how can you reason with a woman who's made up her mind? And at any rate, they could at least escape undue harassment and the risk of arrest from someone taking a dislike to your face. There was one more rule for how to keep safe during a 'cleansing op', which the old men would often teach the defiant youth, particularly on public transport: 'Never look those dogs in the eye. If you stare at them, you'll only provoke them.' It is well known that staring into the eyes of dogs will provoke them to attack, and perhaps these elderly men were right to call the soldiers 'dogs'. Meanwhile, the 'targeted special operation' continued. The soldiers sealed off a small area and swarmed over the damaged former House of Fashion store, while their comrades stood at the cordon. As a rule, they all wore balaclavas. One of them stared a long time into my eyes. I forgot about the rule not to look them in the eye and I gazed hard at him like a rabbit staring at a boa. Several long minutes passed. There was no doubt about it: this was one of my friends and he had recognized me. And he must have been trying to decide what to do next: should he turn me in or say nothing. 'Do we know each other?' I asked, to provoke a response – I was getting tired of waiting for him to decide what to do – but he walked away without a word. So he hadn't lost all his humanity.

During the brief day that I spent in Grozny I made a frightening discovery. What brings a city alive is not the simple arithmetic of how many souls live and go to work there. A city is brought to life by the existence of a rough equilibrium between happiness and misery, sorrow and joy, pain and delight, fear and confidence. Disrupting this harmony in either direction – for excessive happiness and excessive misery are equally lethal for the soul and heart – will end up killing the city. Just six months ago we were happy in our burning city. We were alive, free and fighting for the city. But we were miserable to an equal degree. We were freezing and dying, every day we were losing comrades and we were cut off from our usual living conditions. We were afraid too: of being killed or maimed, of freezing to death or falling sick, but our fear was transitory and emotional and it passed as soon as the threat had gone. Here, fear was something quite different. It was constantly present. Everyone was afraid. People were afraid of the night. It was at night that most of the civilians would disappear. The officials were afraid of the Russian secret services and the resistance. The soldiers and secret services were afraid of the guerrilla attacks and the land mines. Some of the ministers would spend the entire week working and sleeping in their offices and coffee rooms in the government compounds (as people discovered later), then at the weekend they'd travel to their families somewhere in Russia. The only people who felt they were hunters rather than victims were the guerrillas. I ran into some guerrillas of my acquaintance on that day. You could find fear everywhere, there was plenty of it. And that was why the city was not alive. It never returned to life after being burnt to death.

As I left Grozny the next morning, I noticed that my mental state was worse than on the night of the breakout, when we were leaving the city to the barbarians. Back then we had left the city alive. Mortally wounded, torn to pieces, dying, yet alive. Of course the city even now was not entirely dead, but nor was it living. It felt somehow suspended in timelessness. Despite this sadness, I didn't get the feeling that the people of Grozny, the ordinary people, had been broken or subjugated. You could tell the general mood of the people by watching the women. They sensed with their hearts the state of their men and they mirrored it. They could intuitively feel when their men were broken in spirit, when they were buckling. That's why I placed more trust in the attitude of the women to any given event (meaning women in general, not as individuals) than I did in the propaganda and the official press. There was one particular stray dog, a very affectionate white bitch, that acted as a clear demonstration of the people's attitude; the Chechen women trading at the market used to feed her scraps. The women had named this dog 'Putin', to which she'd respond happily, wagging her tail.

20

The military camp and the autumn forest. It sounds like a painting by an artist with an unhealthy imagination. How could a camp filled with men armed to the teeth and dressed in camouflage pop up amid the magical beauty of the autumn forest? The dull lustre of tempered steel weaponry and clothing the colour of toads do not harmonize with the sad honking of the cranes flying in formation, the buzzing of the wasps and autumn's purest gold. It is a violation of the natural order. Surrounded by such beauty, when every living thing is at peace, you feel more like living than fighting. But man is not just another living creature: he is lord of all creation, he is homo sapiens, to whom God, or nature if you're an atheist, has granted vast power and authority over the rest of the living. The peacefulness in nature does not apply to him, and that's why we set up a military camp in the autumn forest. And this is not the fantasy of an abstract artist: it is reality. But we're not here from a desire to kill and be killed. The cruel and powerful enemy has forced this fight upon us, and we have accepted it. The enemy has one goal: to destroy us as an ethnic entity. No, not through the physical murder of every member of the nation, but through the destruction of a specific category and age range of its male population, through psychological oppression and through physical extermination, through a linguistic and cultural genocide. And our goal is to stop the enemy from achieving his goal. That's why we, intelligent beings, have dressed in camouflage and set up camp in the autumn forest. And we are disturbing the primeval sounds and rustlings of the forest with the click-clack of rifles being cocked and with human speech. We have gathered for a fight with other intelligent beings who've come to this ancient land and declared themselves our enemies. And our hatred for each other is so immense that this hatred alone ought to be enough to make us see, if we really are intelligent beings, that we cannot live together as one people in a single country, nor as friendly nations, or at least our generation cannot. Men who, at the start of the 1990s, had been romantics absorbed in the war games they played at summer camp, were reborn just a few years later as professionals of war, trying to kill each other in cold hatred. One side was seeking dominion over the other; the other side was refusing to acknowledge anyone's dominion. The enemy did not want a friendly nation; they wanted a nation that was submissive. And so from time to time you came together in mortal combat with the foe. It didn't matter that you lost. Losing the battle, you won the war. You didn't become one of them; you saved yourselves from assimilation. And there's nothing the enemy wants less than for you to keep your Chechen spirit alive. For it is your Chechen spirit that allows you, time after time, to meet in battle with an opponent you know to be powerful. And the enemy knows that he will keep on losing for as long as your Chechen spirit is alive. That is why he's launched a wide-ranging war against your culture, your language, your way of thinking. After all, those are the things that make up your national spirit. But once again the enemy is doomed to lose.

The camp is set up in a good location, in a good type of forest – a beech forest. Beech trees are particularly tall, and this has advantages. The smoke from the campfires diffuses among the trees before floating above the crowns of these slender giants. You can cook food in safety without the need for additional camouflage measures. The enemy air reconnaissance will not notice the smoke. This is a temporary camp. So we won't be here for long – a week at most. We have to head out on a three-day march through mountainous terrain to reach our permanent base. And there we'll join up with other units to carry out our mission, though we don't yet know what that will be. Only the leader of the operation knows. Two of us are journalists. We are here to film everything that takes place, if we're in luck and the weather and the conditions allow. No, we're not hired cameramen taking footage for video reports. One of us works for a world-famous news agency; the other is a freelance journalist. Apart from a small core constantly maintaining the main base, all the other fighters in the unit have gone legal. They come from the ranks of students, the middle classes, and even the creative intelligentsia, and they have gathered together for a specific operation that has been planned by the command headquarters. After the operation, those who survive will return to their legal occupations until the next time. This tactic is one of the secrets of the partisans' invincibility. The unit has quite a few young guys setting out on the warpath for the first time, which brings its own problems for the commander and the veterans. These young kids are too sure of themselves. They think that sitting out some airstrikes counts as participation in combat, and they're raring to fight, not satisfied with twiddling their thumbs in the forest. On the very first day of the march, they'll tear off as if they're competing in a hiking contest and try to overtake even the group of scouts who are moving ahead of us along the route. We constantly have to rein them in. They don't seem to have a clear picture of what combat is like, and of the state it leaves you in when you experience it for the first time; they laugh a bit at the caution shown by the seasoned veterans. There is no way to express in words what the first taste of battle is like; you need to go through it yourself, and only then can you call yourself a warrior. So nobody bothers to explain it to them, to prepare them psychologically for their first fight; they just keep an eye on them so their actions do not give the camp away to enemy reconnaissance, who are constantly prowling the forests.

Camouflage is as precious in the forest as water in the desert. There are always a lot of enemy agents in the forest. And they're not necessarily armed reconnaissance and sabotage units. Anyone who looks like a civilian could be an enemy agent, whether it is an old man or a teenager, a shepherd or a beekeeper, a hunter or a woodcutter, not to mention the foresters, who have been used for such purposes often enough. If any person wanders near the camp and sees just one fighter, he cannot be released. Even if he is not an enemy agent, there is no guarantee that the enemy won't notice him and get him to talk. Indeed, the enemy are expert at forcing people to talk, and they're likely to keep the people who go into the forest under some degree of observation. In the Soviet Army they trained the reconnaissance fighters and special forces to kill any voluntary or involuntary witnesses. And to kill them quickly and without sentiment, though not before putting them through aggressive interrogation. But we are not the Soviet Army. We are fighting to protect our nation from just such practices carried out by just such an army. We cannot go around shooting innocent people. But nor can we simply release them … It's not a problem if the unit is on the march. By the time the intelligence gets to the enemy, we'll already be out of their reach. But when we're at the base, it would be tantamount to death. And it would be absurd and pointless to drag an arrested civilian around wherever you go. You'd be releasing him after the operation in any case, and by that time he'd have learnt a whole lot more than an ordinary guy is supposed to know. Perhaps you'll be lucky if he's just a civilian. But what if he isn't? And so the only solution is to become just as invisible to civilians in the forest as to the enemy. Naturally in these conditions camouflage plays a crucial role.

After a few days waiting for all the units to arrive and stocking up on food and ammunition, we set off. For most of the way we need to negotiate long ascents up steep mountainsides. Coming back down these mountains is more difficult and dangerous than climbing up, especially when you're carrying a heavy rucksack, which pulls back when you're climbing and pushes you forward as you descend. It is easy to strain a tendon or get some other injury during the descent – all it takes is one wrong move. On the first day of the march, before you reach the mountains proper, the young guys rush on ahead. But by the second and third days they begin to lag far behind, unaccustomed to such strenuous exertion. And their zeal gradually subsides. We arrive without incident at the main base, and the fighters settle down to rest while we wait for the other units to join us. The only men not to rest are the scouts who, a day after reaching the base, are already beginning their main duties. We have our scouts in the village, of course, but it is the armed reconnaissance who must act from this side.

In war it is the scouts who generally get the least rest of all. The start and outcome of any military operation hang on how well they perform their job. If planted agents provide information about the enemy's structure and plans, that is, strategic information, then it is the tactical intelligence, the armed reconnaissance, that obtains information about the strong and weak points in the defence or the disposition of enemy troops, their firing positions and tactical rules. And it is the tactical intelligence that will identify the avenue of approach to the enemy site; they'll identify the enemy's vital points to be attacked first and the potential routes for reinforcements sent to the enemy. If the operational environment requires it, the scouts can and should conduct prisoner snatches and sabotage operations at key enemy installations. They must act within the boundaries of their unit's area of operations. The scouts also have to prevent stealth entry to the base by enemy units or reconnaissance. This means they must closely scan the area within a certain radius of the base to detect the slightest sign of human or animal tracks. If tracks appear, the scout must have at least a rough idea of when they appeared and, after sifting through the evidence, he must lay an ambush to destroy or capture the unwanted guests. When the unit is on the move, the scouts always walk on ahead. In an army, the remit of the reconnaissance unit is narrower; scouts in a guerrilla unit have, if anything, a wider range of tasks. And this leaves them little time for rest. Scouts are the aristocrats of war: only the finest get chosen. They need to have stamina, quick wits and the guts to be always in the most dangerous sector.

And here they are this morning, preparing to head out. They need to cover a good distance and return before dawn. They take ammunition and provisions to last a week, because a scout can never be sure where an ambush might lie, and how many enemy fighters he might have to engage. They set out at midday. By evening they need to have checked all the approaches to the base for tracks, as well as noting anyone visiting the forest by chance or design. And they need to do this without betraying their presence. They are looking out not only for human but also for animal tracks. If an animal has been here, it means there are no humans. When twilight comes, the group will embark on their main mission. Only a few men from the fairly sizeable reconnaissance group will enter the village. The rest will lay ambushes on the most dangerous sections of the road to provide cover for the men entering the village. They'll be dressed in Russian uniforms and armed with Russian weapons. The enemy don't always use patches and rank insignia themselves. The village contains several enemy bases: the military commandant's office, the police and the FSB, a company of Internal Troops, an OMON company and a unit of Spetsnaz GRU. There are checkpoints at all the entrances to the village that control the roads day and night. But the guerrillas can always find a way to slip into any village or town, and this one is no exception. The group is posing as a patrol. Ahead of the group is a man wearing a bandana (the standard headdress for the enemy's special forces and reconnaissance troops); everyone else wears military caps. The man at the front has a vital role. He has to convince all the civilians and servicemen who pass that they are Russian Army soldiers. He doesn't have any special ID to flash if they run into the enemy. And he can't just say, 'We're Russian Army servicemen.' But what he can do is speak perfect Russian. All the men in the group can speak Russian without mistakes, but speaking without mistakes is not the same as speaking Russian perfectly. And this man's Russian is perfect. That is, every other word is a swear word, making it the authentic, living language used by the vast majority of Russians. He speaks in the dialect of a particular Russian provincial town and uses army slang. The team's objective is to identify infiltration routes into the village and places where the enemy have congregated. They walk down the street in full view, fairly relaxed, exactly the way a patrol moves about the area they're guarding when they feel sure of their safety. The civilians hide indoors as soon as twilight descends and the only signs of life are the glowing windows of the houses. Three policemen are approaching. They are Chechens. They stop when they see the group. The scout in the bandana is walking ahead; the others stop a little way off in the shade of a tree. There's a chance that some of the policemen might know them by face.

'Got a fag?' the scout addresses them.

'Where are you from?' the policeman asks, holding his pack out.

'Kostroma,'[50] he replies, knowing perfectly well what the question is getting at.

'What unit are you from?' the policeman tries again. 'Why won't your friends come over?'

'They're shy.' The scout grins. 'You want to know our unit? Maybe you'd like us to show you our papers? Or you want our home addresses?' he asks with undisguised sarcasm. 'Who are you?' His speech is thickly peppered with profanities, adding weight to the effect.

'We're on patrol here.'

'Congratulations! We're also on patrol.'

'Well, if you're really on patrol, no worries. It's just, you know … There are all these guys going on night raids, and by the morning people are missing.'

'Yeah, but they go about in armoured personnel carriers. We're just kicking about on foot. Thanks for the smoke. Come on, guys, let's go.' And the scout walks off with the group. His lippy attitude, idiosyncratic accent, lively Russian rolling off the tongue, everything about his appearance has reassured the policemen and they've left.

A few days later the scouts run into a group of Russian soldiers in the same village. This time they can't pull off the patrol trick because they'd probably be asked for a password. So they play the part of a group returning tired and irritable from a dangerous mission. As a rule, when you're out on a high-risk mission you don't carry ID. And a commander worth his salt will barely use his radio – the channel can be hacked into. But, to be on the safe side, the scouts have their radios tuned in to the FSB. They carry it off with great success and this story is the one they adopt. Every other night the scouts return to the village, until they've discovered the entire layout of enemy positions, their key installations and hidden approaches to them, along with a quick exit route for after the battle.

A few days before zero hour, two hundred metres from the base, a man in his fifties is detained. During the search they find a pound of marijuana on him, but no ID. In Chechnya, civilians do not venture anywhere without their passport, and certainly not into the forest, where at any moment they could run into an armed unit of Russians or guerrillas. Once they've found out who you are, the guerrillas would most likely let you go, but there is little chance of the Russian tactical intelligence doing that. So the appearance of this man near the camp seems a little suspicious. He answers our questions vaguely and incoherently. He gets his story mixed up. The only thing he tries consistently to lead us to believe is that he's a drug dealer on his way to his marijuana plantation in the forest. He has not said it openly, but he keeps on softly hinting at it. But here he's slipped up. If he was on his way to the plantation, why was he taking the end product with him? It would be more usual to take the crop from the plantation to sell it. And in any case, there is no plantation anywhere within a five-kilometre radius of the camp. The scouts would have seen it. Another cause for suspicion is the fact that he is from the village which any day now we're planning to attack. If he is an enemy agent, then his handler was none too clever. And he probably is an agent: it can't have escaped the notice of Russian reconnaissance that there has been increased movement of guerrilla units in recent days. Whoever has told this agent to play the part of a drug dealer hasn't rehearsed all the possible scenarios with him. He hasn't worked out the details of his cover story, what answers he should give and how he should give them and so on. After weighing up the factors for and against, the command of the operation conclude that he is indeed an enemy agent. But they don't shoot him. He may have strayed from the right path, but he is still a Chechen. This argument, of course, has lost weight for both the guerrillas and their Chechen opponents, but on this occasion it plays a positive role in the fate of this man. The guerrillas simply decide to hold him at the camp until zero hour, and after the operation to let him go. At that point he can do no damage. Naturally enough, they take his dope away, but they return it to him when they release him. Why they return it remains a complete mystery to me – although the commander does explain that it is out of a desire to keep the men from temptation.

Life in the base is not particularly different from life in an army field camp anywhere in the world. The scouts return to camp each night in the early hours and they set out each afternoon. Now and then they have a day off. The rest of the men live the usual guerrilla lifestyle. They keep guard of the camp, take turns to cook, clean their weapons and replenish their ammunition stocks, dig trenches and dugouts in case there's a sudden enemy airstrike or an unexpected fight with the enemy attacking the camp. The latter is unlikely – the scouts are hard at work – but if you don't want to get caught out in the forest, you have to live by the principle: 'Hope for the best but prepare for the worst.' There is at least one hot meal a day. Life in the autumn forest with its incessant rain would be hard without hot food. We cook using an earth oven. It is well concealed; even with the help of thermal imaging, no air reconnaissance could detect its flame. The guerrillas have got camouflage down to a fine art. And of course fuel is no problem in the forest. There are various ways to maintain bodily hygiene: the more hardened men who can handle the cold bathe in the icy water of a mountain stream – even in the summer the temperature never rises above eight or nine degrees Celsius – while the less hardy heat up their water. In the usual camp setting everyone is equal. It is only during an operation or combat, or at a meeting, that the commanders emerge as leaders. The discipline is enviable. The detained man isn't left to sit in some pit. He lives with everyone else in the camp, but any attempt to leave the camp would be abruptly terminated. He knows that very well and he doesn't provoke the men. A few places in the camp are categorically off limits for him. During the day he is under the responsibility of the guards on duty. Living in wait is getting rather tedious, you are yearning for action, but patience is one of the key ingredients of the guerrillas' success. And everybody understands that. The only men who don't get bored are the scouts. The quality of their work could greatly increase our chances of avoiding losses. And then finally, zero hour arrives.

21

On a gloomy day boding foul weather, a major guerrilla formation, made up of several units that have joined together for the upcoming mission, heads out from the camp. It sets off early from the temporary base so as not to tire the men with too swift a marching pace. Passing through a small clearing near the base, the first to hide among the golden leaves of the autumn forest are, as ever, the scouts. The main column waits for a while, then silently moves on, winding in a dark ribbon. A couple of hours later, the scouts stop the slowly advancing column, having spotted some woodcutters ahead on their path. Soon everyone can clearly make out the whine of a chainsaw. These are peaceful villagers gathering firewood for the winter. The fact that they are civilians does not ease the dilemma for the command: it only complicates matters. The column cannot pass by them unnoticed, but nor can we allow them to see us. And if they do see us, we can't let them go home before we've carried out our mission, that is, before we've arrived at our destination. While the column stops for a rest, the scouts consult with the commander then walk on ahead. Several men are busy felling trees when they notice the scouts. They are startled to see armed men in balaclavas (the entire column is in balaclavas, including the scouts) racing towards them. They mistake the group for Russian soldiers and, anxiously throwing down their saws, they hasten to speak: 'Guys, we're peaceful woodcutters. We're just gathering firewood for the winter.' But when they notice that one of the scouts has a black headband with a surah from the Quran over his balaclava, they cry, 'Oh, it's our side! Everything's OK.' And they calm down.

The commander of the group finds out which villages they come from and asks, 'How long were you planning to fell timber today?'

'We're more or less done. And if there's anything we can do to help, we'd be happy to.'

'No, thanks, we don't need your help. Although if you'd like to help, we suggest you join us on your way home. The place we're going to is not far from where you live. Don't get me wrong, it's not that we suspect you, but …'

'Of course we'll go back with you. We understand,' the wood-cutters say.

And one of them, a young guy, adds, 'Even if they torture me I won't tell them a thing. If you knew how those bastards treat us civilians. But when they're up against you, they're not the big men they pretend to be in the movies.'

The scouts lead them over to the column, then walk on ahead. The woodcutters go with the main formation, but not under guard like the man detained at the base. Seeing the number of guerrillas, the young guy turns to his companions: 'If only those bastard traitors could see them now! Always talking about "a few dozen bandits in the forests". In their dreams!' The approaching dusk quickly turns into dense darkness as rain begins pelting down. The guerrillas stop in a forest clearing and set up a watch; they begin the late-afternoon prayer. There is no pressure on anyone to pray or perform religious rituals. We are all free to choose how deep our faith goes and how much to follow the rituals and rules. In Islam there is no compulsion. And this tenet is confirmed in the Quran. Anyone who forces a person into faith is violating this sacred rule, thereby showing disrespect for the

Quran. But the overwhelming majority of the Chechen resistance fighters are deeply religious. Everyone believes in his own way, but the majority are believers. And faith can help a man cope with the stress which he faces every hour in those conditions. Watching the silhouettes of the fighters prostrated in prayer in the pouring rain and the intense darkness, men who in an hour's time will be engaging in a battle with an unknown outcome, you feel sure that those who fall in the war will find their eternal rest in a better world. They are protected from hell as surely as gold is protected from rust.

The entire column of guerrillas silently enters the quiet but not yet sleeping village. The rain that has been falling now suddenly stops. The woodcutters have already been released, but the man detained near the base is still being guarded by one of the groups. He will be set free after the operation. No matter how silently the men try to walk, they cannot prevent the slurp of mud under multiple feet from being heard and people begin popping their heads over the fences, but a menacing holler at them in Russian is enough to make them vanish. For some reason today there are no patrols in sight. In fact there are no armed men at all. Could we have a traitor among us, could the enemy already know everything?

When all the groups have taken up their initial positions at the designated facilities, the command to attack comes over the radios. The cry 'Allahu Akbar!' flies from every throat as a tremendous salvo of fire bursts through the stillness of the night. But in response comes silence. Not a single shot or shout. The enemy are hiding in their shelters, behind concrete blocks and trench lines, and they remain silent. Silent in response to the guerrillas' barrage of fire raining upon them. There is only one heavy machine gun firing from the roof of the FSB building; a shot from a grenade launcher silences it. The guerrillas spray the enemy-held buildings from their grenade launchers, machine guns and other small arms, but the enemy responds with stubborn reticence. They are incurring no appreciable losses and they won't engage in combat. The guerrillas hadn't been expecting to get much reaction from them. And they don't have much need of an enemy sitting in shelters. If they start fighting, the guerrillas will of course fire at them and perhaps even start storming the buildings they're holding. But that is not what really matters. The guerrillas have carried out operations like this plenty of times. This tactic was devised by the President and it has always brought guaranteed success. That is, until this night.

The guerrillas' primary target is not the enemy forces in the village. They are essentially bait. The primary target is the forces in the fortified bases nearby. The tank regiment, the artillery battalion, the airborne battalion and the motorized infantry brigade, all based a couple of kilometres from there. And maybe somebody else will come blundering to the aid of their comrades. But they'll only be playing into the hands of the guerrillas. If you attack a village, they're supposed to come running to the aid of those under attack. And until now they have always done so. But here comes the big surprise: along all the routes available to them, the guerrillas have set up ambushes. What's more, among the attackers are groups ready to split off and join the ambush units at the first sign of the enemy's approach. Usually it takes an hour of fighting before the reinforcements rise to the bait. And it is when the tanks and the rest of the armoured vehicles head out to help their comrades that the bloodbath begins. Any unit on the move is particularly vulnerable. While deploying for combat in the open field, before they've even reached their comrades, it will all be over for them. The elite groups will ambush them from positions which have already been picked and prepared. But today, the guerrillas have been firing at the enemy for several hours and there is no sign of help being mobilized. Even the artillery remains silent. Civilians are popping out of the houses and trying to put food into the hands of the fighters, wishing them luck and victory. But the fighters coax them back indoors.

Nobody knows why the enemy are silent and what they might do next.

If you analyse the enemy's behaviour and inaction, it gives reasonable grounds to suspect that we do indeed have a traitor in our midst and he has managed to warn them in time about the operation. Otherwise how can you explain the extra defences around the facilities marked for attack that were not there yesterday? How can you explain their dogged reluctance to engage in combat and enjoy the advantage of defence? How can you explain the silence at the enemy base just two kilometres from the site where you've been clobbering their comrades for hours? And all the Chechen police and special forces have been secretly holed up for the past two days in their barracks. That is, they too have already taken shelter behind concrete blocks, which the guerrillas cannot destroy without time and special weapons. But time is just what they don't have. Nor do they have heavy artillery. And the existence of a traitor is later confirmed when, through his fault, one of the best unit leaders, who also takes part in this operation, is ambushed near his base and dies in an unequal fight. Later they work out who betrayed them. After that ambush he openly goes over to the Russian side. When the enemy fail to rise to the bait (perhaps they've finally seen through our scheme and aren't going to fall for it this time), the guerrilla formation slowly begins their withdrawal. They depart in several directions, but the bulk of the fighters need to get back to the main base. To throw the enemy reconnaissance off the track, we wade through the river. We have to walk waist-deep in icy water for the several hours left until dawn. And as dawn breaks over the forest, reconnaissance aircraft appear. When they fail to find any obvious signs of the guerrillas, they drop their bombs on the forest roads and tracks and fly off.

Despite the minimal losses to the enemy, the operation proves a huge propaganda success. The daring attack by guerrillas on a village considered one of the most secure in the republic, and around which are clustered, in addition to those already mentioned, several other formidable Russian Army forces, has demonstrated the strength, ability and morale of the resistance fighters. And although this time we haven't managed to lure the enemy into our trap, the operation nevertheless has a surprising result. It spurs the enemy towards a peace initiative. Not long after, a team of mediators makes contact with the Chechen side to sound out the possibility of negotiation. But as has happened many times before, this attempt is thwarted by the Russian security services, who have no interest in ending the war. After all, this war has made them all-powerful. And some bastard with an inferiority complex – for the secret police across the world generally attract this sort – is feeling like a superman and glorying in that sensation of power.

The time has come for the guerrillas to split up until they meet again for the next operation. Those who've gone legal return to their legal life, the others go to their bases. The group I've come with has to retrace their steps along the route they took. But I'm not going with them. My knee is injured, which means I can't negotiate difficult mountain tracks and I have to take an easier route. But the only easier route goes through Russian checkpoints, which in turn pose an enormous risk. Unable to find an alternative, I decide to give it a shot.

When a man spends weeks in the autumn forest under almost constant rain, no matter how carefully he has prepared for this, he'll always end up freezing and soaked. His only salvation is fire. And in the forest the benefits of fire are exploited to the full. We too made use of them. On a clear day we could only have a concealed earth oven, but on a foggy, overcast day we would light several fires at the camp. In any case the smoke wouldn't be seen. We would dry and warm ourselves at these campfires; sometimes we just sat admiring the flames and chatting away. Of course we all absolutely reeked of smoke. The smell impregnated our clothes, hair and skin. Prepared for every contingency, I had in my rucksack a fresh set of civilian clothes, wrapped in several layers of plastic bags. I never once pulled them out to air, knowing only too well the effects of campfire smoke. And I was wearing a pair of leather hiking shoes. But here's the thing: once while drying myself at the campfire, I inadvertently brought my feet too close to the fire and the tips of the soles got burnt and melted. Any fool at the checkpoint could guess where these shoes had been. To disguise them, I had to carefully trim away part of the sole, making them look as if they'd always been this ugly. At first glance, you wouldn't notice, but if you looked more attentively ...

I took all this into account while staying in the house of one of the fighters in the nearest village. Trying to wash away the smell of campfire, I spent several hours in the bathhouse, got changed into my civilian clothes and felt somewhat calmer. Before leaving in the morning, I doused myself liberally in aftershave. I decided to go by bus. After so much campfire smoke, my nose was immune and I thought I'd got rid of the smell. But I hadn't. My suspicions were first aroused when the passengers on the bus kept looking me over. The smell of aftershave wouldn't have elicited such attention. In Chechnya, plenty of men use aftershave; some practically bathe in the stuff. So it had to be something else. And that something could only be the aroma of 'Forest Fresh'. Perhaps it would be a good idea to get off the bus right now ... But, wise as that idea might have seemed, it wouldn't have helped. It would have been dangerous to stay in the village until the smell of smoke had gone. At any moment there might be a 'cleansing op', with a predictable outcome for me and the hosts giving me shelter. So I decided to go on with my journey. The thought that people were maybe just staring because I was a stranger calmed me a little.

Having passed all the other checkpoints smoothly, we drove up to the main one: Checkpoint Caucasus on the border between Chechnya and Ingushetia, a checkpoint that had brought plenty

243

of heartache to peaceful and not-so-peaceful civilians. To go through this checkpoint you had to walk (if you were male) along a narrow corridor of barbed wire in single file holding your passport out. It was still early morning and so the soldiers weren't especially foul-tempered: they still had the prospect of making some money ahead. They could get nasty towards the evening, if they'd had slim pickings. I was standing in line as the two guys in front were showing their documents. And here the man behind me said something to me in Chechen. Lost in reverie, I didn't hear him, but my thoughts were interrupted by the officer. 'Speak Russian!' he addressed my fellow passenger. 'Or else I won't understand.'

'I wasn't saying anything. Just commenting on the weather,' he replied.

'Maybe. But then you could have been saying, "Let's attack now." I mean, this guy stinks to high heaven of smoke, as if he's straight out of the forest.'

At these words I turned cold. It took a monumental effort for me to preserve an air of unfazed surprise on my face: 'Nonsense! It's autumn. Well, everyone's burning leaves in their gardens. Of course I'm going to smell of smoke. If I was straight out of the forest, I'd hardly turn up at your checkpoint.' I smiled wryly, trying to keep my heart from leaping out of my chest.

'Yeah, you got a point. You don't look like some suicidal idiot who'd come straight from the forest right into our hands. Particularly after the latest events ... Go on through!'

He handed me my passport. The whole time he didn't once look down at my shoes. If he had, I would never have left the checkpoint. For, coupled with the distinct smell of forest smoke, the shoes would have been grounds enough for me to join the ranks of the 'disappeared'. People had gone missing at that checkpoint on far flimsier evidence. I only understood the true extent of the risk I'd taken a bit later, when I dropped in on some friends. They could hardly believe that I'd passed through

Checkpoint Caucasus. According to them, you could smell my intense forest campfire aroma from several metres away. Most of the other fighters also returned without incident.

22

It is an early morning in March. The weather is cool. March in the Caucasus is not quite spring, but it is no longer winter. The first flowers appear; the Cornelian cherry comes into blossom. It is the first tree to blossom and the last to produce its harvest. But the sowing season has not started, meaning it is not yet spring. That is how we have thought in the Caucasus since time immemorial. According to the old Chechen calendar, sowing begins when the rooks return, and it ends without fail when the cuckoos arrive. This year, spring has come a little early, and so the snow has melted, although there's still some frost at night.

I'm standing at the appointed place on the outskirts of Nazran, in Ingushetia, along with my go-between. He got in touch with me yesterday through another intermediary, someone I trust, and he told me the location for the meeting. Today I have a long journey ahead, one not without risk. I'm travelling to Georgia. Under normal circumstances the risk might not be particularly high, but so far in the last six months I've taken part in two guerrilla operations, changed apartments several times in the hope of a quiet life, thwarted an attempt by an 'old friend' to turn me in to the Ingush branch of the FSB, and I've shown up in certain circles. Thanks to these considerations and certain persons, lately I've been gaining experience of life underground, a skill that will come in handy in the future. And now, finally, I have a real chance (albeit a risky one) to slip for a while under the radar of certain parties who are after me. At the appointed time, a car should be arriving to take me into neighbouring Georgia through the Verkhny Lars border post in North Ossetia.

Soon two cars stop near us, and no one gets out. The go-between walks up to the first car and beckons me over. Throwing my holdall into the boot, I get in and we pull away. There's a full crew of Chechen resistance fighters in the car behind us; in this car there are four of us. I'm next to the commander of one of the guerrilla squads, in the front is the man responsible for ferrying people there and back, and sitting in the driver's seat is a young guy with classically Slavic looks. He is Russian. He's an FSB officer. And he's helping the resistance fighters. Of course, he's doing this out of the goodness of his heart. The sum he receives is meagre recompense for risking his life and career. He is close friends with one of the Chechens – their friendship goes back to those happy days when they were both eighteen and war belonged in the history books. His friend is a commander in a guerrilla squad. It is his belief in his friend that motivates him. I find all this out from a conversation during the journey. He comes straight out with it: 'If my friend, whom I've known half my life and whom I'd trust with my life, has chosen to join the fight for freedom, then as far as I'm concerned that's a pretty powerful argument that you're on the right path.' Perhaps just lofty words, or perhaps not. Only he knows the truth. He will later die in a firefight against FSB officers, which suggests we should believe him, as he is no longer alive. We don't introduce ourselves and don't ask questions. As you'd expect. It isn't done to ask for names here – it only makes everyone uncomfortable. His task is to provide us with safe passage through the police and army checkpoints along the road as far as the border post. And, once there, he is to get the group past the border guards without having their passports checked. Of course this involves paying the guards.

At Checkpoint Chermen, between Ossetia and Ingushetia, they stop us to check our passports. But our ally – let's call him Oleg – shows them his ID and presents us as officers in his organization. We arrive without incident at the Verkhny Lars border post. Oleg goes into an office and he soon emerges, having agreed a deal. Of course the guards realize who these guys in the cars must be, seeing as they don't want to produce their passports. But this does not stop them from coolly taking their bribe and making things easy for all of us. After all, if they tried to detain us, we'd have no option but to attack them. And there's no telling how that would end.

Having taken us just over the border, Oleg returns while we drive on in cars that have come to meet us. In the depth of the night we arrive in the capital of Georgia and the next day we go our separate ways. Each of us has his own mission, and we each now embark on it. I have no alternative but to ply my trade as a journalist, so I busy myself in these new conditions. And, thanks to the large number of Chechen refugees, there is plenty of work.

23

Today, I'm dying. No, not from wounds; from stupidity. From my own unforgivable stupidity. I let myself be tricked and broke my resolution. I drank water. Not much – just a few sips. But it was enough to make me collapse on my way up from sheer exhaustion and with the bitter feeling that this folly had brought death upon my soul. No, the water isn't poisoned. Yet this pure, life-giving moisture, which I once craved more than life itself, has now turned into a poison, slowly killing me. And this has never happened to me before, in all my long years at war, where I've often covered vast distances in speed marches with the Chechen fighters. What a strange, unpredictable trick of fate! That same substance that can save your life at other times can kill you. Whatever made me drink it? I've never drunk water while climbing up a mountain. But today the mountains deceived me. Looking up towards the summit, I decided there must be five hundred metres left at most. Meaning as the crow flies – along the track it would, of course, be further. Five hundred metres is nothing, and it is a very hot summer day. So I had a sip of water from the flask. But when I'd climbed those five hundred metres, I discovered that I still had a steep ascent of several kilometres ahead of me. It was five hundred metres only to a bend in the ridge. You should never trust your eyes in the mountains – you need to double-check everything in sight.

We have been on the road for a week. We're a guerrilla formation under Angel's command.[51] And I'm with them from force of habit. They are returning to Chechnya, and I'm returning with them. After around a week of speed marching, we rest for a few days, setting up camp in some remote spot where people prefer not to venture. We cannot travel like normal people: we are guerrillas. So the roads are off limits to us. The enemy air reconnaissance is almost ever-present in the sky. Our enemy is cunning and wily. And so we have to be even more cunning and wily. They have planted agents among us. We don't know who, but we know for sure they're among us. This means only a very restricted circle can be told the next day's route. This is the key to our success. The agents in our midst can only send their masters information about the ground we've covered, not about the route ahead. They can also pass on intelligence about our weaponry, but this intelligence is rarely accurate. Whenever there's a skirmish the guerrillas invariably seize trophy weapons, and so the quantity of arms is always in flux. We need to take particular care: we know the enemy are waiting for us. Only recently another guerrilla group was travelling along one of these routes when they were ambushed, surrounded, and almost completely wiped out. And the fact that they fell as warriors and sold their lives dearly was cold comfort to us. Now the enemy are waiting for us in several locations. But the bulk of their forces are concentrated on the same route that the ambushed group were taking. They think this route holds the greatest strategic value for us and they're expecting us to repeat the mistakes of the first group. And their agents are encouraging them in this belief, having been cleverly hoodwinked by Angel's commanders just in time.

For the moment we are moving towards where the enemy are waiting for us. The enemy have underestimated us and this is good. If your enemy is laughing, laugh with him. But do not laugh like him. For he is laughing at his own carelessness, while you are laughing at his weakness. Rejoice with him, only rejoice at the unexpected gift which this powerful enemy has handed you by making you stronger through his carelessness. A complacent enemy is a weak enemy. He thinks himself smarter and stronger than you, and that makes him weak. This description fits our enemy perfectly. Having masterminded a top-secret operation under the self-congratulatory name 'Snare' in the direction of the 'probable enemy breakout' and laying small ambushes in a few other areas that he knows about, our enemy has relaxed, thinking that victory will now come running to him on our legs. But alas! Once again his hopes will be bitterly dashed. We will perform our mission and grant him no such joy.

So that's how I've come to be lying in a forest halfway to the top of a mountain pass. And all I need now is to sleep for at least fifteen minutes. I feel intuitively that sleep will restore my strength, and I have some time to spare. In around fifteen minutes the rear guard will arrive. But no matter how I try, I just can't get that sleep. Every fighter thinks it his duty to wake me up to check what's happened, offer me some water or food and try to help me walk on further. I try to explain to them that all I need is fifteen minutes' sleep and I'll catch up with them when the rear guard reaches here. But the men are used to seeing me in the advance guard and they're not too impressed by my explanation. How galling to be dying from such folly and how ashamed I feel of my own body. The sensation that I'll die if I don't get some sleep is very real. I don't dare move out of the way for my sleep – the rear guard might not notice me. My survival instinct is ordering me to sleep and heal myself. But I yield to the fighters and stand up with one of them. Remembering the maxim, 'Work your hardest, then work harder,' I walk on ahead. I conquer the mountain and make it to our overnight camp. It has been very difficult walking. The heavy rucksack has been cutting into my shoulders and something bad is going on with my feet inside the army boots. My right foot feels particularly sore. I only get a chance to examine it properly two days later, when we stop for the next break in a deep ravine. And once I've seen it, I have to go to great lengths to get hold of a pair of civilian mountain boots, and the front of my ankle, rubbed raw by the army boots, takes a long time to mend. The abrasion is fairly deep, and the daily wading through the many fords does not speed its recovery. So I have to tend it for quite a while before it heals. But never again! Never will I drink water while climbing a mountain.

Our journey is not without curious episodes. One day we had set up camp in the forest to rest. We needed several days to refresh ourselves. After a couple of days the guards apprehended a man heading towards the camp on a three-wheeler all-terrain motorcycle. Astonished by his answers to their questions, the guards came and reported to the commander. It turned out the man was from a nearby village. He had fitted his three-wheeler with a refrigerator and was selling ice cream from it. And this is what brought him to the forest: he wanted to sell the fighters ice cream. He knew that guerrillas were staying in this forest, and he knew the area well. But, unaware of the location of the camp, he decided to try his luck. Angel asked him why he needed to travel into the forest to sell his ice cream, and the elderly man replied bashfully, 'See, what happened is I lost my job. Well, I have to feed myself somehow, so I took up selling ice cream. But these days I can't shift it. Too many competitors. After all, they've got to eat too. So I thought maybe the fighters would buy some of my ice creams.'

Angel bought the whole lot and advised him not to sell his wares in the forest any more and to keep quiet about what he'd seen (though he only saw a few fighters standing guard). When I asked if he would indeed keep quiet and whether he wasn't an agent, Angel replied, 'He won't talk. Why risk being charged with supplying us with "articles of food"? And he doesn't look like an agent, just a man in desperate need. But even if he is an agent, it doesn't matter. We'll be gone from here in two days' time.'

It's a brutal night. And I'm frozen stiff. This is summer, but at an altitude of 3,700 metres above sea level there are constant blizzards, interspersed with occasional hail. My torso and feet aren't freezing – I'm in a warm Gore-Tex jacket and boots – but I'm bitterly cold from the waist to the ankles. I have thin summer trousers on. Who knew we'd have to spend the night at such an altitude? And intensive walking in warm trousers is an absolute curse. A little below, at an altitude of 3,500 metres, amid the rocks and glaciers, is our camp. We've been camped there a week, under camouflage capes stretched across the rocks and invisible to enemy aircraft. We haven't lit fires. In any case, there's nothing to burn. Here, besides the glaciers all we have is the most astonishing rock formations, which are breathtakingly beautiful. The only vegetation is moss and edelweiss. These beautiful, strange flowers remind us that we're still on earth. No mosquitoes or gadflies annoy us here, no blood-sucking insects of any sort; there aren't even snakes. Nor is there water, but we do have glaciers. During the day they start slowly thawing in the sun and from under the ice mass water trickles out. That's what we use for our needs. And the sun shines every day here – at least in the summer. Below is a sweeping panorama of magical beauty. Just beneath you the clouds are drifting gently, showering rain upon the earth that is ready to spring to life. And all around are mountains. My camera clicks away tirelessly. I photograph the extraordinary landscapes.

We camp here longer than usual to allow the enemy's alarm at our sudden disappearance to subside. Here at the summit the enemy's agents are automatically neutralized: they cannot send intelligence from here. We're maintaining absolute radio silence, and if anyone were to turn on his radio, he'd blow his cover. The enemy have been shadowing us for a long time with their agents and air reconnaissance. At one point we drew close to the ambush laid for us (we were just an hour's journey from the site) in order to register on their radar, that is, to flag up our presence at that location to the enemy reconnaissance, then we veered sharply to one side and walked all night in a forty-kilometre speed march before vanishing into a remote ravine. There we had to wait a few days for our battered and chafed feet to recover. After spending two more nights marching almost as fast, we find ourselves at the foothills to the glaciers. We climb up to the glaciers in a day. Along the way the guerrillas have to perform two rescue missions. A fighter falls from a precipice, catches hold of the rock and is left dangling over the abyss. They haul him up by lowering a volunteer on a rope to rescue him. And then two guerrillas get stuck on a thin ledge over an abyss. For their rescue a narrow path has to be hewed out in the rock – luckily not a long one. We hoist our pack horses up the mountain, after unloading the MANPADS, the Russian-manufactured Strela man-portable air-defence systems, which we now have to carry ourselves. The only animals in these parts are the Caucasian tur and the snow leopard. Our horses are visiting these glaciers for the first time. We've been surviving all this time on field rations. And we have with us a fellow member of my profession, although communication is somewhat tricky because of the language barrier. But sometimes we talk through an interpreter. This is British journalist Roderick John Scott, known simply as Roddy. Along with everyone else, he endures all the hardships of this trying journey with remarkable stoicism, which fills me with pride; my fellow journalist is a match for the seasoned partisans. He never complains and he dismisses any suggestion that he should turn back. His only complaints come when he is not allowed to film the fighters' faces on his video camera. But he shows understanding of the rules of guerrilla warfare, where not everyone likes to give interviews with their faces on show. Whenever he is asked, 'How are you?' he always replies, 'Good.' He works unceasingly. Despite our large supply, the video camera batteries go flat. Our solar-powered chargers are effective for the radio sets, but the cameras are far more power-hungry. At one point, defying the danger of detection, I have to take several days out to travel from the camp to a friend's house to recharge our batteries.

Today I've climbed ahead with the advance-guard scouts, who will be the first to descend from the glaciers. On the whole, I prefer to go with the reconnaissance group, as they are the first to go into action. And I also need to film the skirmishes. If I were at the tail of the column, I might not make it to the site of combat in time. So I need to be something of a scout myself. A fearsome blizzard is howling and the summit, licked clean by the winds and flat as an airfield, offers no place to shelter. There are not even glaciers or snow here – everything has been blown away by the powerful winds. Neither the thermal insulation mat nor the sleeping bag can save me. It occurs to me to get up and walk round in circles until morning. But I quickly realize this idea wouldn't work. First, I'd waste a lot of energy – and there's no telling what lies ahead on the journey. And second, I'd start to freeze, not from the low temperature, but from the icy winds – the wind chill would cancel out any chance of warming myself by moving about. If I take off my jacket and wrap it round my legs, I'll soon feel like a lump of ice, because all I have under the jacket is a thin polo neck. But praise be to God! The summer nights – it's August – are not very long and I'm still alive by dawn. And at dawn the group continues on its dangerous journey.

If you look up to the summit from which we've just descended, at the route which barely resembles a trail, it's extraordinary to think we've just travelled this way. And the men were carrying not just their rucksacks and their personal weapons but also the heavy MANPADS missiles. The scene looks so sinister and terrible that a treacherous chill of fear creeps into my heart. The next day, the main column will traverse this route. Despite everything, we won't lose a single man or horse, and not even one cartridge. No matter how tired, a guerrilla never discards any cartridges. A cartridge is your chance to survive the battle, a chance for the enemy to die before you do.

24

I often talk at length with the fighters, trying to understand what makes them endure such inhuman physical and psychological strain. What motivates them to condemn themselves to such a life? After all, despite the Russian claims that only a handful of criminals are left in the mountains, who have nothing left to hope for and nowhere else to go, the vast majority of these men (around 98 per cent) could legalize their positions easily enough and live a peaceful life. From all these conversations one conclusion emerges: they are fighting for freedom. They think it was a mistake for the Chechen volunteers to go to the aid of their 'Dagestani insurgent brothers', believing, quite reasonably, that it was a set-up, a pretext to begin a second war against Chechnya. They criticize Aslan Maskhadov's policies in the three interwar years, but they remain convinced that Russia would have found an excuse to attack Chechnya in any case. I marvel at their profound, sincere faith in God. No, they don't smack of radicalism, and they're not fighting for their faith. I have met very few people in this war who are fighting for their faith. It's simply that Islam says it is the duty of every Muslim to defend his home against aggressors. Russia has never felt like a home to the Chechens. A home is not about state boundaries or political ideologies. It is something that lives in the heart, something a person is born with and dies with. In the entire history of Russian-Chechen relations, the only time the Chechens viewed Russia as a common home was during the Second World War – and we all know what came of it.

I had many conversations with Angel. He was a man whose reputation remained spotless, despite all the enemy's efforts. Even his bitterest enemies acknowledged the sincerity of his motives and his military prowess. He had made no enemies among the Chechens during all these bloody years, while continuing to be the gravest of enemies to the Russian Army, and he intrigued me. We'd known each other since the late 1980s and my interest had not faded. From my numerous conversations with him, there was one short monologue that succinctly summed up his stance towards what was happening in Chechnya.

'If a man's dangling over an abyss, clinging only to a branch, it doesn't matter who saves him. All that matters is for someone to reach out his hand and pull him up. The Chechen people today are dangling over a physical and spiritual abyss and they need to be saved. It doesn't matter who saves them – Maskhadov, Kadyrov[52] or somebody else. The enemy has come to our land and now they're violating our most sacred concepts of honour and dignity. The enemy is like a slave who has suddenly found power over free men, and now he's madly imposing his slave values on them, destroying the very spirit of freedom. And whoever is on the side of such an enemy cannot be the one to reach out his hand and help. If someone says, "I'll save the people from their physical and spiritual destruction," then I'm ready to follow him and help him. Whoever he might be. But he has to prove beyond doubt, by his actions, that his motives are pure, so the people will believe him. I'm not a politician – I'm a warrior. I don't want to delve into all of the political intrigues, but one thing is clear to me: the Chechen people have a right and duty to live by their culture, their beliefs and national spirit. And yesterday's slaves (it wasn't long ago that the Russians were serfs, the chattels of their own masters)[53] cannot lord it over this land with their slave mentality. In any case, I believe in the Chechen people and in our victory. I believe that our people will survive and keep their spirituality alive, just like they've done so many times in history.'

As I listened to this man, I realized the secret of his strength. Why the men trusted him implicitly and why there was nothing and nobody who could dent his reputation in their eyes. He had a clear sense of his role and was fully focused on his mission, something that was true only of a select few. He was sincere not only with his friends, but with the whole world, with his enemies too. He never deluded himself or tricked others. The fighters could see this, and that was why they believed in him. And it was this – the men's trust in him – that made him a grave enemy to the Russian Army. He was almost unknown to the world at large as he did not court attention through sensational actions. But the Russian generals who met him in battle knew him well and respected him highly.

25

Your mighty enemy has caught you by surprise. That enemy is hunger. You walked for a week without field rations. And then in the ravine where you stopped, you slaughtered a horse. Angel had foreseen this moment and brought more horses than were needed to transport the MANPADS. You were blessed with fog and so you were able to grill the meat on hot coals. There wasn't much – you each got a small cube. But for hungry stomachs even that was plenty. Under these circumstances, the stomach digests foods with almost no waste. The body's defence mechanisms take over in extreme conditions. Then you followed the river downhill, but your scouts were spotted by a Russian covert observation post as they were clearing the path of mines. Observation-post soldiers don't generally enter into battle; their task is to detect their adversary and report back to headquarters. But your scouts also spotted them. They even observed them radioing their sighting to base. The only comfort was that they didn't know who you were or the size of your group. They realized that you were guerrillas, of course, but didn't know who your commander was. And so you've deviated from your course, climbing up a mountain that forms the left slope of a ravine. On your way out of the ravine there's a single checkpoint. That is not too formidable an opponent; it can easily be eliminated. Especially if you attack at night, when they are more or less helpless. But your purpose is not to eliminate this checkpoint. You should not engage the enemy unless strictly necessary. Your primary concern is to reach your destination without incurring losses. What's more, if you go into combat, it will be difficult to avoid casualties among the civilians in the nearby villages. In fact it will be impossible to avoid, because your opponents are particularly proficient at fighting peaceful civilians. And they might even deliberately fire at the villages. So you shelter on a wooded mountainside overhanging the ravine. You can only move at night. You need to sit out the day, but the enemy's swift response means you'll be holed up here for longer. Here two rivers meet, forming an angle, and in this angle stands your mountain. The days are fine and hot. Soon your hunger is joined by an agonizing thirst. And this is harder still to cope with. One day you are lucky: a mist settles on the mountain. You all come down the treeless slope of the mountain and begin eating the bilberries that grow here abundantly. Bilberries are rich in vitamins and they quench your thirst. But soon the fog disperses and you have to return to the shade of the forest, where no fruit grows. Meanwhile, a huge number of troops flow into the ravine. They stretch for kilometres along the narrow mountain road, packed so densely that if you'd wanted to attack them, it would be hard to imagine a more convenient target for a swift blitz of the column without suffering losses. Their advance units are already conducting a fierce battle in the ravine, using all manner of small arms and light artillery. Only they are engaging not with you, but with the traces of your presence. Traces such as the animal bones stripped of meat or a ripped rucksack discarded by somebody from the unit. Judging by the intensity of their fire, you would think they're in a fierce, arduous battle, but watching the whole performance from above, we merely laugh at their 'bravery'. In the four or five days while you're biding your time to leave, they do not summon the courage to venture deeper into the forest and comb it.

You are suffering from the hunger and thirst along with everyone else. But the harder it becomes to survive, the more interest you take in the behaviour of the partisans. Here they are pulling up grass, wrapping it in a strip of bandage from their first-aid kits and squeezing it. This produces a murky green liquid. If you sweeten it liberally with saccharine, which we're carrying due to its lightness, and if you're desperately thirsty, you can drink this stuff. Even with the addition of saccharin, it tastes unimaginably foul, but it's better than total dehydration. There is cast-iron discipline. A few hundred metres below the camp flows a river and we can constantly hear its tantalizing babble. But not one fighter tries to visit the river in violation of their commander's orders.

A group of five men are calling you over. Someone pulls a single rusk out of a bag, divides it into six equal pieces and offers you one. You are as hungry as the rest. You've finished your field rations, which you also shared with the others. So without compunction you gratefully accept what is probably the man's last piece of rusk. You go over to check on your colleague Roddy. He is hungry, thirsty and tired, but content. The fighters have managed to find him some berries, and the chief of staff shares his last Snickers bar with him, included in the fighters' field rations. You chew on slender twigs plucked from the trees, which taste more or less acceptable, and they somewhat dull your hunger and thirst with the saliva produced. But the effect does not last for long. Your thirst even makes you forget the hunger. At night a group of scouts goes down to the river and they bring back a little water in flasks. Everyone receives a few sips. You cannot slaughter a horse here, either – the risk of exposure is too great. You're interested in the morale of these men of iron, and you try to get interviews, though you always end up with a monologue instead. Despite the arduous conditions, almost all of them are filled with optimism. And this is hardly surprising. For all the men in this unit are seasoned, battle-hardened warriors, who have been through far worse with their commander. You'll find no casual novices, seduced by the romance of war. Here every man knows why he's here and what he's fighting for; he is fully focused on his objective. It is this moral and psychological state that gives the men such strength and stoicism. And it is the dream of every military commander to have an army in this state. Before he set out with them on this journey, Angel subjected his men to a rigorous selection process that might have seemed extreme. He made them run for extended periods along paths that even the beasts preferred to avoid. When I enquired about the reason for such a harsh regime, he replied, 'It'll either break them or harden them. And anyone who breaks won't cause us problems. Because he won't be going with us.' And his tactics are now beginning to bear fruit. It was only now, when the men were pushed to the brink of human endurance, that the true value of this selection process became clear.

The men's speeches are often turned inward, as if they're talking to themselves. And in these extremely candid monologues you glimpse their infinite weariness with this unending war, their yearning for a life of peace. They dream of never carrying a weapon, of never having to use it. They never talk of the war itself. This is the wisdom of men who have looked many times into the empty, bottomless eyes of death. In conversations among themselves, they often talk about the past. All their memories are of peaceful life before the war, when they were ordinary guys in the countryside or city, studying and working, having friends and falling in love. There are plenty of conversations about memories and just as many about future plans for a peaceful post-war life. They dream of ordinary bread as if it were the most exquisite of dishes. They name the precise addresses of cafés and restaurants and the time of day they plan to visit them, listing what they'll order after the war. It is, of course, a very bad idea to think about food when you're hungry. It only makes you hungrier. But then again, these dreams help them live, striving towards an objective that perhaps seems prosaic: eating. Yet was it not through mankind's desire to eat nice food and work less hard that modern progress was born? Strange as it may sound, I sense no malice towards the enemy. Hatred of course is present, but malice – the insatiable, senseless malice that generates yet more senseless, cruel malice, which their opponents demonstrate so often in life, on the television and in the press – is not. There is only cold, controlled hatred and each man views his participation in the war as a necessity.

Tonight we are leaving. We are sealed in, but not so tightly that we cannot find a passage out. Below, on the bank of a roaring mountain river, the enemy have placed checkpoints spaced a hundred metres from each other. Tonight we shall pass between them. The river is shallow, it only comes up to the waist. But it is a mountain river, and it flows very swiftly. In profound silence and darkness, you cross it in groups, clinging to each other to avoid being toppled and swept away by the current. During the crossing you lose two MANPADS, which the water tears from a horse that falls in, and two fighters. They are swept along the river and two days later the enemy will fish out their bodies downstream. By crossing the river at this point, you are clearly giving away your location, but you have the entire night ahead. And you will make full use of this night. Angel once again pulls off his favourite manoeuvre. You make a sudden sharp turn to one side that comes as a surprise even to you, and, going flat out all night, by the morning you find yourselves in a deep ravine far removed from where you passed through the checkpoints. Along the floor of the ravine flows a nameless little river. The morning mist allows you to roast another horse. In the daytime you ought to catch up on sleep, but it is sunny and so you spend the day washing, laundering your clothes and tidying yourselves up. You didn't wash at all during the entire week you were on the mountainside. Neither enemy air reconnaissance nor anything else disturbs you. Nobody is expecting you to be here. So you can travel on safely even by day. But you are utterly drained by hunger and you cannot walk fast. You observe the commander. He is heaving a rucksack which holds his personal belongings plus extra supplies of ammunition and he is armed with a heavy, large-calibre RPK machine gun. He goes forward to the head of the column, puts his rucksack down and walks to the back to take a rucksack from a fighter who's fallen behind. Day after day he moves up and down the column like this. Occasionally you slaughter a horse, but there is barely enough meat to give you a taste. Often you have to eat it raw. Now and then you manage to pick some forest fruits and berries. You pass so close to the enemy that you have to gesture to each other with signs. The enemy are oblivious to your presence here, but you can see and hear them perfectly. The fog, though, does not always come to your aid.

26

You've always suspected that it is only his living conditions that prevent man from going back to his roots. After all, no matter how loudly modern man might crow about his achievements in equality and humaneness, we are the sons of Cain, who murdered his own brother. Or, according to Darwin's theory, so popular among atheists, we're just ex-monkeys. Our distant ancestors did not stop to think when they faced the question of survival. And when modern man falls under the influence of an urge such as hunger, thirst, sexual arousal or greed, he makes a leap back to the psychology of his ancestors, triggering his instinctive survival mechanism; we term this 'going wild'. Given the right conditions, modern man can undergo something akin to becoming 'wild', although he is stopped from truly returning to a wild state by a number of factors.

You have been moving slowly for several days through the dense mountain forest and gradually going wild. There isn't so much as a crumb left from the field rations. You've polished off even the saccharine. You cannot use all of the horses for meat – nobody has the strength to carry the extra load of the heavy MANPADS, and discarding weapons and ammunition goes against the guerrillas' principles. Sod's law dictates that there is no wild fruit in this forest. And there is no chance of hunting successfully; there are too many of you and the wild animals can scent you from afar. Of course, not all of you go wild, not even most of you: only those weakest in spirit. It's true they can't seize anything from the others by force. There's nothing to seize. But even if there were something, it wouldn't happen. There is no 'fittest' here. Everyone is armed, and everyone knows how to shoot. Here strength means only fortitude of spirit. Everyone's nerves are strained to the limit. But only the weak of spirit have reached nervous meltdown. No, they do not try heroically attacking the enemy singlehanded – their survival instinct is still functioning. They simply make life miserable for the rest of their comrades. They pick a fight over the slightest thing; the tiniest trifle makes them lose their temper. Their more restrained comrades, who make up the vast majority of the fighters, put up with their behaviour and do not succumb to the same temptation. You watch these people and can barely contain a fierce wave of anger welling up from somewhere deep inside. You wonder, *Why exactly should we tolerate them?* This use of the collective 'we' helps you position yourself mentally as upholder of the common interest. But then it dawns on you that you too are simply turning into one of them, and you summon up the strength to restrain yourself. Generally speaking, a man who is weak of spirit will be a danger in any abnormal situation. Whether it's hunger, exhaustion or any serious threat to life. You once saw a soldier who found himself near a large number of enemy forces, and thus close to death, almost lost his mind with fear. Like a dog backed into a corner, he was picking fights with his comrades over the most trivial things, threatening to give them away to the enemy and get them all killed. It was only when one of his comrades-in-arms rather elegantly conveyed a genuine death threat that he pulled himself together and stopped endangering the entire group. Afterwards, when the terror of death had passed, he apologized to everyone with whom he'd been spoiling for a fight. Now, as you watch the fighters similarly afflicted, you realize that if any of them were given the chance of surviving alone, they would seize it without a second thought. But even in their present state, they can see that survival alone would be impossible. They would have nowhere to go: the enemy are all around. Their only option is to stay with the group. And so that's what they do, while they grumble, bark at everyone and lose their temper. You draw your own conclusion from this somewhat subjective analysis, and it is clearly not in their favour.

Today one of the groups went to a nearby farm hoping to buy some animals. The watchman refused to sell them a couple of bulls and they ended up taking them by force. As the group left, they ran into some armed men who were out hunting. The men turned out to be police and FSB agents. The guerrillas proposed they hand over their weapons and leave in peace, but instead the men tried to open fire. As a result, three of them were killed and two were captured. But when it emerged that the men they'd taken prisoner were Ossetian hunting guides rather than secret-service officers, and they hadn't tried to shoot, they were released on the spot.

As soon as the group returned with the animals, you slaughtered the two bulls but you could not cook them, for you had been discovered. You were listening in on the enemy radio channel and heard all their communications. They didn't know the size of your group or who you were. But some modest police and army units, far too small for you to bother with, were sent out to the forest. They thought there must be a dozen of you at most. You left an ambush along their path and moved on ahead. They were about to give up and turn back when one of the fighters fell into their hands. He had not wanted to eat his chunk of meat raw, so he'd decided to grill it a little. To do this, he slipped back from the unit and began making a fire – and that's when an enemy search team stumbled across him. Of course, there was nothing he could do and they took him. They soon got him to speak – at the first high-speed interrogation he told them everything he knew. To be fair, it was his only way to avoid an agonizing death and it would be heartless to reproach him for it. In no time they'd surrounded the forest with a huge mass of troops. Just like before, you knew how many men they'd deployed and where they were heading. To give credit where it is due, they acted with skill and professionalism. They began expertly blocking all the routes out of the forest, trying their best to cut off your route, which they had learnt of from their prisoner. But Angel would not have been Angel if he hadn't foreseen this. Without a word, he simply adjusted the route and the unit again veered to the side. Of course, you are unlikely to find a clear path out of the sealed-off section of the forest, but the most poorly controlled sector has been identified. The enemy are zealously assisting you with the heavy use of their radios. Helicopters are circling the forest like a murder of crows on the scent of carnage – they're disturbing you badly and so you decide to give them a fright. A shot from one of the Strela MANPADS has proved fatal for one of them. And now the others become so wary that you can continue your journey safely. You can even light campfires. They don't dare come in close enough to fire their rockets at the smoking fires. And their artillery doesn't work all that accurately. You come to the edge of a fairly sizeable village and stop to rest for the day. The hunger is agonizing. You eat all the old nettles growing on the bank of the brook where you've stopped. You're constantly chewing on twigs. But you dispose of the chewed twigs carefully so as not to leave traces. Out of reflex. Angel calls you over. He has grown gaunt, but he's as composed as ever.

'Do you have any civilian clothes?' he asks.

'Yes. I always carry a set.'

'And what about your passport?'

'I've got it.'

'Today we're going to get out of the encirclement. If we can, we'll leave without firing. If not, we'll fight our way out.'

'OK. My camera batteries still have plenty of life. I'll film it.'

'No, you won't be filming this time.' He half-smiles. 'I've got another job for you. Today, just before we go, a group of five fighters are leaving the forest. They have a mission, which you don't need to know about. They're armed. You need to change into civilian clothes and leave with them.'

'But I can't leave when there's going to be a breakout. How can I abandon my comrades at a time like this? Without knowing what will happen to you.'

'You're not leaving to save yourself. You'll have a mission of your own. But your comrades aren't to know that. Part of their mission is to help get you out. I've already spoken to them.'

'But they can do the mission instead of me. Let me stay one more night with you. I'll go tomorrow if you need me to.'

'Tomorrow the group won't be here. And in any case, we don't know what will happen to you once you're out. You've got to break out of the encirclement too, after all. And if you're discovered, none of you will have any chance of surviving. So it's hard to say who's taking more of a risk. To say nothing of how important your mission is. So hand over your weapons and get changed. You can take the video camera with you but leave the cassettes and films here. Just in case you're killed or fall into their hands.'

'Can I at least keep the knife? It's a gift from a friend.'

'OK. But no other weapons.'

'So what's my mission?'

'It's to do what you do best. You've been with us all this time. Seen everything and been through it yourself. Your mission now is to tell our story. Not right away, of course, but you have to tell it. And it must be the truth. You can do that.' He pauses.

How strange … Why has Angel started speaking like this to me today? For the first time in the many years we've known each other, and in all the time I've spent in the war and with his people.

Angel breaks your chain of thought: 'But the main thing is you must meet a certain person – and this is very important – someone you know quite well, and pass on a message from me. You must make sure no one else hears what you tell him. You're the only person here who knows him. So you can safely meet him and talk with him. He's waiting to hear from me so it's important. And you must not, under any circumstances, ever mention this to anyone.'

'OK. And how will I find you afterwards?'

'We'll get in contact. Soon. Do you have a reliable channel we can communicate through?'

'Yes. I'll give you a phone number. You can call this number any time of day or night, and when you hear "hello", say a phrase which we'll agree on now, then hang up. It'll take half an hour at most for me to get your message. Let's say that two hours from your call a contact will wait for me at some place which we'll decide on now. We can pick a number of places just in case. The contact will repeat the phrase that was used on the phone. It should be someone I know by sight.'

'All right.' He smiles. 'You choose the places and tell me the phrase for me to memorize. We'll do it that way. I knew I could rely on you to come up with something good. We don't know what we'll be facing next, so I can't even give you a rough idea of when we'll make contact. But I promise we'll get in touch. Just go about your business and wait for us. You need to get ready now.'

You join the group which is preparing to leave. It hasn't occurred to you that you are seeing Angel for the last time. You're not familiar with this village and you don't know anyone in it. Everyone else in the group has friends or relatives here. You watch the movements of the enemy soldiers from your hiding place on the edge of the forest and wait for dusk. On the outskirts of the village lives a friend of one of the men and your goal is to reach his house. Leading up to the village is an open field with mown grass which you need to cross. Ahead of you, where the field meets the road, there are enemy armoured vehicles and checkpoints. You will have to pass between them. This is the only option that offers some small hope of success. At nightfall, you run out of the forest and make a headlong dash straight for the enemy vehicles.

When you get five or six metres from the vehicles, you fall to the ground and freeze. The soldiers are listening to pop music on a stereo in one of the armoured personnel carriers and they don't notice you. They don't have any night vision goggles. Your main advantage is that they aren't expecting you to get so close. They cannot imagine such audacity, and this plays to your advantage. You cannot run any further – they'd be sure to see you. All you can do is crawl. On your stomachs. So that's what you're doing. You're crawling and crawling. Sometimes you switch to lizard crawls. You crawl for a kilometre and a half, hidden by the neat rows of freshly mown grass. You crawl right past the enemy and you're out of the ring. Coming through the back gardens, we approach the house and one of you goes into it. Soon he returns with the owner. The first thing his wife does is bring out food. It feels a little strange to be eating normal human food, but you manage to polish off a big pan of rice. Then your comrades hide their weapons and change into civilian clothes. You go to stay the night with the relatives of one of the men. Tomorrow you need to travel on. If all goes well …

Meanwhile, your comrades also come out of the encircled forest through the southern part of the village. As they pass through, they ask the villagers to sell them something to eat, but the people offer them food without taking payment. Almost all of them have crossed the village without hitch when the rear of the unit catches the eye of the local policeman. He runs over to the commander of the battalion covering the sector and addresses him: 'What's this, Comrade Major? Can't you see there are rebels sneaking right past you?'

'I noticed them a while ago. Well, what of it? Let them go. They're not after a fight, so that's OK,' the major replies. But the policeman does not let it rest and he runs off to complain to the colonel. The colonel arrests the major and gives orders for an ambush to be set up on the path of the resistance fighters. And it is the rear of the unit that runs into the ambush. In the brief battle, they lose eight men and several are wounded and taken prisoner. The enemy loses three armoured personnel carriers, two infantry fighting vehicles and their fatalities alone number thirty. At dawn the guerrillas shoot down a second helicopter. Among the dead is the British journalist, Roddy. Usually they wouldn't allow him to stay in the front or rear, as these are the most dangerous places. He was meant to stay in the middle of the column. But it seems he got a little confused in the dark and fell behind. He died instantly. Such an easy death is what every warrior dreams of.

The events of that night were retold from the accounts of eyewitnesses: the villagers and the fighters breaking out of the encirclement. The policeman was later found and dealt with. In the morning you left the sealed-off village in the car of a policeman who was on your side. His ID carried sufficient weight that at the checkpoint they didn't bother to check your papers or search you. Only now that you were in relative safety did you realize how thin you'd become: in the two months you'd been on the move, you'd lost twenty-two kilos. You were perpetually hungry, but you couldn't manage to eat a normal portion. Your stomach started to hurt unbearably from even a small amount of food. Your body had grown unaccustomed to food and it violently rejected whatever you tried to eat. And you suffered for a long time before you could feed yourself properly and without upsetting your stomach. You still didn't know that it was the last time you'd take to the forest and you lived in the hope of seeing your comrades. And that hope dragged on.

27

Then the long, agonizing days of waiting began. The attempts to find temporary work to bring in at least some kind of income. You came to the realization that nothing you'd experienced so far could compare to the agony of sitting around and waiting, feeling redundant. Accustomed to living an active life, you found it extremely hard to take this enforced idleness. Then came the news of Angel's death. Alongside him died the finest fighters and some of your closest friends. Over the past few years you were always trying to keep some distance, not to get too close to anyone. You'd learnt to know, through some sixth sense, when a particular fighter was doomed. You could tell who would die soon – you didn't know how, but you could feel it. And that's why you tried to stay aloof. You were tired of losing friends and comrades in this war. There had been many occasions when a fighter you hardly knew had come and bared his soul to you, as if saying farewell to the world. And soon after, that fighter would die. Listening to his dreams, his childhood, his plans for life, you would keenly sense that he had been marked by the Angel of Death. And you didn't want to get close to those fighters. In a situation where the team means pretty much everything, it's too easy to make close friends. And so hard to lose them. You too had a small circle of friends, and now you've lost even them. Their deaths shocked you so deeply that it took you a long and painful time to emerge from a profound depression.

You had your work for the official Chechen press, first with a newspaper and then with a magazine, that you only found thanks to your writer friends. You led an underground, semi-legal existence. You constantly had to change address – every two or three months, following the age-old rules of underground life – and, given Grozny's catastrophic shortage of housing, this was not easy. You lived in fear of running into old acquaintances – with the exception of a narrow circle of friends – and particularly former brothers-in-arms who, for whatever reasons, had switched sides to join the occupying authorities. You lived in more or less round-the-clock expectation of arrest or of simply being shot on the spot, which nowadays was common practice. Faced with the choice between arrest and being shot, of course you'd have chosen the latter, like many of your comrades had done. But now you were unarmed, so even that option had gone. Your articles in the newspaper, written under a pseudonym, had led to accusations that you were inciting war against Russia. Then there was hope. The hope that the Chechen people would find the best way to escape from the Russian bone-crushing machine. And there were the dreams where you'd meet your dead brothers-in-arms and occasionally some of the few who were still alive.

The war went on. More comrades and enemies fell. The land continued to be too hot under the feet of the occupying troops. The guerrillas carried out ever more daring operations, and the enemy again began to feel its impotence in the face of the Chechen people's hatred. And, along with their people, Chechen presidents were killed. And the enemy knew they were doomed to lose this war. Like all the wars that had come before, they would lose this one too. The people, whose finest sons had sacrificed themselves, managed once again to preserve their Chechen spirit. They did not bow down before their nation's butcher. Your people defeated the enemy, as they had done so many times in history. This great battle was still raging, but for now you had stepped back a little from the thick of it. You were waiting. And you kept waiting and waiting, until you realized there was nobody left to wait for. You had been waiting for someone to contact you on behalf of a warrior, and you remained faithful to this mission till the end.

All your fallen brothers-in-arms had won their battle. They'd departed this world as victors. Those who fall in battle have not lost; it's only the survivors who lose battles. On both the winning and losing sides. All the survivors have lost. They all die over and over again in their subsequent lives, whereas the fallen die only once. And that's how you too lost your battle. The fallen were consumed in the sacred flame of battle and they won. While you will continue to glow like an ember of that fire for the rest of your life. And not because you couldn't die or you were too fond of life, but because you hated life too frequently to let her be rid of you so easily and simply. Too often life for you was worse than death yet you kept on stubbornly choosing it. Now you have to continue running across the blade of the knife and dying every day in your memories. Dying along with all your fallen brothers-in-arms, with each one separately and all of them together, until the Angel of Death comes for you. What form he takes doesn't matter. It doesn't matter at all.

Epilogue

I often come here to the rocks. I come to listen to the sea. And the sea talks to me. I listen for ages to its unhurried tales of something of its own, something eternal. Thoughts come easily to the sound of its sad whispering; its grandeur cleanses me, freeing me of earthly troubles. To the sound of the slow, pensive whisper of the sea, I often go back there, into the past. I now live in a small, quite beautiful town on the edge of the sea. Here, in the Land of the Midnight Sun, there is peace and calm. Once it was like that in my country. But that world was so long ago that sometimes I wonder whether it existed at all. From here, from the vantage point of time, so distant from those events, I keep running over and over in my head the happenings of the past couple of decades. Trying to understand what our generation did wrong. Was there really no way to avoid bloodshed? Can our generation be to blame for this carnage? There was another way. It was slavish allegiance to the Empire. That's right, slavish. Not to be a people with rights in a democratic country, and not even to be second-class citizens – to be third-class citizens, 'persons of Caucasian ethnic origin'. You can only solve the issues of self-determination for nations and peoples in a civilized way if you live in a civilized world. But the world of those peoples who had the cruel misfortune to live on the one-eighth of the earth that was under the patronage of Russia can hardly be called civilized. And our generation bears no guilt for that. We simply acted as our fathers and grandfathers had over the centuries. We had the chance to break free from the deadly friendship that the rulers of Russia had foisted upon our people and we seized that chance. And if it were to happen all over again, none of us late-twentieth-century idealists who believed in the centuries-old dream of our people would choose a different path. We would once again step into the fire and blood, even knowing that we would lose the battle. The Empire won all the battles, yet it could not conquer us, assimilate us and make us its slaves. Winning the battle, it lost the war. The Empire never did manage to obliterate our spirit of freedom And so we were doomed to be free.

There is no other course for the Empire and us. We know each other too well to stay together. Our people know the true meaning and value of all the ideals proclaimed by the Empire: 'democracy' and 'equality of nations', while the Empire understands the depth of our people's loyalty and obedience. And that mutual knowledge ruins any chance of us staying together as one country. Only by bleeding and crushing us can they keep us within the boundaries of the Empire. Even those Chechens who serve Russia faithfully would rise up against her at the drop of a hat if they believed victory would be theirs. They are loyal not from love, but from a lust for money and power. And some of them out of fear too, of course. But all hate the Empire. No, they don't hate the Russian people, who suffer at the hands of the Empire no less than the rest. Just the Empire itself and its ambitions. And in this hatred lies the spectre of the Empire's defeat.

My life now does not compare with the stormy adventures and risks of my past. Here I can plan my time as much as a week or – amazing! – a month in advance. Back then I could not be sure what would happen even an hour ahead. Here people feel confidence in the future. They even feel confidence in life. Their safety is granted and guaranteed by the state; that's the true role of the state. I know here nobody will come for me in the night and I won't disappear without trace. Nobody will discriminate against me on any grounds. Nobody thinks I'm a potential murderer or terrorist just because my small homeland was attacked by an empire and we had to defend ourselves. And here nobody shows me any condescending, mawkish pity. I am one of the many free people who live in this wonderful country. Any person of any colour can live in and travel around whatever part of the country they like.

Yet my entire present life – and future life – is set against the backdrop of my past. My memories refuse to follow the rules of chronology. All I can do is receive them in the order in which they are revealed. When I come here to the rocks, to the deserted shore, I begin long conversations with myself, with my memories and the ghosts of those who fell undefeated. What is missing here is that love of life, that desperate joy from the sensation of life that I once had there. I am learning how to smile again. How to smile just like that, without any particular reason. I'm getting used to living in a world where the air isn't poisoned by danger. I realize that I'll never truly come out into the world, but I'll try. I am fated to long, endless conversations with the ghosts of my memories. And these ghosts will only die when I die. Unlike the characters in so many films and books, I don't want to forget the past. For there is nothing degrading in it, and it deserves to be remembered. This is not only my past: it is also the past of those who will never be able to talk about it or return to it in their memories. Their pains and hopes are reflected in me as in a mirror. Since it was my lot to survive, I have a duty to remember the past of those who burned in the nation's sacrificial fire. And not just to remember, but to tell their story as best I can. That's what I have tried to do in this chronologically messy, stylistically imperfect but true and honest account. I have tried to recount the war without recounting the fighting. To describe the transformation that a man undergoes in such an inhuman situation. My experience has convinced me that in war there are no heroes in the clichéd sense. In war a man becomes the person he truly is. War, this hell incarnate, mercilessly reveals the essence of each person who finds himself there. That is why war is terrible and wonderful at the same time. It is only there that you can see with your own eyes the depths of man's fall and the heights of his nobility both at once. War is the concentration of all man's animal passions and all his noble yearnings. Those who dream of being a hero don't last long in a real war. Heroes are created merely for the parades. And this flawed story is not about heroic war, or high-flown war, but real war. War seen through the eyes of an ordinary civilian. It is a fragment from my never-ending conversations with the ghosts of my memories.

Acknowledgements

I wish to express my special gratitude to the following people: Kjell Olaf Jensen, Moris Farhi, Ros Schwartz, Apti Bisultanov, Eliza Musaeva, Aage Borchgrevink, Ekaterina Sokirianskaya, Arve Solbakken, Terje Hellesen, Britt Vårvik, Gry Elise Albrektsen, Alexander Gunin, and I'd particularly like to thank my talented translator Anna Gunin and publisher Philip Gwyn Jones.

I thank you with all my heart!

Notes

1   Ruslan Labazanov was a colonel in the Russian security services. Following a mass breakout which he organized from a detention facility in November 1991, he infiltrated Dudayev's entourage. Labazanov was responsible for the deaths of a considerable number of innocent civilians. He styled himself as a 'Chechen Robin Hood'. Later he openly switched sides, joining the opposition. His armed group was defeated by Chechen government forces in the summer of 1994. Labazanov was killed by his own bodyguard in the summer of 1996.

2   Pavel Grachev was Russian Defence Minister from May 1992 to June 1996. He was the architect and director of the unsuccessful assault on the Chechen capital Grozny on the night of 31 December 1994.

3   Sergey Yushenkov served as a deputy in Russia's State Duma. In the first Duma, he was Defence Committee chairman. In 1995 he quit the army due to his objections to the war in Chechnya. He was shot dead in Moscow on 17 April 2003.

4   On the northern fringes of Grozny.

5   Hamzat Gelayev was a prominent Chechen field commander. From 1995 he was Brigadier General in the Chechen Armed Forces. In February 2004 he was killed in action.

6   Shamil Basayev was a Chechen field commander. From 1995 he

was Brigadier General in the Armed Forces of Chechnya. He was appointed Vice President of Chechnya. He died in July 2006.

7 Gennady Troshev was a Russian general. A native of Grozny, he fought in both the First and Second Chechen Wars. He is the author of *Moya voyna. Chechensky dnevnik okopnogo generala* (Vagrius, 2001).

8 In *Chechnya: A Small Victorious War* (Picador, 1997), Carlotta Gall and Thomas de Waal give this account of events: 'The New Year's Eve battle seemed at first a great Chechen victory. A small band of Chechen fighters had humiliated a superpower, deflecting the assault of Europe's largest army and turning on its head the Cold War assumptions that made Russia's armed forces the most feared in the world. By one estimate Russian forces lost more tanks in Grozny than they did in the battle for Berlin in 1945. The Chechens had seized countless weapons and ammunition and gained a breathing space as the Russian command slowly took in the scale of the catastrophe on their hands. Jubilant, the Chechen fighters roared around the city centre on captured tanks, flying the green Chechen flag. Basayev was one who did not brag. "It was a senseless battle, without logic," he said. "They just threw their men in." But as if he knew what was to come, he said the Chechens had shown they were deadly serious. "It is not an empty threat that we will fight to the death."'

9 See *Chechnya: v kogtyakh d'yavola ili na puti k samounichtozheniyu* by Akhmed Kelimatov (Ekoprint, 2003).

10 Sydnocarb is a stimulant drug adopted by the Russian military during the 1980s. Its use is intended to boost soldiers' levels of energy and aggression for six to eight hours. It comes with side effects in the form of increased excitability and hallucinations. Users will see the enemy everywhere, with all the consequences that entails.

11 In 1944 Stalin deported the entire Chechen people to Central Asia and Siberia on a false charge of collaboration with the Nazis, despite the Chechen-Ingush Autonomous Soviet Socialist Republic not

coming under German occupation. More than half the nation died in exile from cold and hunger. The exile lasted until 1959.

12 Oleg Gazmanov is a Russian pop singer.

13 In January 1995 the streets of Grozny were strewn with the many corpses of Russian soldiers killed during the storming of the city. The abandoned corpses of soldiers and officers were eaten by feral cats and dogs. Only two weeks later did the Russian commanders agree to a temporary truce to remove the corpses from the streets of the city.

14 'Nakh' is the ancient name for the Chechens, the Ingush and the Batsbi, who are a Christian community of Chechen origin living in Georgia.

15 Dadi-Yurt was a large village, the site of a bloody battle in September 1818 between the Russian occupation forces led by General Alexei Yermolov and the Chechen resistance. The village was totally annihilated; almost all the inhabitants were killed, including the women and children. Legend has it that the girls of the village danced for their male defenders to raise their morale. And then these girls fell too, charging at the Russian soldiers with daggers. Among the few captives were two boys who were taken to Russia. One grew up to be the famous artist Pyotr Zakharov-Chechenets. The second, Bata Shamurzayev, became a Russian officer who crossed over to the Chechen side and fought against the Russians. In 1851, he sided once again with the Russians and fought against his former comrades. The Tsar rewarded him for his loyalty with 600 hectares of land.

16 Alexei Yermolov, the Russian infantry general, appointed Proconsul of the Caucasus by decree of Alexander I on 6 April 1816. A bloodthirsty tyrant and slaughterer of the Chechen people.

17 Alkhan-Kala is a small village not far from Grozny.

18 Around seventy kilometres south-west of Grozny.

19 Usman Imayev was the Prosecutor General for Chechnya. He was a field commander and engaged in combat against the Russian Army. He went missing in action in the spring of 1996.

20 Vedeno is a district centre in eastern Chechnya.

21 It so happens that the very same clever question, 'Why aren't you at your place of work?' was put to me in December 1994 at the height of the war by Abu Arsanukayev, head of Dudayev's security service, thereby demonstrating his somewhat modest intellect. And all that stopped him from answering my sarcasm with a demonstration of his power, too, was the explicit intervention of the fighters with whom I'd just returned from the front line. Generally speaking, you'd seldom encounter men of intellect in the Soviet military. The generals, though – Dzhokhar Dudayev, Boris Gromov, Aleksandr Lebed, Aslan Maskhadov – were the exception. Nevertheless, it was Lebed who offered the most vivid portrait of Soviet Russia's top brass: 'A general who is not a thief is a contradiction in terms,' he said in an interview.

22 Zelimkhan Yandarbiyev was Vice President and later President of Chechnya. He was a poet. He was assassinated in 2004 in Qatar.

23 The residents of Bamut, Stary Achkhoy and Yandi deserted the villages, leaving behind all their belongings for the use of the resistance. The villages were defended until the end of the first war, in April 1996.

24 Movladi Udugov was Dudayev's Information Minister and Deputy Prime Minister under Yandarbiyev and Maskhadov. He set up the website Kavkaz Center.

25 In May 1995 this bunker-buster was dropped in Shatoy, killing more than fifteen civilians who were hiding in the bomb shelter.

26 On 14 June 1995 a group of Chechen fighters led by Shamil Basayev crossed into the Stavropol territory in southern Russia and captured the town of Budyonnovsk. They held over a thousand civilians hostage and demanded an end to the war. The operation resulted in a ceasefire and peace talks.

27 Sheikh Kunta-Haji Kishiev was a peacemaker and Sufi saint, famed throughout the North Caucasus, who opposed the destruction of the Chechen people in the nineteenth-century Caucasian War. He was arrested by the tsarist authorities on 3 January 1864 and exiled for life.

28 This song is from the 1981 Soviet film *Karnaval*.

29 Khankala is a ravine at the entrance to Grozny.

30 Konstantin Balmont (1867–1942) was a Russian Symbolist poet. These lines are from his sonnet, 'The Scorpion'.

31 *Kontraktniki*, or contract soldiers, are professional servicemen who serve in the Russian Federation military on a contractual basis.

32 The notorious camp PAP-1 (Passenger Bus Garage No. 1) was located in the Leninsky district of Grozny. It was in operation from February 1995 until the end of the first war.

33 Situated in the high mountains near the border with Ingushetia, the village of Bamut became the site of a battle that lasted for fourteen months. Chechen singers wrote songs celebrating the Battle of Bamut.

34 In March 2000, a major battle took place in Komsomolskoye, with the Chechen resistance suffering heavy losses. Large numbers were killed, wounded and taken prisoner. 'White Swan', or Solikamsk Prison, is a Russian penitentiary in the Urals.

35 General Pulikovsky delivered an ultimatum giving the resistance fighters forty-eight hours to evacuate the captured city. Otherwise, the general promised to use all available means to liberate the city by force.

36 In July and August 1999 to support the Dagestani guerrillas.

37 A district centre in Dagestan.

38 Vladimir Putin was appointed Acting Prime Minister on 9 August 1999 and became Acting President on 31 December 1999.

39 The three Yamadayev brothers – Sulim, Ruslan, a former deputy in the State Duma of Russia, and Dzhabrail, all decorated Heroes of the Russian Federation – were former field commanders who in 1999 went over to the Russian side.

40 On 4 October 1993 Russian troops, with tanks and special forces, stormed the Russian parliament building. The Speaker of the Russian Supreme Soviet, Ruslan Khasbulatov, and the Vice President, Aleksandr Rutskoy, were arrested and later pardoned by Boris Yeltsin.

41 'Angel' was the call sign used by Hamzat Gelayev. See note 5.

42 Shamil Basayev.

43 The battle for Grozny lasted from November 1999 until February 2000.

44 According to the human-rights organization Memorial, on 5 February 2000, in just one small village, Novye Aldy, on the outskirts of Grozny, Russian soldiers killed over fifty civilians during a 'cleansing operation'.

45 It is worth stressing that the Russian General Staff had no operational plan called Wolf Pit, as their generals subsequently claimed. If such a plan had been carried out, the losses during the breakout would have been 30 or 40 per cent of the men, if not more, given that for most of the way we were moving through occupied territory. In reality, though, we lost less than 5 per cent during the entire two-week march towards the mountains, which reflects the flawlessness of the operation from a military perspective. The Russian generals, as always, were simply trying to explain away their incompetence retrospectively. They have traditionally been great strategists of their battles after the event.

46 The route for the breakout from Grozny ran through the following villages: Alkhan-Kala, Zakan-Yurt, Shaami-Yurt, Katar-Yurt and Gekhi-Chu in western Chechnya. From Gekhi-Chu the route swerved sharply into the mountain forest, which extended all the way to the mountainous Shatoy district, where we arrived from 12 to 14 February 2000.

47 Shali is a town in eastern Chechnya; at this time it was under pro-Moscow control. It had a large market where you could purchase food and essentials.

48 The battle of Komsomolskoye took place in March 2000. The Chechens suffered heavier losses in this battle than in any other during the first and second wars.

49 In the Russian Federation, all citizens were required to have internal passports officially recording their place of residence. Any Chechen caught without the right stamps in his passport would immediately arouse suspicion. Legalization was essential for

freedom of movement, as the Chechens could be asked for their ID in random swoops or at checkpoints.

50 Kostroma is a city in Russia.

51 This journey is the return to Chechnya of Hamzat Gelayev's guerrilla unit. Until this time, he was based in the forests of eastern Georgia.

52 Akhmad Kadyrov, who changed sides and became President of the Moscow-appointed Chechen administration. He was the father of Ramzan Kadyrov, who succeeded him as President.

53 In Russia, serfdom was abolished only in 1861.